PHYSICAL ACTIVITY
& Behavioral
Medicine

Behavioral Medicine and Health Psychology Series

SERIES EDITOR

J. Rick Turner
SilverCreek Health Associates

Behavioral Medicine and Health Psychology brings the latest advances in these fields directly into undergraduate, graduate, and professional classrooms via individual texts that each present one topic in a self-contained manner. The texts also allow health professionals specializing in one field to become familiar with another by reading the appropriate volume, a task facilitated by their short length and their scholarly yet accessible format.

The development of the series is guided by its Editorial Board, which comprises experts from the disciplines of experimental and clinical psychology, medicine and preventive medicine, psychiatry and behavioral sciences, nursing, public health, biobehavioral health, behavioral health sciences, and behavioral genetics. Board members are based in North America, Europe, and Australia, thereby providing a truly international perspective on current research and clinical practice in behavioral medicine and health psychology.

EDITORIAL BOARD

Books in This Series

PHYSICAL ACTIVITY
& Behavioral Medicine

James F. Sallis | Neville Owen

Behavioral Medicine & Health Psychology 3

SAGE Publications
International Educational and Professional Publisher
Thousand Oaks   London   New Delhi

For information:

SAGE Publications, Inc.
2455 Teller Road
Thousand Oaks, California 91320
E-mail: order@sagepub.com

SAGE Publications Ltd.
6 Bonhill Street
London EC2A 4PU
United Kingdom

SAGE Publications India Pvt. Ltd.
M-32 Market
Greater Kailash I
New Delhi 110 048 India

Printed in the United States of America

Library of Congress Cataloging-in-Publication Data

Sallis, James F.
    Physical activity and behavioral medicine / by James F. Sallis
and Neville Owen.
        p.   cm.— (Behavioral medicine and health psychology series;
v. 3)
        Includes bibliographical references and index.
        ISBN 0-8039-5996-6 (cloth: acid-free paper)
        ISBN 0-8039-5997-4 (pbk.: acid-free paper)
        1. Medicine and psychology.   2. Physical fitness—Physiological
aspects.   3. Physical fitness—Psychological aspects.   4. Health.
I. Owen, Neville.   II. Title.   III. Series.
R726.5 .S25 1998
613'.7—ddc21   98-25362

This book is printed on acid-free paper.

98   99   00   01   02   03   04   7   6   5   4   3   2   1

Acquiring Editor:	C. Deborah Laughton
Editorial Assistant:	Eileen Carr
Production Editor:	Sanford Robinson
Copy Editor:	Linda Gray
Editorial Assistant:	Denise Santoyo
Designer/Typesetter:	Lynn Miyata
Cover Designer:	Ravi Balasuriya

Contents

PART I: INTRODUCTION

PART II: PHYSICAL ACTIVITY AND HEALTH

PART III: DEFINING AND MEASURING PHYSICAL ACTIVITY

PART IV: UNDERSTANDING AND INFLUENCING PHYSICAL ACTIVITY

PART V: CONCLUSIONS AND FUTURE DIRECTIONS

J.F.S.: To Shemi (asante sana, again)
and the Saturday morning jogging group:
Bob Kaplan, John Martin, John Elder, Al Litrownik

N.O.: To Sue, Alice, Cate, and Eric; to Alan, Linda, and Ruby

Series Editor's Introduction

Physical Activity and Behavioral Medicine is the third volume in this series, following *Stress and Health* and *Understanding Caffeine*. It is appropriate and timely to include a volume on the health benefits of physical activity since it is now clear that physical *inactivity* is an important risk factor for many diseases, including cancer, cardiovascular disease, diabetes, and osteoporosis. The timeliness is underscored by the recent publication of the first Surgeon General's report on Physical Activity and Health. The Senior Scientific Editor of that report, Dr. Steven Blair, has kindly written a foreword for this volume.

Dr. Jim Sallis is Professor of Psychology at San Diego State University. A couple of years ago I heard him give a fascinating talk at his alma mater, Memphis State University (now The University of Memphis). He not only provided compelling evidence of the benefits of physical activity, but also described research exploring the most effective ways to increase people's participation in sports and other physical activities. Following this talk, I invited Dr. Sallis to contribute a volume for this series. He subsequently joined forces with his colleague Dr. Neville Owen, head of the School of Human Movement at Deakin University, Australia, to write this outstanding book.

My thanks are expressed to both authors. Their international collaboration and perspectives have clearly enhanced the presentation of this topic, and I have no doubt that you will find their writing highly accessible and most informative.

—J. Rick Turner
Chapel Hill, North Carolina

Foreword

When I started my academic career more than 30 years ago, the term *exercise science* was not used. Indeed, if you had used it, academic colleagues would have thought you pretentious. Individuals investigating the effects of exercise generally were not taken seriously, and few exercise studies were published in highly ranked biomedical journals. The status of exercise science clearly is different today, and there are numerous highly productive and respected scientists who study exercise, such as the authors of this book.

Exercise science is now accepted as a legitimate, even important, area of investigation. There are few things that perturb as many body systems as exercise; and use of exercise as a stressor is common in many types of physiological investigations, ranging from studies of the immune system to bone. Physical inactivity is recognized as a major health issue in most industrialized countries. In the United States, several major scientific and medical organizations, along with public health agencies, recently issued statements on physical inactivity as a public health problem. One of the first key statements was published in 1992 by the American Heart Association, and with this statement, physical inactivity was recognized as the fourth risk factor for coronary artery disease, along with cigarette smoking, high blood pressure, and high cholesterol. In 1995 the American College of Sports Medicine and the U.S. Centers for Disease Control and Prevention issued public health recommendations for physical activity. Two major reports were issued in the United States in 1996, one by the National Institutes of Health from a consensus development conference on physical activity and cardiovascular health, and a second by the office of the U.S. Surgeon General. All of these reports conclude that physical inactivity contributes to the development of several chronic diseases and other health problems, that too many individuals are sedentary, and that efforts to promote increased physical activity must be increased.

Early research on physiological responses to exercise date to the first part of the 20th century, and systematic evaluations of the relation of inactivity to disease began in the 1950s. Accumulated findings from these areas of research greatly accelerated over the past 25 years, and the body of evidence relating inactivity to increased health problems led to the recent consensus documents mentioned above. My own scientific career parallels the development of exercise science over the past several decades. My early interest was in physiological responses to exercise, and later I focused on the relation of inactivity to morbidity and mortality. Most recently, my research efforts expanded to develop and evaluate different models and programs for promotion of physical activity, and I consider this latter area the most challenging, and perhaps most important.

We can now be certain that inactivity contributes to health problems and that modern life is becoming increasingly sedentary. What to do about this problem is less clear. Controlled research on physical activity interventions is a relatively new area of investigation for exercise scientists. Drs. Sallis and Owen are leaders in these efforts, I have learned a great deal from them, and I am privileged to collaborate with Jim on a randomized clinical trial of physical activity interventions in primary health care settings. Both Jim and Neville have been involved over the past 20 years in various interventions for individuals across the age range and in clinical settings, schools, and in entire communities. They bring a fresh and creative perspective to the field, and we can all learn from them.

This book will be useful to scientists and clinicians in many disciplines who are interested in physical inactivity as a public health problem. I am impressed with the broad range of topics included in the book. It is clear that the public health issue of sedentary living requires a multidisciplinary approach, and the authors are masters at using information from many areas of research and practice to present a comprehensive behavioral medicine strategy. There has been much recent progress in understanding physical activity behavior, and what types of interventions are useful in promoting physical activity. Much remains to be done, but a crucial step is for many more in science and medicine to become involved in developing, implementing, and evaluating physical activity interventions. This book will be helpful to them in enhancing their knowledge and skills about how to promote physical activity more effectively. I recommend it highly.

—Steven N. Blair
Cooper Institute for Aerobics Research
President, American College of Sports Medicine, 1996-97
Senior Scientific Editor, *Physical Activity and
Health: A Report of the Surgeon General*

Preface

We wrote *Physical Activity and Behavioral Medicine* because it became clear to us that there was a need to consolidate and integrate the now extensive body of knowledge on health-related physical activity with an emphasis on a behavioral science perspective. Although both of us are trained in psychology, we believe this book is true to the spirit of behavioral medicine. We have attempted to integrate theory and research from several disciplines to provide a broad coverage of the issues related to physical activity and health. We have both worked closely with professionals from multiple disciplines, and we hope we have learned enough from our colleagues to adequately synthesize multiple viewpoints and approaches in this book.

This book can be used in training students in a variety of disciplines, including psychology, exercise sciences, nutrition, medicine, nursing, and public health. However, our emphasis is clearly on behavioral aspects of physical activity. We adopted this emphasis deliberately, not only because of our backgrounds but also because we strongly believe the most important challenges in the field deal with intervening on physical activity. Many of the health benefits are widely known, but we are much less advanced in our knowledge of how to help people become active enough to enjoy these benefits. We see promoting physical activity as one of the major public health tasks of our time, and we hope this book makes a positive contribution to this effort.

Many of our colleagues in the disciplines of epidemiology, psychology, exercise physiology, the other human movement sciences, preventive medicine, and public health have relatively recently become involved with promoting higher levels of physical activity in specific groups and whole populations. Because of our long-term involvement in applied physical activity research, we find ourselves providing advice to practitioners and policymakers in the government and private sectors on ways to promote higher levels of physical activity. It has become increasingly clear to us that the field of physical activity and health would benefit from a book that draws together the major strands of knowledge from the relevant disciplines to develop a systematic approach for applying high-quality research and theory to physical activity promotion. We hope this book clearly explains our empirically based approach to physical activity and public health.

Because of its behavioral emphasis, this book will be worthwhile reading for exercise scientists and other interested professionals with training in the biological sciences. Both researchers and practitioners should find the material in this book useful for providing an overview of the field as well as for stimulating new questions for research and new directions for programs.

We decided early in the planning of this book to make it international in scope. We have monitored and edited each other so the material has as wide a relevance as possible. Physical inactivity is a problem in all industrialized nations, and we hope readers in many countries will find this book useful.

The writing of this book started on the first day of Jim Sallis's sabbatical with Neville Owen. Books inevitably take more time and effort than is anticipated at the start, but our task was made more enjoyable by working in pleasant environments as often as possible. We wrote part of this book on the coast of Victoria, Australia, as parrots and cockatoos fed outside the window. During breaks, we saw koalas as we walked and jogged through a nearby park. On another occasion we spent a couple of days writing in the Anza-Borrego desert in San Diego County. To get warmed up, we took a hike at dawn through stunning desert scenery.

Health-related physical activity is a new and exciting frontier in behavioral medicine. The publication of the first U.S. Surgeon General's report on

Physical Activity and Health in 1996 is an indication that the area of physical activity and health has achieved a status similar to that achieved by the smoking field on the occasion of the first U.S. Surgeon General's report on *Smoking and Health,* published three decades earlier. Interest in a scientific approach to physical activity and health has never been higher, and we hope this book inspires students, scientists, and practitioners from many disciplines to join in the effort to improve health through the promotion of physical activity.

Now we have done our part. The book is written. Your part is to take this book, learn how you can be part of the solution to the epidemic of physical inactivity, and take action through research and practice.

Acknowledgments

We both express our gratitude to Rick Turner and C. Deborah Laughton for their patience and encouragement during the writing of this book.

James Sallis

Over the years I have had the pleasure of collaborating with many wonderful people on a variety of projects related to physical activity. These collaborations have not only provided me with the chance to enjoy the company of these people, but I have also learned much about physical activity, research, health, and life. I want to thank many of the key people, with apologies to others not named. I also acknowledge my students who keep my brain active and help me stay young at heart.

I got my start in physical activity research during my postdoctoral fellowship at Stanford by tutoring from some of the best: Bill Haskell, Peter Wood, Nathan Maccoby, Barr Taylor, Steve Fortmann, Jack Farquhar, and

Ralph Paffenbarger. During this time, Neville Owen and I began periodic discussions that eventually led to this book.

My colleagues on the San Diego Family Health Project introduced me to research with pediatric populations: Phil Nader, Tom Patterson, Cathie Atkins, and Mike Buono.

The group working on physical activity determinants in community samples has had a long and fruitful collaboration: Mel Hovell, Dick Hofstetter, John Elder, and several very competent staff and students. I also want to thank our CDC colleagues Carl Caspersen and Ken Powell.

The continuing work on San Diego SCAN is still stimulating, due to the interdisciplinary team: Phil Nader, Thom McKenzie, John Elder, Chuck Berry, Michelle Zive, Shelia Broyles, and Tricia Hoy.

The SPARK team has worked together on a particularly close basis: Thom McKenzie, Paul Rosengard, Bo Kolody, John Alcaraz, Nell Faucette, and Julia Roby Cuban.

The PACE group has provided me with a very supportive environment for working on difficult problems: Kevin Patrick, Karen Calfas, Barbara Long, Wilma Wooten, Denise Wilfley, Jodi Prochaska, Marion Zabinski, Mike Pratt, and Greg Heath.

The GRAD study has benefited from a cohesive and talented group of investigators: Karen Calfas, Jeanne Nichols, Julie Sarkin, Susan Caparosa, John Alcaraz, and Sheri Thompson.

The multicenter ACT study allows me to work with some of the best people around the country: Steve Blair, Abby King, Andrea Dunn, Bess Marcus, Denise Simons-Morton, Jack Rejeski, Bob Klesges, Cheryl Albright, and Stuart Cohen.

Although separated by great distances, the Cowles Media Foundation project team has worked well together: Russ Pate, Patty Freedson, Wendell Taylor, and Diane Hermann.

The energetic M-SPAN group is stimulating some new approaches to measurement and intervention: Thom McKenzie, John Elder, Marianne Wildey, Terry Conway, Paul Rosengard, Michelle Zive, and Simon Marshall.

Extra thanks to the Aussies who made my sabbatical a very special time, especially my gracious hosts Neville Owen and Brian Oldenburg. I also benefited greatly from my contacts with Adrian Bauman, Christina Lee, Mike Booth, Ron Borland, Jack James, the whole group of Italians at Deakin University, the staff at QUT, the National Workplace and Health Project staff at Sydney University, and wonderful people in several offices of the Australian Heart Foundation.

I want to thank Nick Cavill and Stuart Biddle for involving me in the "Young and Active?" symposium in London.

My international collaborations have been very meaningful, and I hope they continue. In the Czech Republic Josef Hrebicek was my closest collaborator and friend, and I am saddened by his death in 1997. Other valued colleagues in the Czech Republic are Jiri Novosad, Hana Valkova, Karel Fromel, and Milan Horvath. In Brazil, I have enjoyed getting involved with Agita Sao Paulo and working with the very impressive CELAFISCS team, headed by Victor and Sandra Matsudo. In Portugal: Luis Sardihna, Margarida Gaspar de Matos, and Jorge Mota.

It is clear that many people have contributed to my work, and I hope this book does not embarrass any of them. However, I want to single out a few people who have played very key roles in my development over the years and have been supportive beyond reasonable expectations: Ken Lichstein, Bill Haskell, Elaine Stone, Bob Kaplan, Steve Blair, and Thom McKenzie.

Special thanks to Kecia Carrasco for managing the office and keeping so much information in her head. Thanks to Susie Newmiller and Helen Hayden for their futile attempts to organize my office.

Finally, I want to thank Walter and Joan, a retired couple who really enjoy taking brisk walks on the beach every morning. They remind me that physical activity can always be a fun part of your day, and it leads you to meet very nice people.

Neville Owen

Since I first started to do research on physical activity, I have worked with many excellent colleagues and students. I owe a great deal to them all for the knowledge, skill, enthusiasm, patience, and commitment that they brought to the research we did together.

Some particular colleagues have helped me to map and build the conceptual and scientific pathways that have led to the writing of this book. Adrian Bauman has been an inspiring, prolific, and cordial collaborator, as have Michael Booth and Christopher J. Gore. Ron Borland and Brian Oldenburg have also been inspiring and energetic collaborators on my research in tobacco control, workplace health promotion and behavioral epidemiology, as have Melanie Wakefield and Lyn Roberts.

Particular thanks also to those who inspired and supported my early efforts at physical activity research: Christina Lee, Tony Sedgwick, Kevin Haag, Wayne Coonan, and Terry Dwyer. For their support and productive involvement in my overall portfolio of behavioral and public health research, I am indebted to many colleagues and former and current students: David Hill, John Pierce, Wayne Velicer, Stephen L. Brown, Alison Smith, Penny Kent, Philip Vita, Herbert Severson, Mario Virgili, Rob Donovan, Judy Simpson, Anne-Louise Ewins, David Edwards, David Wilson, Colin MacDougall, Arul Mylvaganam, Kristyn Willson, David Weller—and particularly Andrew Gilbert. I learned some very useful nuances of epidemiological and occupational health logic from my associations at the University of Adelaide with Tony McMichael, Alistair Woodward, Janet Hiller, Dino Pisaniello, and Richie Gun.

My approach to physical activity research has been influenced significantly by the exceptional scholars whom I met during my time as a Kellogg Foundation fellow in behavioral epidemiology with the Stanford Heart Disease Prevention Program—particularly Nathan Maccoby, John W. Farquhar, C. Barr Taylor, William Haskell, Todd Rogers, June Flora, and David Abrams. I first met Jim Sallis at Stanford, and the Stanford connections led me to a most productive collaboration with Bess Marcus.

The staff of the National Workplace Health Project at Sydney University deserve special thanks. Under the skillful management of David Harris, they have all helped me to be part of an excellent workplace health study.

The inspiration and personal generosity of international colleagues have been very important to me over the years, particularly Alan Marlatt and Judith Gordon, Stan Maes, David Russell, Gerjo Kok, Amanda Killoran, and Nick Cavill.

When I moved from the University of Adelaide to Deakin University in 1995, I took up the unique and challenging opportunity of setting up a new human movement department. The support of my senior academic colleagues at Deakin, particularly Kerin O'Dea and Lawry St Leger, has been invaluable, as has been the excellent support of Robert Price, Judy Ann Jones, Peter Le Rossignol, Tony Sparrow, and Mark Hargreaves. I must thank all the staff of the School of Human Movement at Deakin University for their loyalty and support.

    Thanking some people generally and some specifically never seems quite right. Very special thanks to Sharon Melder, who has protected my time, given me very good advice, and had an invaluable role in the production of this book. Special thanks also to Lyn Golder, Judy Crowe, and Jenny Rosengrave, and to Shayne Cox and David Owies. The Physical Activity, Fitness and Health research group at Deakin University and our associates have been very good colleagues—thanks to Jenny Veitch, Eva Leslie, Jo Salmon, Sue Mounsey, Jane Burns, Sing Kai Lo, Bill Bellew, Phillip Vita, and Ian Kett. David Crawford's breadth of knowledge, scientific judgment, research skills, patience, and energy are greatly appreciated. James Sallis's presence at Deakin University in 1995 was a most enjoyable, inspiring, and productive episode for all of us. Jim and I started this book at that time. He has written more than his envisaged half share and has been a great coauthor and companion, especially during our bursts of writing and outdoor activity on the wet southern coast of Australia and in the dry Californian desert. I look forward to more of the same and some equally enjoyable future variations.

PART
I

Introduction

Section Introduction

The purpose of this book is to review research and theory on physical activity and health, with an emphasis on integrating behavioral and physiological sciences. Appropriately for a book in a series on behavioral medicine, the facts and ideas we describe here are drawn from a number of research fields, particularly epidemiology, exercise physiology, and health psychology. So that the reader is clear about our approach from the beginning, we state two principles that guided the writing of this book. First, we want this book to contribute to improvements in public health. Physical inactivity is a mass phenomenon in industrialized nations, so our ultimate goal is to learn how to increase physical activity in entire populations as a way to improve public health. Second, we emphasize a scientific approach to public health interventions, because we believe physical activity programs are most effective when they are based on the best available data. Because the evidence is incomplete, we also describe how promising theories can be used to develop better interventions.

In *Physical Activity and Behavioral Medicine*, we attempt to answer four questions that are central to understanding the causes and effects of physical activity and to using that knowledge to improve health of people through participation in physical activity.

1. What is known about the physical and mental health benefits of physical activity?
2. How is physical activity defined and measured for the purposes of health-related research?
3. How can we understand factors that influence the physical activity habits of individuals and whole populations?
4. How can we modify the physical activity habits of individuals and whole populations?

These domains of research and theory are covered in the three central sections of the book:

Part II: Physical Activity and Health
Part III: Defining and Measuring Physical Activity
Part IV: Understanding and Influencing Physical Activity

These sections describe how we see the current state of research evidence and what we believe to be the most relevant theories and the most important contemporary applications of this research and theory.

The organizing framework of "behavioral epidemiology," described in Chapter 1, comes out of our work as behavioral scientists with long-standing interests in understanding the multiple influences on physical activity and how an understanding of these influences may be put to good use in helping people lead more active lifestyles. The behavioral epidemiology framework can be applied equally well to other health-related behaviors—cigarette smoking, food choices, weight control practices, sexual habits, or drug and alcohol use. The reader might usefully pause at some points and consider how the behavioral epidemiology framework can be applied to other health behaviors that are relevant to his or her professional life.

As we show in Part II, studies of the behavioral epidemiology of physical activity build strongly on a base of fundamental epidemiological and biological research. This research has, particularly over the past 10 years, made major strides in identifying the types and amounts of physical activity necessary for maintaining good health.

As Chapters 1, 4, and 6 make clear, we are in the midst of an epidemic of sedentary behavior. Government and private sector bodies are now trying to come to grips with effective strategies for promoting higher levels of physical activity participation in whole populations. We hope the integration of theory, research, and applications in this book can lead to better solutions for this worldwide epidemic. Chapter 1 describes how research, theory, and applications can be integrated within the behavioral epidemiology framework. The usefulness of the framework should be made clear in subsequent chapters.

Introduction, Definitions, and Plan of the Book

Generally speaking, all parts of the body which have a function, if used in moderation and exercised in labors to which each is accustomed, become healthy and well developed, and age slowly, but if unused and left to idle, they become liable to disease, defective in growth, and age quickly.

—Hippocrates

Throughout virtually all of human history, physical activity was an inevitable part of people's days. When they wanted to go somewhere, they walked. When they wanted to move something from one place to another, they carried it. It required effort to gather, grow, or hunt food. Almost all forms of work required physical exertion or movement of some kind.

Most people sought relief from all of this physical activity, and they welcomed the conveniences supplied by the industrial revolution. In the last two centuries, an extraordinary burst of invention has created an immense number of "laborsaving devices" that have become part of our daily lives. Late 20th-century life in industrialized nations is vastly different from life in past times. We transport ourselves primarily by automobile or other motorized means. Machines do much of the labor of growing, harvesting, packaging, and transporting food, so individuals spend little energy getting food. Work around the home is assisted by power lawn mowers, power tools, food processors, and washing machines. For most people, "work" is now mainly mental rather than physical. Hard labor typically pays the least, so it is avoided as much as possible. Sedentary entertainment through television, movies, videos, and computers fills much of people's leisure time.

These changes have created a situation in which it is possible to go through each day being almost wholly sedentary. For the vast majority of people in industrialized nations, hardly any physical activity is needed to put in a day's work, feed oneself, or be entertained. This is a unique situation in human history, and we are now finding that there are severe health consequences from the current epidemic of sedentary lifestyles.

The value of exercise for health and well-being has been recognized throughout recorded history, as illustrated by the quotation at the beginning of this chapter. Active people have been admired for their discipline. Participants in sports have been celebrated for their physical prowess and attractive bodies. Exercise has been used for centuries as medical treatment for various maladies. The profession of physical education was developed over 100 years ago to promote physical activity in youth, and there is a long history of research on the physiological effects of exercise.

Despite this illustrious past and high public regard, leisure exercise was not a mass phenomenon for most of the 20th century. Although children are frequent participants in active games and sports, a minority of adult enthusiasts engage in amateur sports and vigorous exercise. Widespread interest in physical activity for health and well-being, or the so-called fitness movement that was in full swing by the 1970s, grew out of three distinct sources in the 1950s. First, modern scientific studies connecting physical activity with improved health were published in the 1950s. Second, a few visible leaders such as Jack LaLanne brought exercise to the consciousness of millions of people. Third, concern about the apparent lack of physical fitness of military recruits in World War II stimulated action on the part of the U.S. government.

The first study that helped kindle the current worldwide interest in the effects of physical activity on important health outcomes was conducted in the 1950s in England. Dr. Jeremy Morris (Morris, Heady, Raffle, Roberts, & Parks, 1953) studied the frequency of heart disease in employees of the London bus companies. He found that drivers had significantly higher rates of heart attack than conductors. Although it was originally thought that differences in stress could explain the results, it is now widely believed that differences in daily physical activity on the job was the most critical factor. Drivers sat all day, but conductors constantly walked the aisles and climbed the stairs of the double-decker buses collecting fares.

This landmark study stimulated other investigators to examine physical activity on the job and during leisure time to determine its effects on health. As described in Chapters 2 and 3, there is a large body of evidence supporting the beneficial role of physical activity in preventing and treating a wide range of physical and psychological disorders. These studies, conducted throughout the industrialized world, have placed physical activity prominently on the health agendas of many nations, stimulated many other studies on physical activity, and prompted the need for this book.

Plan for This Book

The field of behavioral medicine is characterized by the close collaboration of interdisciplinary teams for research and intervention, and physical activity has become an excellent example of productive behavioral medicine research. The best physical activity research is often the result of partnerships among biomedical and physiological scientists, behavioral scientists, and public health professionals. The amount of research on physical activity has increased dramatically in the past 15 to 20 years, as epidemiological research has documented its strong influences on health. This research covers a wide range of issues, uses a variety of methods, and is far too extensive to cover in this small volume. Our plan for this book is to selectively highlight some of the best and most important research in physical activity rather than attempt to be exhaustive. This research is leading to changes in medical practice, public health programs, and government health policies related to physical activity, and we will describe some current approaches used to encourage people to be more physically active.

Because physical activity research covers a broad range of topics, from basic laboratory research to public health practice, we use a framework to help us understand the purpose of each phase of the research. We have used a behavioral epidemiology framework to organize this book. The purpose of traditional epidemiology is to understand the distribution and causes of diseases. Epidemiologists study who is most likely to have a disease and what factors cause the disease or place a person at risk for the disease. Traditional epidemiological research established that physical inactivity is a risk factor for heart disease and other conditions. Behavioral epidemiology is concerned with the distribution and etiology of behaviors linked with disease, so it takes up where traditional epidemiology leaves off (Jeffery, 1989). In the case of physical activity, we are interested in who is active, why they are active, and how we can use this information to help others be more active.

The Behavioral Epidemiology Framework

We propose five main phases of behavioral epidemiology research, as they may be applied to physical activity and health.

Phase 1: Establish the links between physical activity and health. This phase is complex, because different types and amounts of physical activity are probably related to different health benefits and risks (Haskell, 1994b). Once traditional epidemiology studies document the association between behavior and health, the research can proceed to the other phases of behavioral epidemiology. Phase 1 research is covered in Chapters 2, 3, and 4.

Phase 2: Develop methods for accurately measuring physical activity. Measurement of physical activity behavior is an ongoing challenge, but high-quality measures are essential for all types of research. Several types of measures are described in Chapter 5.

Phase 3: Identify factors that influence the level of physical activity. Describing the characteristics of those who are most and least active can be helpful in deciding which groups are most in need of interventions. Chapter 6 summarizes the physical activity patterns of important population subgroups. Chapter 7 reviews the research on physical activity determinants, which focuses on modifiable factors that may influence physical activity. The modifiable factors that are identified can then be targeted for change in interventions.

Phase 4: Evaluate interventions to promote physical activity. Because so many people in industrialized nations are not physically active enough, intervention programs need to be developed and tested. Chapter 8 contains examples of interventions designed for individuals and small groups, and Chapter 9 reviews interventions for communities.

Phase 5: Translate research into practice. In theory, each phase of the behavioral epidemiology framework builds on the previous phase. Phases 2 and 3 study the types of behaviors identified as most closely associated with health in Phase 1. Phase 4 targets the most sedentary groups and tries to change influences found to be most related to physical activity, identified in Phase 3. When interventions are shown to be effective in Phase 4, it is hoped that they will be used in worksites, schools, health care settings, fitness facilities, and the broader community environment. The use of effective programs in practice is discussed in Chapter 10.

If you have done much reading in physical activity, you have no doubt come across contradictory advice about training regimens, conflicting statements about the effects of exercise, and statements about benefits and risks that seem to be exaggerated. Some of the writing in the popular press on physical activity, exercise, and fitness is based on bad science, old science, or no science. In this book, we focus on the most influential and widely recognized studies as well as the most respected consensus statements about physical activity.

After reading this book, and some of the suggested readings, you will be well informed so you can judge the accuracy of statements made in magazines or on television. Although new findings about physical activity are released every week, and startling or controversial stories are emphasized in the press, certain basic principles and findings have been extensively studied over decades, and these basic facts are unlikely to change in the near future. Keeping these basic facts in mind will help you make your own assessment of headlines such as, "Too much exercise can kill you," and "New form of passive exercise is guaranteed to make you thin."

Early research on physical activity was guilty of being a "white man's science," because most of the research was conducted on middle-aged, middle-class white men or white college students. The composition of study samples has changed enormously over the past few years and now usually reflects diversity in gender, age, and ethnic group. In each chapter, we attempt to draw from studies of women, children, the elderly, and people from a variety of ethnic backgrounds and socioeconomic levels. Physical inactivity is a major health problem in most industrialized nations, so we have drawn examples of studies from multiple countries, primarily in North America, Australia, and Western Europe.

Terminology

As in any field, it is necessary to be clear on the meaning of key words. Table 1.1 contains the definitions most widely accepted in the field, as they

Table 1.1 Key Terms Used in This Book

Physical activity	"Any bodily movement produced by skeletal muscles that results in energy expenditure" (Caspersen, Powell, & Christenson, 1985)
Exercise	A subset of physical activity defined as "planned, structured, and repetitive bodily movement done to improve or maintain one or more components of physical fitness" (Caspersen et al., 1985)
Physical fitness	"A set of attributes that people have or achieve that relates to the ability to perform physical activity" (Caspersen et al., 1985)
Health-related fitness components	a. Cardiorespiratory endurance (also known as aerobic fitness) b. Muscular endurance c. Muscular strength d. Body composition e. Flexibility (Caspersen et al., 1985)
Performance-related fitness components	a. Muscular power b. Speed c. Agility d. Balance e. Reaction time (U.S. Department of Health and Human Services, 1996)
Moderate intensity physical activity	For young adults, activity requiring approximately 3 to 6 times as much energy as rest. Equivalent to brisk walking.
Vigorous intensity physical activity	For young adults, activity requiring 7 times as much energy as rest, or greater. Equivalent to jogging.
MET	Metabolic equivalent. Used as an index of the intensity of activities. 1 MET is resting energy expenditure (3.5 ml $O_2 \bullet kg^{-1} \bullet min^{-1}$), so 4 METs = four times the resting rate.

are used in this book. The terms *physical activity, exercise,* and *physical fitness* are often used incorrectly, so their differences need to be emphasized.

"Physical activity" is any bodily movement, but in this book, usually we are referring to the movements of large muscles, such as arms and legs, because these kinds of activities are most closely associated with health outcomes. Physical activity can be performed at a wide range of intensities. Physical activity is the primary topic of this book.

"Exercise" is a subset of physical activity distinguished by being done with the purpose of improving or maintaining physical fitness or health. Exercise can also be performed at a variety of intensities, although in popular use, exercise often means "vigorous exercise." However, walking at a moderate intensity can also be exercise, if it is done for the purpose of improving fitness or health.

"Physical fitness" is a physiological state or attribute, so it is not a behavior and should not be used interchangeably with physical activity or exercise. It is often considered that there are two types of fitness: health related and performance related. As health researchers, we are mainly interested in health-related components, whereas athletes are more likely to be concerned with performance-related components. However, health-related components are also important for performance.

SUMMARY

Probably for the first time in human history, millions of people are able to lead extremely sedentary lifestyles. We no longer have to be active to obtain food, earn a living, or transport ourselves. These lifestyles, however, extract a large cost in reduced quantity and quality of life. We believe that interdisciplinary behavioral medicine research has the potential not only to document the effects of sedentary living on health but also to provide us with the information needed to help people become active enough to protect their health. The behavioral epidemiology framework that we use to organize this book shows how research can help us move from identifying physical inactivity as a problem to understanding influences on behavior to developing and implementing effective interventions.

FURTHER READING

Bouchard, C., Shephard, R. J., & Stephens, T. (Eds.). (1994). *Physical activity, fitness, and health: International proceedings and consensus statement.* Champaign, IL: Human Kinetics.

This book is an "encyclopedia" of physical activity research with 72 chapters reviewing the effects of physical activity on many systems of the body and diseases.

Quinney, H. A., Gauvin, L., & Wall, E. T. (Eds.). (1994). *Toward active living.* Champaign, IL: Human Kinetics.

This is an excellent introduction to physical activity and health, covering physiological and behavioral aspects.

PART
II

Physical Activity and Health

Section Introduction

Launched to coincide with the 1996 Olympic Games in Atlanta, Georgia, the U.S. Surgeon General's report on physical activity and health (U.S. Department of Health and Human Services, 1996) has documented the current state of knowledge on the health benefits of physical activity. What is clear from the Surgeon General's report and from other recent authoritative sources, such as the National Institutes of Health Consensus Statement, is that there is now an extensive and scientifically strong body of evidence that physical activity has significant health benefits, particularly in the prevention of cardiovascular diseases, diabetes, and some cancers.

The material covered in Chapters 2 and 3 is the knowledge base on which all other behavioral epidemiology studies of physical activity are built. The evidence on the health benefits of activity makes clear that current efforts to promote higher levels of participation in physical activity are no longer based on wishful thinking. There is a large literature showing that physical inactivity is one of the most important causes of death, disability, and reduced quality of life in industrialized nations. The scientific base supporting physical activity initiatives is crucially important, because it gives credibility to efforts to promote active lifestyles. There is no need to make wild claims about the health benefits of physical activity, because many of the benefits are known and are impressive. We hope advocates who read this section will be able to use accurate scientific data to educate people about the health benefits of physical activity and to make the case that interventions are needed.

Physical Activity, Longevity, and Physical Health

The first step in the behavioral epidemiology framework is to establish the link between physical activity and health. There is no doubt that this has been accomplished. If physical activity did not affect health profoundly, there would be little need for this book. Chapter 2 summarizes current scientific understanding of the effects of physical activity and inactivity on a variety of indicators of physical health. Our intent is to highlight key studies rather than provide an exhaustive review.

Physical Activity and Longevity

Studies of longevity help answer the question of whether physical activity adds years to life. The consistent answer for women and men is that physical activity substantially reduces the risk of dying in any given year. Longevity is a very basic measure of health, and the fact that physically active people live longer than the sedentary means that the health benefits of physical activity outweigh the risks.

The most common type of longevity study assesses physical activity in a large group of healthy adults, then years later uses national death statistics to determine who died and the cause of death. The risk of dying for somewhat active or very active people is compared with the death rate of the most sedentary group, and the differences in rates of dying can be expressed as percentages. For example, the classic study of college alumni by Paffenbarger and colleagues (Paffenbarger, Hyde, Wing, & Hsieh, 1986) showed that mortality from all causes was reduced by 53% among men who played at least 3 hours of sports per week, compared with those who played less than 1 hour. In a finding that indicates important health benefits can be obtained from moderate-intensity activity, death rates were 33% lower among men who walked 15 or more kilometers a week, compared with men who walked less than 5 kilometers per week. When the life spans of active and inactive men were compared, it was found that the active men lived more than 2 years longer.

Because self-reports of physical activity are known to be somewhat inaccurate (see Chapter 5), some studies have examined the effect of cardiorespiratory fitness, usually assessed by endurance on the treadmill, on death rates. The most prominent example of this type of study is the work by Blair and colleagues who have studied a large group of adults who underwent physical examinations at the Cooper Clinic in Dallas. Studies using fitness measures typically show a stronger association between physical activity and health outcomes, probably because there is less error in fitness measures. Blair et al. (1989) found that the most fit men had a 71% lower death rate than the least fit men. It was not necessary to be in the highest-fitness group to have a health benefit. Even men in the next to lowest fitness group had a 60% lower rate of all-cause mortality than the least fit men. The Blair et al. (1989) study is also important because more than 3,000 women were studied. If anything, the protective effect of physical fitness appeared to be even stronger for women: The most fit had a 79% lower death rate than the least fit women. Women in the next to lowest fitness group had a 48% lower rate of all-cause mortality than the least fit women. These dramatic results indicate that physical activity and fitness decrease the risk of dying to a major degree in both women and men. However, these kinds of simple epidemiological studies do not answer all the questions.

The relationship of physical fitness or activity with longevity could be due to some other factor, such as family history of disease or obesity. It is possible that not all people experience the protective effect of physical activity. However, several studies show that virtually all groups of people benefit from being fit and active. Blair et al. (1996) found lower all-cause mortality in higher-fitness groups whether they smoked or not, had high cholesterol or not, had high blood pressure or not, and whether or not they were healthy or unhealthy at the baseline examination. Both men and women in the higher-fitness groups had lower death rates than the low-fit group, whether they were overweight or not, had high blood glucose or not, or had a family history of heart disease or not (Blair et al., 1989). Many years ago, Paffenbarger and colleagues (Paffenbarger, Wing, & Hyde, 1978) published a study showing the benefits of physical activity in reducing risk of coronary heart disease applied to all risk groups. Thus, it is clear that physical activity and fitness can improve health for women and men, regardless of their family history and risk factor status. For example, smokers who are unable to quit smoking can still improve their health by becoming physically active.

Another criticism of the early epidemiological studies was that although physical activity was measured only once, it actually can change over time. Stronger evidence that physical activity and fitness *cause* health improvements would come from studies showing that changes in physical activity predict changes in risk of all-cause mortality. Again, Paffenbarger, Hyde, et al. (1993) were the first to examine this question. The 10,000 men in their study reported their physical activity in the 1960s and again in 1977. Their mortality status was determined in 1985. Compared with men who were inactive at both assessments, those who became active decreased their risk of dying by 15%. Those who were active at the first assessment but became inactive at the second assessment increased their risk of dying by 10%. Men who became active gained, on average 0.72 years of life, and this compared with a gain of 1.46 years for those who quit smoking. These gains in longevity from becoming physically active were seen in all age groups, from 45 to 84. A Swedish study of more than 1,000 women found that those who decreased their physical activity had a 207% higher death rate than those who did not change their activity levels (Lissner, Bengtsson, Bjorkelund, & Wedel, 1996).

Blair, Kohl, et al. (1995) examined this question with their fitness study, and their results confirm the physical activity data. Men who went from unfit to fit between two examinations reduced their death rates by 44%, compared with men who were unfit at both exams. This protective effect of increasing fitness was seen in all ages of men. From these studies it can be concluded that increasing physical activity and fitness in adulthood improves longevity.

This is cause for optimism because it indicates that changes in physical activity at any age can be helpful.

Now that numerous studies have documented that physical activity can reduce all-cause mortality, a remaining question is how much activity is needed for this health benefit. Figure 2.1 summarizes the results of several studies. All of them indicate that the more physical activity one does (or the more fit one is), the lower one's risk of dying. However, almost all these studies demonstrate that the greatest benefits are seen between the least active or fit group and the next most active or fit group. These consistent findings, that even a modest amount of physical activity can be protective, have led to new physical activity recommendations stressing the public health value of moderate intensities and amounts of physical activity (Pate, Pratt, et al., 1995; U.S. Department of Health and Human Services [DHHS], 1996).

Physical Inactivity's Contribution to the Burden of Disease and Premature Death

Another way of putting the health effects of sedentary lifestyles in perspective is to estimate the number of deaths that inactivity is responsible for. This figure, called the "population attributable risk," is based on relative risk associated with inactivity and the prevalence of inactivity in the population. Inactivity is a major risk factor for some of the most common causes of death. For example, being inactive doubles one's risk of coronary heart disease. In addition, physical inactivity is very common, with more than half of the population getting less activity than recommended. Because of the combination of high relative risk and high prevalence, the population attributable risk of physical inactivity is large. Hahn, Teutsch, Rothenberg, and Marks (1990) estimated the effects of several risk factors on death from nine common chronic diseases, such as coronary heart disease, stroke, diabetes, and several cancers. They estimated that 256,686 deaths in the United States in 1986 could have been prevented if the risk factor of physical inactivity was eliminated. This figure amounts to 23% of all deaths. For purposes of comparison, 33% of deaths were attributable to smoking, 23% to high blood cholesterol levels, 24% to obesity, 1% to alcohol, and 1% to not using mammography. This study shows that physical inactivity should be considered one of the most important health problems, deserving the same level of concern as smoking, blood cholesterol, and obesity.

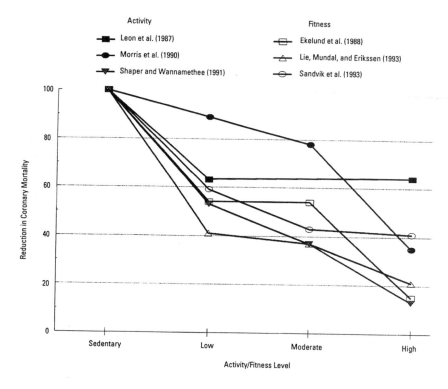

Figure 2.1. Summary of the results from six studies in which fitness level was determined (three studies) or activity level assessed by questionnaire (three studies) in individual populations. Follow-up was generally between 7 and 9 years except that of Sandvik et al. (1993), which had a 15-year follow-up. The *low*-level group for each study represented in this figure was the activity/fitness level next to the least active/fit group. The *high* level represents the group that was the most active/fit for the particular study. If the study participants were grouped by quintile, the *moderate* group is the average of the 3rd and 4th quintiles.

SOURCE: Figure 1 from Blair and Connelly (1996, p. 197). Used with permission.

Physical Activity and Cardiovascular Diseases

Physical activity reduces all-cause mortality primarily by decreasing risk of cardiovascular diseases, which are the most common cause of death in the world, particularly in industrialized nations. The underlying disease process is the buildup of atherosclerotic plaques in the arteries that eventually block blood flow. If blood flow is interrupted in arteries that feed the heart, this is termed *coronary heart disease,* and the result can be a myocardial infarction. If the blocked artery is in the brain, this causes a *stroke,* and if a blockage occurs in the legs, it called *peripheral artery disease.* Twelve prospective epidemiological studies show that physical activity and fitness reduce deaths from total cardiovascular diseases (U.S. DHHS, 1996).

Coronary heart disease is the most deadly form of cardiovascular disease, and there is overwhelming evidence that physical activity is an important protective factor. In the U.S. Surgeon General's report (U.S. DHHS, 1996), 36 studies were reviewed, with almost all showing the protective effect of physical activity. A meta-analysis of this area found that the least active or fit study participants had an 80% higher risk of dying from coronary heart disease than the most active or fit group (Berlin & Colditz, 1990). There is a strong dose-response relationship between activity level and risk of coronary heart disease. With each increase in physical activity, there is a decrease in risk, and the largest risk reduction occurs when moving from the sedentary category to some activity (U.S. DHHS, 1996). It is estimated that 35% of deaths from coronary heart disease are attributable to sedentary living, and if the Healthy People 2000 (U.S. DHHS, 1991) goals for the nation were achieved, the population attributable risk would decline modestly to 30% (Powell & Blair, 1994).

Similar to findings for all-cause mortality, changes in physical activity have been shown to affect risk of cardiovascular diseases. Men who were unfit at baseline but increased their fitness later were found to reduce their risk of cardiovascular diseases by 52%, compared with men who were unfit at both examinations (Blair, Kohl, et al., 1995). Paffenbarger, Hyde, et al. (1993) reported a 41% decline in mortality from coronary heart disease in initially sedentary men who adopted moderately vigorous exercise, compared with men who remained sedentary. These studies provide more evidence for the hypothesis that physical activity causes cardiovascular diseases. However, these studies need to be conducted with women.

Physical Activity and Risk Factors for Cardiovascular Diseases

Some of the epidemiological studies find that statistically adjusting for other cardiovascular disease risk factors reduces the strength of the association between activity and mortality rates (U.S. DHHS, 1996). This indicates that some of the protective effects are due to beneficial influences of physical activity on risk factors.

Prospective studies have shown that participation in vigorous sports reduces risk of developing hypertension by 19% to 30% in men (Paffenbarger et al., 1983), and physically active women were 30% less likely than sedentary women to develop hypertension (Folsom et al., 1990). In studies of the effects of aerobic exercise in hypertensive patients, the average reduction is a substantial 6 to 7 mm Hg in both systolic and diastolic blood pressures (Kelley & McClellan, 1994). Even a single episode of physical activity temporarily lowers blood pressure by dilating blood vessels, and longer-term exercise training lowers blood pressure by reducing sympathetic nervous system activation (Fagard & Tipton, 1994).

There is great interest in the ability of physical activity to affect blood lipids, which are strongly connected with the development of atherosclerotic plaque in the arteries. Physical activity does not reliably affect total cholesterol or low-density lipoproteins (LDL). However, of 60 studies, about half found that physical activity increases high-density lipoproteins (HDL; Stefanick & Wood, 1994). Male and female endurance athletes are typically found to have HDL levels 20% to 30% higher than those of sedentary persons of similar age. HDL reduces risk for cardiovascular diseases by transporting cholesterol from the blood vessels to the liver for elimination. Even a single episode of physical activity can raise HDL for several days (Durstine & Haskell, 1994). A large study of women runners found that HDL was strongly related to the distance run. Thus, the longer these women ran, the higher their HDL levels, so additional benefits were gained from very high rates of exercise (Williams, 1996). Physical activity also reduces levels of triglycerides, fats in the blood that raise the risk of cardiovascular diseases (Durstine & Haskell, 1994).

Physical Activity and Prevention of Obesity

Physical Activity and Body Fat

Overweight and obesity have been linked to a variety of diseases, including cardiovascular diseases, hypertension, and cancers. Although obesity, or excess body fat, is believed to be the most important factor for health effects, most large studies actually assess overweight using some measure of weight adjusted for height. Body mass index, computed as weight (in kilograms) divided by height^2 (in meters), is the most common way of expressing overweight. Obesity is a common health problem, and prevalence rates are increasing worldwide in industrialized nations. In the United States, about 25% of adults were overweight in the 1970s, but that figure rose to 33% in the early 1990s (Kuczmarski, Flegal, Campbell, & Johnson, 1994). Similar changes are seen for children. If the 95th percentile of body mass index for children in the United States in 1963 is taken as a standard, then 10.9% of children in the early 1990s are overweight; more than a doubling of the rate (Troiano, Flegal, Kuczmarski, Campbell, & Johnson, 1995). Studies of Australian school children document a steady increase in average body mass index from 1913 until 1970 (Dwyer & Grey, 1994). These increases in the prevalence of being overweight apply to males and females of all ethnic groups and socioeconomic strata. However, ethnic minority women have the highest prevalence rates, with 49% of African American women and 47% of Mexican American women being overweight (DiPietro, 1995).

Excess body fat is believed to develop from an imbalance of energy intake and expenditure. Genetic and metabolic factors also influence the accumulation of body fat. In children and adults, there are conflicting findings on whether overweight people are less active than normal-weight people (DiPietro, 1995; Grilo, 1995; Stefanick, 1993). The inconsistent results from cross-sectional studies may be due to inaccurate measurement of physical activity, failure to take dietary factors into account, or the fact that many overweight people are using exercise to manage their weight.

Prospective studies generally support the idea that physical activity reduces risk of becoming overweight. In a large Finnish study, men and women who rarely exercised were twice as likely to have a major weight gain over 5 years, compared with frequent exercisers (Rissanen, Heliovaara, Knekt, Reunanen, & Aromaa, 1991). A study of weight gain over 10 years in adults found that men and women who reported physical activity at both baseline and follow-up gained significantly less weight than inactive adults (Kahn et al., 1997). On the other hand, another study of 10-year weight changes in a representative sample of U.S. adults had mixed findings (Williamson et al., 1993). Women and men who were active at baseline and follow-up gained much less weight than those who were inactive at both measurement points. Women and men who decreased their physical activity gained much more weight than those who did not change their activity levels, which supports an interpretation that physical activity protects from weight gain. Surprisingly, both women and men who reported increases in their activity gained more weight than the adults whose activity levels did not change. This last finding does not support the hypothesis and illustrates the difficulty of drawing conclusions from existing studies.

There are many known physiological mechanisms by which physical activity should prevent the development of obesity (Stefanick, 1993). Chronic exercise can improve the body's ability to burn fat as fuel and can reduce fat cell size. Exercise can also stimulate modest increases in metabolic rate following exercise, and it builds or maintains lean body tissue that enhances metabolic rate, but the overall effect of exercise on resting metabolic rate is unclear (Grilo, 1995).

There is more consistent evidence that exercise alters the distribution of fat by selectively mobilizing "central" fat. Regardless of the total amount of body fat, central or abdominal fat is more health damaging than fat stored on the periphery, such as buttocks and thighs. Men are more likely to have central fat, and women tend to store fat peripherally. Waist-to-hip ratio is a common index of fat distribution, with higher ratios indicating higher risk. Epidemiological and clinical studies now show exercise reduces waist-to-hip ratio among women and men (Kahn et al., 1997; Stefanick, 1993).

Fitness or Fatness?

It is well accepted by health professionals that obesity causes a wide variety of health problems and shortens the life span. Intriguing new data have led this truism to be questioned. A study of men examined at the Cooper Clinic confirmed that overweight men died sooner than lean men (Barlow, Kohl, Gibbons, & Blair, 1995). The investigators went a step further than all other studies and examined whether aerobic fitness explained the health effects of obesity. The somewhat revolutionary finding was that fit men had the same risk of dying, no matter what their overweight status was. That means fit overweight men lived just as long as fit thin men. There was a protective effect of fitness within each weight group. Thus, within the overweight group, the high-fit men reduced their risk of dying by 71%, compared with the low-fit overweight men. Similarly, in the lean group, the high-fit men reduced their risk of dying by 66%, compared with the low-fit lean men. It is important to see if these findings also apply to women.

Like other studies of the protective effects of fitness, the authors interpret the findings as suggesting a protective effect of physical activity (Barlow et al., 1995). These provocative results indicate that overweight people can benefit greatly from being active and increasing their fitness, even if they do not lose weight.

Physical Activity and Weight Loss

Grilo (1995) summarized a large literature on the contribution of physical activity to the treatment of obesity. Exercise alone typically produces modest weight loss of around 3 kg. Weight loss is more for males than females. Weight loss from exercise is less than expected, in part because high-intensity exercise increases muscle mass, which weighs more than fat. The small weight loss from exercise can lead to multiple health benefits, but it is unsatisfying to many obese people who desire greater weight loss.

Most studies show that dietary restriction plus exercise produces more initial weight loss than diet alone (Grilo, 1995). However, the exercise component enhances the effect of diet only a small amount. An important role of exercise in weight loss is to preserve muscle mass, because dieting alone leads to substantial reduction in muscle. Exercise also enhances fat loss. Thus, it is well accepted that the combination of dietary restriction and regular exercise should be used in weight loss efforts.

In contrast to the weak effects of exercise on weight loss, physical activity is the best predictor of weight loss *maintenance*. This has been shown in many studies (Grilo, 1995). For example, of the few women who successfully maintained their weight loss, 90% reported regular physical activity (Kayman, Bruvold, & Stern, 1990). Physical activity improves weight loss maintenance in combination with either balanced diets or very low calorie diets. Several impressive studies by Epstein and colleagues (Epstein, Valoski, Wing, & McCurley, 1994) show that physical activity improves weight management more than 10 years after the treatment of obese children.

There is growing interest in the contributions of resistance training (e.g., weight lifting) to weight control, because resistance training increases metabolically active muscle tissue. However, few studies have examined the weight loss effects of resistance training. One study found that women in the strength training group had greater reductions in resting energy expenditure than did those in the aerobic exercise group. However, at the 1-year measurement, there were no benefits of either type of exercise, compared with diet only, on weight loss or fat loss (Wadden et al., 1997).

The key to physical activity's effect on obesity prevention and treatment may be the long-term continuation of even modest activity levels. Walking a mile takes 15 to 20 minutes and burns about 100 calories. This small energy expenditure will not lead to rapid weight loss. However, walking 1 mile per day for a year should lead to a weight loss of about 5 kg (11 pounds) (Stefanick, 1993).

Physical Activity and Diabetes

Diabetes mellitus is a group of diseases characterized by excessive levels of glucose in the blood and inability of insulin to metabolize glucose. Non-insulin-dependent diabetes mellitus (NIDDM) accounts for about 90% of all diabetes cases. In developed nations, between 3% and 6% of adults are diagnosed with NIDDM, but almost as many more may have undiagnosed disease (Kriska, Blair, & Pereira, 1994). Rates are much higher for non-Caucasian populations, and rates are 40% to 80% higher for women than men (Gudat, Berger, & Lefebvre, 1994). NIDDM leads to blindness and kidney disease, but its primary health effect is as a risk factor for cardiovascular diseases. The combination of genetic susceptibility and obesity, especially central obesity, leads to NIDDM, and it can be reversed through weight loss. NIDDM is not a problem of insufficient insulin production. Rather, NIDDM is a problem of inadequate uptake of insulin by receptors, known as insulin resistance.

Physical activity is believed to be useful in the prevention and treatment of NIDDM owing to two mechanisms. First, physical activity reduces blood glucose and enhances sensitivity of receptors to insulin. This is partly because active muscles use glucose as fuel. Second, physical activity can reduce central obesity. Several prospective studies show that physical activity reduces risk of developing NIDDM. An 8-year study of 87,000 female nurses indicated about a 15% reduction in risk for those who exercised vigorously at least once a week, compared with those who did not exercise (Manson et al., 1991). A 5-year study of male physicians revealed about a 25% reduction in risk for those who exercised vigorously at least once a week, compared with those who did not exercise (Manson et al., 1992). In both of these studies, the active group weighed less than the inactive group, supporting this as one mechanism by which physical activity prevents NIDDM. It is estimated that physical inactivity accounts for about 35% of deaths from NIDDM (Powell & Blair, 1994).

Physical activity is part of the accepted treatment regimen for NIDDM, along with dietary changes and weight loss. Physical activity is sometimes said to be as effective in reducing blood glucose levels as a dose of insulin, and physical activity has a particularly important role to play in long-term weight management.

One of the most dramatic examples of a comprehensive NIDDM treatment that included activity was conducted with Australian Aboriginals (O'Dea, 1991). Before European contact, Aboriginals were nomadic hunter-gatherers, so their lifestyles were active and their diets were low in fat. When Aboriginals make the transition to Western lifestyles, they are particularly vulnerable to obesity and NIDDM. Rates for NIDDM are two to six times higher for Aboriginals than for Australians of European descent. O'Dea and colleagues evaluated 10 diabetic Aboriginals as they reverted to traditional lifestyles for 7 weeks. They ate foods such as kangaroo meat, which is very lean, and did physical activity every day. The Aboriginals lost about 1 kilogram per week, and in just 7 weeks, their fasting glucose and insulin levels decreased by about 50%. They also had substantial decreases in blood triglycerides and blood pressure (O'Dea, 1991). This study implies that some elements of traditional lifestyles need to be adopted by people in industrialized nations to reduce the toll of chronic diseases.

Physical Activity and Cancers

Cancer is the second leading cause of death in many industrialized nations. The most common cancers are of the lung, breast, prostate, and colon. Cancer is actually a large number of different diseases, and each is likely to have somewhat different causal factors. Thus, it makes sense to examine any protective effects of physical activity for specific types of cancer. The hypothesis that physical activity has cancer-protective effects has been studied since the early 20th century when it was observed that amount of physical activity on the job was related to cancer risk (Lee, 1994).

Over 30 studies of colon and rectal cancer have been conducted. There is a clear and consistent association with colon cancer, and it has been estimated that 32% of these deaths can be attributed to inactive lifestyles (Powell & Blair, 1994). This is the strongest evidence that physical activity reduces risk of developing a specific cancer. There is no association with rectal cancer (Friedenreich & Rohan, 1995; Lee, 1994; U.S. DHHS, 1996).

There is some evidence that physical activity may protect from breast cancer in women and prostate cancer in men, but either the evidence is too limited or there are conflicting studies (Lee, 1994; U.S. DHHS, 1996). Numerous mechanisms by which physical activity could reduce risk of cancers have been documented in human and animal studies. The existence of these mechanisms justifies further research. There is now a large literature showing that moderate exercise has a beneficial effect on immune functioning (Woods & Davis, 1994), and the immune system is a key part of the body's defenses from cancer. The most likely mechanism for reducing colon cancer risk is that physical activity can reduce the length of time fecal matter stays in the intestines, known as transit time (Oettle, 1991). Reducing transit time means that carcinogenic compounds in foods have less contact with the intestinal wall. Physical activity may reduce risk of reproductive cancers by altering hormone levels, and it has been shown that exercise training can lower estrogen and progesterone levels related to breast cancer risk in women and can reduce testosterone levels related to prostate cancer risk in men (Richter & Sutton, 1994).

Physical Activity and Osteoporosis

Osteoporosis occurs when the bones lose so much calcium that they are fragile and at risk of fracturing. Bone mineral density increases during youth, reaches a peak in young adulthood, and declines during the middle and later adult years. The peak bone mass and rate of decline determine the risk of osteoporosis, and both of these are believed to be affected by physical activity. Osteoporosis is a particular problem in postmenopausal women, because the cessation of estrogen accelerates the loss of bone minerals (Drinkwater, 1994).

It is known that heredity and dietary intake of calcium are related to skeletal health, but there is substantial evidence that physical activity promotes the absorption of calcium by bone tissue (Bailey, Faulkner, & McKay, 1996). To promote bone growth, physical activity must stress the bone by applying loads (i.e., weights) or working against gravity. It is believed that this stress stimulates the bone to absorb calcium to strengthen itself, much as stressing the muscles with weights stimulates muscle development. Thus, weight lifting, running, and aerobics are likely to promote bone growth, whereas swimming and aqua aerobics will not. There is substantial evidence that in women, physical activity does not enhance bone mineral density except in the presence of estrogen. Thus, amenorrheic and postmenopausal women who are not taking estrogen supplements are not likely to strengthen their bones through exercise (Drinkwater, 1994).

There is a great deal of epidemiological evidence indicating that physical activity improves bone density, but there are no experimental studies proving that increasing physical activity reduces risk of fractures. There is reason to believe that physical activity over the lifetime is important for preventing osteoporosis. For example, reported lifetime physical activity was associated with high bone mineral density for older women and men in the hip but not for other bone sites (Greendale, Barrett-Connor, Edelstein, Ingles, & Haile, 1995). Previous physical activity was related to bone density at several sites in young women aged 18 to 31 (Teegarden et al., 1996), supporting the hypothesis that physical activity is important in the development of peak bone mass. A study of older women found that working for 20 or more years in a job requiring moderate to heavy physical activity, as well as current leisure activity habits, both dramatically reduced risk of hip fractures (Jaglal, Kreiger, & Darlington, 1995). In addition to strengthening bones, physical activity, including resistance exercise, may reduce risk of fractures by improving muscle strength and balance, which may act to prevent falls, especially in the elderly (U.S. DHHS, 1996).

Physical Activity and Functioning in the Elderly

Elderly people are most likely to experience the effects of decades of sedentary lifestyles. Long periods of not using muscles is believed to lead to an inability to engage in what are called "activities of daily living." When older people lose endurance capacity and muscular strength, they may have trouble walking enough to do their shopping, climbing a flight of stairs, getting up from a chair, or even carrying bags of groceries. This loss of functional ability used to be thought of as a normal part of aging, but new research is confirming that loss of function is a result of inactivity. More important, exercise can dramatically improve elderly people's ability to do activities of daily living (Green & Crouse, 1995).

DiPietro (1996) reviews several recent epidemiological studies indicating that physically active older people have higher levels of function than those who lead sedentary lives. Active elderly were found to be 20% to 50% less likely to have a decline in functional ability over time. All types of activities helped elderly people retain their function, including walking, gardening, and vigorous exercise.

It used to be thought that it was dangerous for elderly people to do strenuous activities. A landmark study showed that even very old people can make dramatic improvements in functional ability by doing strenuous resistance training (Fiatarone et al., 1994). The researchers randomized a group of nursing home residents, with a mean age of 87 years, to participate in resistance training or other conditions. After only 10 weeks, the weight lifters increased their strength by more than 100%. More important, they had substantial improvements in walking speed and stair-climbing ability. They spontaneously started doing more physical activity. It looks like physical activity can greatly enhance the functional ability and quality of life for older people, so regular physical activity should be strongly promoted for this group.

As well as beneficially influencing aerobic fitness and strength in older adults, physical activity interventions can have beneficial effects on balance in older people, which has important implications for reducing rates of injuries from falls. For example, Hopkins, Murrah, Hoeger, and Rhodes (1990) randomly assigned women aged 55 to 75 years to a control group or to a 12-week exercise program in which they did three 20-minute aerobic dance and stretching sessions per week. The women in the exercise group significantly increased their cardiovascular fitness, strength, balance, and flexibility. Lord, Caplan, and Ward (1993) conducted gentle aerobic exercise classes for 1 hour twice a week over 52 weeks with a group of older women. They found significantly improved quadriceps strength, reaction time, and sway on a compliant surface compared with an age-matched group of sedentary women.

Physical Activity and Low-Back Function

Low-back pain will be experienced by up to 80% of men and women, and for some this is a chronic problem. There is reason to believe that physical activity should reduce risk of low-back pain by strengthening the muscles that stabilize the spine, maintaining flexibility, and reducing body fat to decrease the load on the spine. Unfortunately, the ability of physical activity to prevent low-back pain has not been studied very much, and there is no convincing evidence of a protective effect (Plowman, 1992). Nevertheless, most experts recommend doing exercises to maintain the strength and flexibility of muscles in the abdomen and lower back.

Resistance training, more commonly known as weight training, is effective at increasing muscle mass and strength at most ages. The general recommendation for resistance training is to perform one set of 8 to 12 repetitions of 8 to 12 exercises two or three times per week for persons under 50 years; persons more than 50 years old should do the same regimen using 10 to 15 repetitions (American College of Sports Medicine [ACSM], 1990). Only recently have the health benefits of resistance training been considered, and limited evidence indicates multiple benefits. These are summarized by Pollock and Vincent (1996). Epidemiological studies suggest that resistance training may help reduce risk for falls in the elderly and decrease the extent of injuries from falls. There are theoretical reasons to believe that improving strength of abdominal and back muscles may prevent low-back pain. Both resistance training and weight-bearing endurance exercise increase bone mineral density. Most resistance training programs do not enhance cardiorespiratory endurance at all, mainly because 1 to 2 minutes of rest is taken between each exercise. However, circuit exercise with moderate weights and brief rests (10 to 15 seconds) between each exercise can increase VO_{2max} by 5% to 8%. Several studies show that resistance training leads to a decrease in body fat while increasing lean body weight. Resistance training can also increase resting metabolic rate, which should help control body fat. The effect of resistance training on insulin sensitivity and decreasing blood glucose seems particularly strong, so it may be very helpful in the management of diabetes. Although there are some conflicting findings, it appears that heavy resistance training may improve blood lipid profiles (Pollock & Vincent, 1996; Tucker & Silvester, 1996).

In summary, evidence is rapidly accumulating that resistance training can provide numerous health benefits. This evidence was strong enough to lead to a recommendation in the 1996 U.S. Surgeon General's report (U.S. DHHS, 1996) that resistance training should be included as part of an overall physical activity program.

Physical Activity, Psychoneuroimmunology, and HIV

Psychoneuroimmunology (PNI) is the study of the interrelations between psychological variables, the nervous system, and the immune system

(LaPerriere et al., 1994). The most often studied psychological factors are stress, coping with stress, and emotions or states such as depression and anxiety. Evidence is beginning to emerge that physical activity can favorably affect the immune system to reduce the risk of respiratory tract infections and improve the psychological and physical status of patients with the human immunodeficiency virus (HIV).

Several lines of evidence suggest that physical activity may be an important means for enhancing immune system functioning (LaPerriere et al., 1994). First, negative emotional states are associated with decreased immune functioning, and physical activity improves conditions such as depression and anxiety. Second, stress hormones such as cortisol and catecholamines appear to impair immune functioning, and physical activity is known to reduce levels of these stress hormones. Third, it is believed that endogenous opioids (i.e., endorphins) influence the immune system, and exercise is known to stimulate the release of endorphins. Fourth, exercise itself has been shown to have direct effects on immune functioning. The general findings are that moderate-intensity exercise enhances immunity and vigorous exercise suppresses the immune system.

LaPerriere and colleagues (1994) propose that exercise training may reduce negative emotions, increase endorphin levels, reduce stress hormones, and enhance immunity. These multiple pathways may produce significant improvements in health status and rate of disease progression in patients with HIV infections. A number of studies have been conducted to evaluate the effect of exercise on patients with HIV, but studies have not been conducted on patients with active symptoms of AIDS. In several controlled studies, exercise has improved numbers of immune cells, such as CD4, and improved psychological health. No studies showed any negative effects of exercise on HIV patients (LaPerriere et al., 1994). Physical activity and PNI is a very active area of research, and our understanding of the effects of exercise on immune-related diseases such as respiratory tract infections and HIV is expected to improve greatly in the next few years.

Health Risks of Physical Activity

Like most issues in health and medicine, the benefits and risks of physical activity must be considered. Although it is well established that the benefits of physical activity outweigh the risks (U.S. DHHS, 1996), it is important to be informed about the risks. A range of health problems have been attributed to physical activity and sports, including numerous musculoskeletal injuries, dehydration and hypothermia from exercise in extreme weather conditions, amenorrhea in women, anemia in athletes, and suppression of immune functioning after very high intensity exercise. Cyclists, runners, and walkers who do their activities near traffic are at risk for collisions with vehicles, and attacks from animals and humans are possible. In susceptible people, exercise can trigger asthma attacks and cardiac events (U.S. DHHS, 1996). However, the rate at which these adverse events occur has not been well studied. Although osteoarthritis is frequently attributed to physical activity, especially to jogging, there is no evidence that exercise increases the risk for this condition. On the contrary, physical activity appears to promote normal functioning of joints and help relieve symptoms of osteoarthritis (U.S. DHHS, 1996).

Most of the studies of the health risks have dealt with musculoskeletal injuries and cardiac events (Pate & Macera, 1994). The risk of musculoskeletal injuries depends on the specific activity as well as the frequency, intensity, and duration at which it is performed. Most injuries can be described as overuse injuries, so one way of reducing risk of a variety of injuries is to follow health-related physical activity recommendations (ACSM, 1990; Pate, Pratt, et al., 1995). For example, between 35% and 65% of runners will have some type of injury, mainly to the knee, foot, and ankle. Most of these are minor and self-correcting, and the risk is strongly related to running mileage (Pate & Macera, 1994). Aerobic dance is a popular form of activity, and injury rates are high, with about 50% of participants and 75% of instructors reporting injuries. However, these injuries rarely prevent participation for very long. Aerobic dancers who participated four times per week had higher injury rates than those who went to classes less frequently (Pate & Macera, 1994). Walking is the most commonly reported form of physical activity, and it appears to have a very low injury rate.

In persons with underlying heart disease, physical activity can trigger chest pain or even a myocardial infarction. Risk of cardiac events is increased during exercise, because there is additional stress on the heart and circulatory system. However, because physical activity strengthens the heart and has many other cardiovascular benefits, risk of cardiac events is greatly reduced in nonexercise time, which makes up the great majority of the day. The net result is that physical activity reduces the risk of coronary heart disease by at least half (Kohl, Powell, Gordon, Blair, & Paffenbarger, 1992). Cardiac

Table 2.1 Summary of the Effects of Physical Activity on Health Outcomes in Adults

Health Outcome	Summary of Association
Longevity	⇑⇑⇑
Coronary heart disease	⇓⇓⇓
HDL cholesterol	⇑⇑
LDL cholesterol	0
Blood pressure	⇓⇓
Body fat	⇓⇓
Central body fat	⇓⇓
Non-insulin-dependent diabetes mellitus	⇓⇓⇓
Insulin sensitivity	⇑⇑
Colon cancer	⇓⇓
Breast cancer	⇓
Prostate cancer	⇔
Bone mineral density	⇑⇑
Activities of daily living in the elderly	⇑⇑
Low-back pain	0
Osteoarthritis	⇓
Immune functioning	⇑⇑
Musculoskeletal injuries	⇑

KEY: 0 = no association; ⇔ = inconsistent association or very limited data; ⇑ = some evidence that physical activity increases this variable; ⇑⇑ = moderate evidence that physical activity increases this variable; ⇑⇑⇑ = strong evidence from many studies that physical activity increases this variable; ⇓ = some evidence that physical activity decreases this variable; ⇓⇓ = moderate evidence that physical activity decreases this variable; ⇓⇓⇓ = strong evidence from many studies that physical activity decreases this variable.

patients need to gradually increase their physical activity to train the cardiovascular system and avoid unnecessary risk.

Physical activity has a number of significant health and disease prevention benefits for adults, as well as some risks. It seems clear that the benefits outweigh the risk, particularly if current physical activity and health guidelines (described in Chapter 4) are followed. Table 2.1 provides a summary of what is known about the main effects of physical activity on health outcomes in adults.

Physical Activity and the Health of Children and Adolescents

Physical activity may influence the health of children and adolescents in two ways. First, physical activity could affect causes of morbidity during youth, but physical activity would not be expected to have effects on mortality during youth. Examples of effects on morbidity could be reducing overweight, reducing psychological stress, enhancing athletic performance through increased fitness, and reducing colds through immunologic changes. Second, physical activity during youth could reduce risk for chronic diseases of adulthood. This is a feasible effect, because several common chronic diseases, particularly coronary heart disease and osteoporosis, are known to have their beginnings in childhood. The literature on health effects of physical activity in youth is much less extensive than the adult literature. There are very few studies on health effects in younger children. This section draws on systematic reviews of health effects of physical activity during adolescence, defined here as ages 11 to 21 (Sallis, 1994).

Three health outcomes that have relevance during the teen years have been studied sufficiently to make some summary statements: aerobic fitness, adiposity and obesity, and sports and recreational injuries. Psychological health is also a potential health benefit during youth, but these findings are discussed in Chapter 3.

Aerobic, or cardiorespiratory, fitness has relevance for both current and future health of adolescents. Adolescents value their athletic abilities, so to the extent that aerobic fitness increases these abilities, it contributes to quality of life. As shown earlier in this chapter, aerobic fitness is a potent determinant of health and longevity in adults, so it is possible that aerobic fitness during youth may have some long-term protective effects. However, no long-term effects of aerobic fitness in youth have been documented. Morrow and Freedson (1994) reviewed the association between physical activity and aerobic fitness in youth. They summarized the results of 20 studies that reported 53 correlations between physical activity and aerobic fitness in free-living populations. The median correlation was $r = .17$, indicating that physical activity accounts for only about 3% of the variance in aerobic fitness. This low association may be the result of (a) poor measurement of physical activity, often by self-report; (b) generally high levels of fitness in adolescents, compared with adults; and (c) true lack of correlation. These authors concluded that because of their high levels of fitness, high-intensity regular exercise is needed to increase aerobic fitness in adolescents.

Reducing perceived overweight is consistently identified as a significant concern for adolescents, so this can be viewed as a quality-of-life and a health issue. Adiposity is also related to chronic disease risk in adulthood, so any effect of physical activity on adiposity in youth may have implications for both current and future health. Bar-Or and Baranowski (1994) reviewed observational and intervention studies. Numerous cross-sectional and prospective observational studies show conflicting findings. Some show that adiposity is negatively correlated with physical activity, and some show no relationship. These discrepancies may have to do with poor assessment of physical activity, assessment of only selected activities such as sports, or flawed designs. Several studies reported physical activity only as total energy expenditure. This is a problem because heavier adolescents expend more energy than lighter ones when they do the same activity. Thus, a heavy adolescent could have a higher energy expenditure value than a more active, but lighter, peer.

Although the relationship between physical activity and adiposity of youth is inconsistent, measures of sedentary behaviors and adiposity are very consistently related. Numerous studies show that children who watch more television have more body fat than children who spend less time in front of the set (Andersen, Crespo, Bartlett, Cheskin, & Pratt, 1998; Dietz & Gortmaker, 1985; Robinson et al., 1993). This effect is seen in boys and girls, but it is possible that eating while watching television is partially responsible for the association. Of U.S. children, 26% watch 4 or more hours of television per day, but 42% of African American children watch 4 or more hours of television per day (Andersen et al., 1998). However, none of these studies assessed other sedentary behaviors, such as video games or computer use. To understand children's adiposity, it is important to consider both physical activity and sedentary behaviors.

Interventions with overweight youth that permit a specific assessment of the effects of physical activity typically show poor results on weight loss but modest effects on reduction of body fat, averaging 1.6% loss of body fat. A few studies suggest that physical activity interventions need to be more than 1 year in length to be effective (Bar-Or & Baranowski, 1994). The treatment studies also show that increased physical activity, without changes in diet, are likely to be ineffective. However, adding physical activity to diet programs improves the maintenance of weight loss (Epstein, Myers, Raynor, & Saelens,

1998). There is some evidence that lifestyle physical activity programs that encourage the child to integrate activity into daily routines are more effective in producing weight loss than is structured exercise (Epstein et al., 1998). No studies have examined whether physical activity prevents excess weight gain or body fat gain during youth.

Injuries are the leading cause of death for adolescents, so it is important to investigate the association between physical activity, sports, and injuries. About 75% of deaths of older adolescents are due to injuries, with 5% of those deaths attributable to sports injuries. It is possible that participation in sports and recreational activities increases the risk for injuries, but it is also possible that active youth have less serious injuries because they are in better physical condition than sedentary youth. Macera and Wooten (1994) reviewed this literature and found insufficient data to determine whether sports and recreational physical activity are related to injuries in adolescents. Most of the studies are based on emergency room visits or sports teams, and none have been conducted with population groups. Based on studies of high school and university sports programs, football, wrestling, and gymnastics were found to be the riskiest sports.

Cardiovascular diseases are responsible for more than half the deaths in the United States and other industrialized societies, and it is well established that the underlying disease process, the buildup of plaques in the arteries, begins during childhood and adolescence. Blood pressure and blood lipids during youth predict the extent of this buildup in young adults (Newman et al., 1986), so it is important to determine the effects of physical activity on these risk factors during youth. Alpert and Wilmore (1994) reviewed the association between physical activity and blood pressure in youth. The findings were clear. Among adolescents with normal blood pressure, physical activity usually has no observable effect. This shows that physical activity will not make blood pressure subnormal. However, among those with elevated blood pressures, numerous randomized controlled studies have showed that physical activity consistently led to substantial decreases in systolic and diastolic blood pressures. Physical activity seldom led to completely normal blood pressures.

Armstrong and Simons-Morton (1994) reviewed the relationship between physical activity and blood lipids in adolescents. There is little or no evidence of any association with total cholesterol, LDL cholesterol, or triglycerides in adolescents. The results regarding HDL cholesterol are mixed. Cross-sectional studies often show that active adolescents have higher

HDL levels, but prospective studies show no association. More important, exercise training studies generally show no effect on HDL in the general population. It appears that physical activity will not produce supernormal HDL levels. However, a few studies indicate that high-risk adolescents— identified as obese, diabetic, or with a family history of heart disease—can increase their HDL levels through physical activity. These findings have some parallels with the blood pressure results; during adolescence, only those in high-risk groups show detectable improvements in blood pressure or HDL cholesterol with physical activity.

Osteoporosis, or deterioration of the bones, is a serious problem for elderly women. However, risk of bone loss in older adulthood is influenced by peak bone mass, which occurs during late adolescence or young adulthood. Weight-bearing activities are believed to stimulate increased calcium uptake by the bones during adolescence. Thus, if physical activity in youth is shown to affect bone density, the benefits may last for decades. Bailey and Martin (1994) reviewed the literature on physical activity and bone health in adolescents. Studies show that arms on one side that are used more, such as for pitching baseballs or swinging tennis racquets, than arms on the other side have denser bones in the same adolescent. These data provide convincing evidence that skeletal health is not influenced only by genes or diet. When active and inactive groups are compared, active youth have denser bones at most sites tested. Aerobic and nonaerobic activities, including resistance training, that stress the bones seem to be effective in enhancing skeletal health. Adolescents should be encouraged to do a variety of activities that stress all the major bones. However, excessive physical activity can impair menstrual function in female adolescents. This is detrimental to bone health because calcium is lost from bones, similar to what happens in postmenopausal women.

Table 2.2 provides a summary of what is known about the main effects of physical activity on health outcomes in young people. Only a few potential health effects of physical activity have been studied in young people. Not only is there a need for more studies to clarify the associations with the health outcomes discussed here, but the effects of physical activity on other physiological outcomes should be investigated. Most of the associations between physical activity and health indicators in adolescents are of weak to moderate strength. This may be explained in part by the higher activity and fitness levels of young people, the imprecise measures of physical activity, and the short

Table 2.2 Summary of the Effects of Physical Activity on Health Outcomes in Young People

Health Variable	Summary of Association
Aerobic Fitness	⇑⇑
Body fat	⇓
Blood pressure	⇔
HDL cholesterol	⇑
LDL cholesterol	0
Bone mineral density	⇑
Musculoskeletal injuries	⇑

KEY: 0 = no association; ⇔ = inconsistent association or very limited data; ⇑ = some evidence that physical activity increases this variable; ⇑⇑ = moderate evidence that physical activity increases this variable; ⇑⇑⇑ = strong evidence from many studies that physical activity increases this variable; ⇓ = some evidence that physical activity decreases this variable; ⇓⇓ = moderate evidence that physical activity decreases this variable; ⇓⇓⇓ = strong evidence from many studies that physical activity decreases this variable.

duration of studies. However, there is at least suggestive evidence that physical activity during youth has benefits for current and future health.

SUMMARY

Regular participation in physical activity extends life, prevents multiple diseases, and has beneficial effects on many systems of the body. These conclusions are supported by thousands of studies. Because sedentary lifestyles are common, about 200,000 deaths in the United States each year can be attributed to physical activity, making it one of the leading causes of death. Physical activity protects from some of the most common deadly diseases: coronary heart disease, colon cancer, and non-insulin-dependent diabetes mellitus. There are some health risks associated with physical activity, but they can be greatly reduced by making gradual increases in activity level and avoiding overexercise. There is promising evidence that physical activity has multiple benefits for children and adolescents, but the evidence is not as strong as it is for adults.

The literature on physical activity and health fulfills the requirements for the first step of the behavioral epidemiological framework. Physical inactivity is a major cause of morbidity and mortality, so there is ample justification for moving on to the remaining steps in the framework.

FURTHER READING

Biddle, S., Sallis, J., & Cavill, N. (Eds.). (1998). *Young and active? Young people and health-enhancing physical activity: Evidence and implications.* London, England: Health Education Authority.

This book has an up-to-date review of physical activity and health in young people, with an excellent discussion of the difficulties of documenting these associations. Other chapters survey determinants of youth physical activity and interventions. (For ordering information, write Health Education Authority, Trevelyan House, 30 Great Peter Street, London SW1P 2HW, England).

Bouchard, C., Shephard, R. J., & Stephens, T. (Eds.). (1994). *Physical activity, fitness, and health: International proceedings and consensus statement.* Champaign, IL: Human Kinetics.

This is truly an encyclopedia of research on physical activity and health. It contains surveys of the effects of physical activity on virtually every disease and physiological system.

Paffenbarger, R. S., & Olsen, E. (1997). *Lifefit: An effective exercise program for optimal health and a longer life.* Champaign, IL: Human Kinetics.

This book summarizes for the layperson current knowledge of the health effects of physical activity. In addition, it contains a well-designed behavior change program for people of any age wanting to start an active lifestyle.

U.S. Department of Health and Human Services. (1996). *Physical activity and health: A report of the Surgeon General.* Atlanta, GA: Centers for Disease Control.

This landmark volume is essential reading for anyone with a serious interest in any aspect of physical activity and health. The centerpiece of the book, however, is an extensive chapter on the effects of physical activity on health and disease.

Physical Activity, Psychological Health, and Quality of Life

Mental health is an essential component of overall health and must be considered in understanding the relationship between physical activity and health. Mental illnesses are found in all populations. They cause much human suffering, consume vast amounts of health care resources, and create economic burdens on individuals and societies. The most common mental disorders are depression and anxiety disorders. More than 10% of U.S. adults suffer from depression in any given year, and annual prevalence rates for anxiety disorders are between 13% and 17% (Kessler et al., 1994).

Associations between physical activity and psychological health have been written about since ancient times, but systematic research on the topic did not appear until the 1930s (Morgan, 1994). Since that time, research has flourished, and there is a sizable literature on the relationship between physical activity and psychological health in clinical and nonclinical samples. In this chapter, we summarize the findings of some of the many previous reviews of this area, but we also describe studies that illustrate typical findings.

There is a great deal of interest in finding out whether physical activity is effective in preventing or treating psychological disorders, and there are well more than 1,000 studies on this question. However, many of them are simply cross-sectional comparisons of psychological variables in physically active or fit groups versus inactive or unfit groups. These studies are likely to have serious problems with self-selection, so it is not clear whether physical activity leads to psychological health or whether psychologically healthy people take up physical activity. It is a particular problem to compare depressed and nondepressed samples on physical activity, because the symptoms of depression include fatigue and inactivity. Thus, whenever possible, we rely on controlled experiments and prospective studies in discussing this issue.

Physical Activity and Psychological Health of Adults

There is interest in the effects of physical activity on substance abuse, hostility, sleep disorders, and schizophrenia, but there are too few studies to draw conclusions. In this section, we discuss the effects of physical activity on a range of psychological disorders and on mood and quality of life in the general population; we also discuss mechanisms by which physical activity may influence psychological health.

Physical Activity in the Treatment of Depression

Everyone experiences depressed moods occasionally, but depressive disorder can be very debilitating and sometimes leads to suicide. Depression disrupts work, family, and social activities. Common treatments include medication, psychotherapy, hospitalization, and electroconvulsive treatments. About 10 experimental or quasi-experimental studies have been conducted to assess physical activity as a treatment for depression (Martinsen & Stephens, 1994; Morgan, 1994). In the first controlled study, 28 depressed patients were randomly assigned to one of two forms of individual psychotherapy or to running for 12 weeks (Greist, Klein, Eischens, Gurman, & Morgan, 1979). At posttest, all groups decreased depression, but running was as effective as one form of psychotherapy and significantly more effective than the other. At the 12-month follow-up, the best maintenance effect was found in the running group (Morgan, 1994). This study stimulated numerous others.

All of the nine other studies confirmed that exercise was at least as effective as a variety of other treatments in reducing depression. Other treatments included relaxation, meditation, group psychotherapy, cognitive therapy, and wait-list control. Martinsen and colleagues in Norway conducted a series of studies on hospitalized depressed patients that demonstrated the effectiveness of exercise even in those who were taking medications. They also found that aerobic and nonaerobic exercise (i.e., strength and flexibility exercises) produced similar results (Martinsen & Stephens, 1994).

These studies consistently show that physical activity is an effective treatment for mild to moderate unipolar depression. The antidepressant effect has been observed to have some effect in as little as 2 weeks' time and to persist as long as 1 year.

Physical Activity in the Treatment of Anxiety

Anxiety is a symptom of being in a state of overarousal. It is common for people to refer to anxiety as "stress." Mild anxiety is common and may be experienced as worry, racing heart, or cold hands. Extreme anxiety problems include agoraphobia (i.e., fear of open spaces) and panic attacks, both of which can disrupt many aspects of life. Anxiety is usually measured by questionnaires, and it can be differentiated as state (i.e., current feelings) or trait anxiety (i.e., general tendency to be anxious). Anxiety has many physiological components, such as muscle tension, increased heart rate and blood pressure, and vascular constriction, known to be influenced by physical activity. Thus, there is a good rationale for testing physical activity as a treatment for anxiety.

Unfortunately, only a few controlled studies have evaluated the effects of physical activity in anxiety patients. The results are encouraging. According to the review of Martinsen and Stephens (1994), one controlled study found walking and jogging to reduce anxiety symptoms, and one study found aerobic and nonaerobic exercises to produce similar improvements. Further studies are needed to compare physical activity with other common treatments, such as relaxation therapy and medication.

Psychological Effects of Acute Physical Activity

Many studies have examined changes in state anxiety and mood before and after a single session of physical activity lasting from 5 to 30 minutes. Most of these studies show that anxiety is reduced by exercise (Landers & Petruzzello, 1994). In general, physical activity produces similar reductions in state anxiety as do relaxation and quiet rest (Landers & Petruzzello, 1994), but the effects of physical activity may last longer, up to 2 to 4 hours (Raglin, 1990).

Steptoe and Bolton (1988) had several critiques of these studies, including the possibility that study participants might be biased to report improved psychological states following a session of exercise. Thus, they disguised the purpose of their experiment and compared the effects of high- and low-intensity exercise, with the low intensity being a control condition. They found that anxiety scores increased during and 1 minute after exercise in the high-intensity group but decreased continually in the low-intensity group. They argue that high-intensity exercise may have a short-term negative psychological effect. Any negative effect is short-lasting, because by 15 minutes after exercise, the high-intensity group had anxiety levels significantly below baseline.

Virtually all of this research has been conducted with aerobic physical activity, so O'Connor, Bryant, Veltri, and Gebhardt (1993) conducted a study of resistance exercise. Each female participant completed a 30-minute session of weight training at 40%, 60%, and 80% of their 10-repetition maximum, as well as a control session with no weight lifting. Only the 60% condition produced significant reductions in state anxiety up to 2 hours after the exercise. This study suggests that resistance training does not necessarily lead to decreases in anxiety. More studies are needed to confirm if only certain intensities of resistance training reduce anxiety.

It is encouraging that physical activity can reduce anxiety symptoms, but it is also important to determine whether physical activity can help people cope with stressful events more effectively. Stress responses include psychological and physiological reactions, and the ability of acute exercise to reduce both types of stress responses has been assessed. The cardiovascular system is highly responsive to stress, with heart rate and blood pressure being the most commonly studied responses. Rejeski and colleagues (Rejeski, Thompson, Brubaker, & Miller, 1992) studied the effects of acute exercise on responses to mental stress in white and African American women. Each woman participated in a control condition, which was quiet rest, and an exercise session, which was 40 minutes of aerobic exercise. Blood pressure, heart rate, and psychological responses were monitored during and after a mental stress task (i.e., the Stroop test) and an interpersonal stressor (i.e., public speech). Thirty minutes following the experimental procedures, exercise reduced blood pressure and psychological responses to the interpersonal stressor, and psychological responses to the mental stress task were also reduced by exercise. This study is important because it shows that even a single session of vigorous exercise can improve one's ability to cope with stress, psychologically and physiologically.

Evidence of a variety of acute psychological benefits of physical activity suggests that maximum benefits can be obtained by doing frequent physical activity. If the benefits last only a few minutes or hours, and this has not been thoroughly defined, then physical activity must be done regularly. Haskell (1994b) has shown how some of the physiological effects of physical activity are acute. These effects may be analogous to taking blood pressure medication. You have to take the medication every day to keep blood pressure under control, because there is no chronic adaptation. There appear to be acute psychological effects of physical activity, but it is unknown whether there are also chronic adaptations by which regular exercisers get a bigger psychological boost from each session of physical activity.

Physical Activity and Psychological Health in the General Population

The possibility that physical activity could improve the psychological health of the population and prevent mental illnesses has considerable public health implications. If the linkage is confirmed, the potential impact is large because both psychological disorders and sedentary lifestyles are very common. Population-based studies provide encouraging results. Stephens (1988) reported on four national surveys from the United States and Canada. Although each survey used different measures of physical activity and different measures of psychological health, they all showed significant associations. Leisure time physical activity was correlated with general well-being and mood and negatively correlated with depression and anxiety. These results were found for men, women, younger adults, and older adults, even after adjusting for potential confounding variables. A further finding was that leisure activities were more strongly related to psychological health than were household chores. This suggests that it is not just the energy expenditure but also the perception or meaning of the activity that may be related to its effects on psychological variables (Stephens, 1988).

These suggestive cross-sectional results are supported by three prospective studies. Two U.S. studies and one Canadian study showed that physically active adults at baseline were less likely to become depressed at follow-up.

Depressed sedentary adults were more likely to stay depressed than those who were active at baseline. For example, the Canadian study had a 7-year follow-up of about 2,500 people. Baseline physical activity predicted mental health at follow-up in five of eight comparisons. Because the analyses took into account age, sex, educational level, physical health, and baseline psychological status, the results provide strong evidence that physical activity predicts positive mental health in the future (Martinsen & Stephens, 1994).

Randomized experimental studies provide the strongest evidence that physical activity improves psychological health. A study conducted in England showed that moderate-intensity physical activity improved tension/anxiety levels after 12 weeks of training, and perceived ability to cope with stress was improved 3 months later. However, vigorous exercise was not significantly more effective than control conditions in improving any measure of psychological health (Moses, Steptoe, Mathews, & Edwards, 1989). More studies are needed to confirm the psychological effects of different intensities of physical activity.

A controlled study of a 6-month aerobic training program also found a number of psychological benefits. Psychological variables were rated every 2 weeks, and significant results were found on 3 of the 11 items (King, Taylor, Haskell, & DeBusk, 1989). Physical activity had significant effects on rated fitness, satisfaction with weight, and satisfaction with shape and appearance. The failure to find exercise effects on items such as depressed mood, tension/anxiety, and stress is a concern, because this is inconsistent with previous studies. A controlled study with older adults also had mixed results concerning psychological effects (Blumenthal et al., 1991).

Results of observational studies show a consistent association between physical activity and psychological health. Experimental studies also show some psychological benefits of physical activity, but there is no consistency across the few studies on the types of variables affected. None of the studies show detrimental effects of physical activity. Taken together, this is strong evidence that physical activity improves psychological health in psychologically healthy populations. More experimental studies are needed to clearly define the psychological benefits for different population subgroups and for different types and intensities of physical activity.

The U.S. Surgeon General's report (U.S. Department of Health and Human Services [DHHS], 1996) also concluded that physical activity can relieve symptoms of anxiety and depression and may help prevent psychological disorders. These data provide yet another rationale for making serious attempts to promote physical activity in the general population and for considering physical activity a valid intervention option for treating mild to moderate anxiety and depression.

Physical Activity and Quality of Sleep

Sleep problems, such as sleep-onset insomnia, are common and lead to daytime sleepiness, which plays a role in many automobile collisions and injuries. Epidemiological studies indicate that physically active people report better sleep quality than the sedentary. It has also been shown that acute exercise results in increased overall sleep time and changes in sleep parameters, such as decreased rapid-eye-movement (REM) sleep (O'Connor & Youngstedt, 1995). To determine whether moderate-intensity physical activity improves sleep quality in sedentary people who complained of poor sleep, King and colleagues (King, Oman, Brassington, Bliwise, & Haskell, 1997) conducted a controlled trial. Forty-three elderly adults were randomly assigned to moderate exercise for 16 weeks or to no intervention. At the end of the study, the exercise group reported higher quality of sleep, shorter time to fall asleep, and longer sleep duration. This study indicates that moderate-intensity physical activity, such as low-impact aerobics, walking, or cycling, can improve sleep in sedentary older adults, a group that commonly reports trouble sleeping.

Physical Activity and Quality of Life

Improving health-related quality of life (HRQL; Kaplan & Bush, 1982) is widely accepted as one of the major goals of the health care system. HRQL can be thought of as a person's satisfaction with life in general, although it is also possible to assess cognitive, physical, and emotional dimensions of HRQL (U.S. DHHS, 1996). Self-esteem is a general evaluation of oneself, and studies consistently show that physically active people have higher levels of self-esteem than do the sedentary. This has been found with children and young adults (McAuley, 1994) as well as with older adults (McAuley & Rudolph, 1995). The longer a person engages in physical activity, the higher his or her self-esteem and psychological well-being.

HRQL is strongly influenced by one's ability to complete activities of daily living. Healthy people have high levels of functioning, but people with diseases may have great difficulty taking care of personal hygiene or transporting themselves. Elderly or ill persons with functional limitations who increased their endurance exercise experienced improvements in psychological well-being and physical functioning (Stewart et al., 1994). Those who initially had the most functional limitations made the most improvements.

Mechanisms by Which Physical Activity May Influence Psychological Health

There is a great deal of theorizing and speculating about the mechanisms by which physical activity improves psychological health, but surprisingly few studies have specifically addressed this question. McAuley and Rudolph (1995) reviewed several frequently discussed mechanisms. A prominent psychological explanation is that physical activity enhances perceptions of mastery and control, and these are incompatible with feelings of anxiety and depression. Although it is known that physical activity enhances perceptions of self-efficacy and well-being, it is not known whether these mediate changes in psychological symptoms. Another hypothesis is that physical activity provides a "time-out" from worry about the stresses of life. Physical activity may distract one from the negative ruminations that are common in anxiety and depression. A third psychological hypothesis is that physical activity is often done in social settings, and social interaction is known to reduce symptoms of psychological distress.

The most popular hypothesis about biological mechanisms deals with endorphins, opium-like compounds produced in the body. Endorphins are released during physical activity, but it is not known whether they mediate psychological improvements. It is also believed that stress-related hormones such as cortisol and catecholamines may be involved, because physical activity and fitness may lead to decreased hormonal responses to stress. The only biological mediator that has been extensively evaluated is aerobic fitness. The data provide little or no support for this hypothesis, because changes in fitness and improvements in psychological health are rarely correlated (McAuley & Rudolph, 1995). Thus, the search for mediators continues.

Detrimental Psychological Effects of Physical Activity

The considerable evidence for multiple psychological benefits of physical activity must be balanced with an examination of possible detrimental effects. Several negative psychological effects have been proposed and evaluated. The most prominent concern is that physical activity can become an addiction, referred to as exercise dependence, obligatory exercise, and compulsive exercise (Davis, Brewer, & Ratusny, 1993). Excessive commitment to physical activity can interfere with social and work activities. It may cause health problems, because one of the defining characteristics is continuing to exercise when injured. Exercise dependence is usually defined by a combination of high levels of physical activity and a strong perceived need to exercise despite all obstacles (Coen & Ogles, 1993; Davis et al., 1993). Another necessary feature of addiction is a withdrawal syndrome. Not only has a syndrome of withdrawal from exercise been documented in mice, but several experimental studies of humans have shown that when habitual exercisers are deprived of exercise, they experience an increase in depression, anxiety, and somatic symptoms of emotional distress within a day or two of stopping exercise (Mondin et al., 1996). Psychological status returns to baseline levels when exercise is resumed (Mondin et al., 1996; Morris, Steinberg, Sykes, & Salmon, 1990). Although negative psychological effects of stopping exercise appear to be common, it is unknown what percentage of exercisers suffer adverse consequences from being dependent on exercise.

A related issue is the hypothesis that exercise addiction shares many characteristics of anorexia nervosa. Yates (1991) proposed that compulsive exercisers and anorexics were both attempting to define their identity through running and excessive dieting, respectively. This hypothesis has generated a great deal of debate. Several studies have found that obligatory exercisers have less psychopathology and less body image distortion than anorexics (Coen & Ogles, 1993). Obligatory runners were not found to have a less developed sense of identity than controls, as predicted by Yates (Coen & Ogles, 1993). However, obligatory exercisers were found to be more perfectionistic than controls (Coen & Ogles, 1993) and to be preoccupied with weight and diet concerns (Davis et al., 1993), as predicted by Yates (1991). The meaning of these mixed results is not clear. An excessive commitment to physical activity does not have nearly the extent of harmful medical or psychological consequences as anorexia nervosa, but obligatory exercisers and anorexics do share some characteristics.

An effect that is contradictory to the exercise addiction hypothesis is that excessive exercise leads to a condition termed "staleness" by Morgan (1994). Staleness is similar to depression and has symptoms of decreased performance, chronic fatigue, muscle soreness, insomnia, and disturbed mood. This effect has been reported only in athletes, and it is apparently the result of overtraining. When swimmers, skaters, wrestlers, and rowers train excessively, they can experience staleness, which is relieved by a decrease in physical training (Morgan, 1994). The extent of exercise necessary to produce staleness, the percentage of athletes who are affected, the risk indicators for vulnerable subgroups, and whether this syndrome is experienced by noncompetitive athletes remain to be determined. Another fundamental question is, Why do some people develop a tolerance for high levels of physical activity and need it for good mental health and others develop symptoms of depression from too much exercise?

There is substantial evidence of detrimental psychological consequences of physical activity. For some individuals, problems associated with compulsive exercise or staleness are clinically meaningful. However, to keep these problems in perspective, one must weigh the beneficial and adverse psychological consequences of physical activity. In the absence of epidemiological data on the prevalence of negative effects, logic dictates that "exercise addiction" is not a common problem, because less than 15% of U.S. adults participate in vigorous exercise (U.S. DHHS, 1996). We argue that addiction to sedentariness is the much more serious problem.

Physical Activity and Psychological Health of Children and Adolescents

Mental health is a serious issue for children and adolescents, because there are disturbingly high rates of depression and suicide in young people. Children and adolescents suffer from a wide range of diagnosable mental and emotional disorders, including anxiety, depression, and substance abuse, and it is possible that physical activity could contribute to the prevention or treatment of these disorders. It is also possible that physical activity can improve psychological health in the general population of young people by affecting variables such as mood, perceived stress, self-esteem, self-concept, hostility, and intellectual functioning.

A recent review by Calfas and Taylor (1994) identified five controlled studies conducted with a variety of adolescent high-risk groups, including those with depressed mood, incarcerated delinquents, those with learning disabilities, and autistic youth. The lack of multiple studies of any one group, and other limitations of the studies, prohibit drawing any conclusions about the effect of physical activity on psychological health in high-risk groups. This is an important area for further research. In an earlier review, Gruber (1986) found a consistent association between physical activity and self-esteem in a variety of handicapped groups, including emotionally disturbed and mentally retarded teens. Physical activity is an effective treatment for depression and anxiety among adults, and it needs to be evaluated in young people. The role of physical activity in the treatment of young substance abusers is also a high priority for research.

There are more studies of the general population of young people, and the results indicate multiple benefits of physical activity (Calfas & Taylor, 1994). Most of these studies used the best available standardized measures of psychological outcomes. Eight of 11 studies reported significant associations or experimental effects of physical activity with anxiety and stress outcomes. Nine of 10 studies supported a relationship between physical activity and self-esteem, self-concept, or self-efficacy. These self-perceptions are core aspects of young people's identity and have been related to many other outcomes, including academic performance and antisocial behavior. Nine of 11 studies found a positive effect of physical activity on depressed mood, with a mean effect size of .38, which is a moderate effect. No conclusions could be developed for anger/hostility or intellectual performance, because there were too few studies.

The consistency of the supportive findings across several psychological outcomes enhances confidence in the conclusion that physical activity improves psychological health in young people. Confidence is further enhanced because most of the studies were controlled trials, and the results of experimental and observational studies were consistent.

Although there is strong evidence that physical activity has important psychological benefits for adolescents, it is also known that excessive physical activity has negative psychological effects. Excessive exercise is a component of several eating disorders, notably anorexia nervosa (Yates, 1991) and may interfere with social relationships in some cases (Calfas & Taylor, 1994). The negative psychological effects of physical activity are real, and they need to be defined further, but they are likely to be experienced by only a small minority of teens. The existence of a small proportion of adolescents suffering adverse psychological effects of excessive exercise should not detract from the main finding, which is that the vast majority of teens can gain important psychological benefits from engaging in more physical activity.

SUMMARY

Many studies of the effects of physical activity on psychological health have been cross-sectional comparisons of physically active versus inactive groups. These studies are difficult to interpret, but a variety of better studies generally show positive effects. Prospective population studies demonstrate that physical activity decreases the risk of becoming depressed. Treatment studies of anxious and depressed patients indicate that physical activity is as effective as standard therapies. Physical activity can enhance self-esteem and reduce symptoms of depression and anxiety in young people. There are some negative psychological effects of excessive exercise, but these appear to be uncommon. Further research is needed to examine the types and intensities of physical activity that are most psychologically beneficial and to identify mechanisms by which physical activity improves psychological health.

FURTHER READING

Biddle, S., & Mutrie, N. (1991). *Psychology of physical activity and exercise.* London: Springer-Verlag.

An excellent textbook on all psychological aspects of physical activity.

Martinsen, E. W., & Stephens, T. (1994). Exercise and mental health in clinical and free-living populations. In R. K. Dishman (Ed.), *Advances in exercise adherence* (pp. 55-72). Champaign, IL: Human Kinetics.

A comprehensive review of the scientific literature on this topic.

McAuley, E. (1994). Physical activity and psychosocial outcomes. In C. Bouchard, R. J. Shephard, & T. Stephens (Eds.), *Physical activity, fitness, and health: International proceedings and consensus statement* (pp. 551-568). Champaign, IL: Human Kinetics.

An excellent scientific analysis of a variety of psychological effects of physical activity.

Morgan, W. P. (1997). *Physical activity and mental health.* Bristol, PA: Taylor & Francis.

This book is a comprehensive account of current scientific understanding of the various effects of physical activity on mental health, including a consideration of mechanisms.

PART
III

Defining and Measuring Physical Activity

Section Introduction

Physical activity, as we have shown in Part 2, has many important physical and mental health benefits, as well as some health risks. Although it has many biological effects, physical activity is a behavior. This section begins the emphasis on the "behavioral" aspects of behavioral epidemiology. Because the behavior of physical activity is shown to be strongly related to health, the next step is to focus on identifying and measuring health-related behaviors, and this allows us to determine who is active enough and who is not.

Health authorities in industrialized countries such as the United States, England, and Australia have developed physical activity recommendations that are being promulgated as part of national health promotion strategies. These recommendations are summarized in Chapter 4. If physical activity is adopted as a public health priority, it is necessary to have accurate measurement methods that can be used to monitor physical activity habits of individuals in programs, special groups, and whole populations.

Key measurement issues such as reliability and validity of the many ways of assessing physical activity are considered in Chapter 5. In Chapter 6, we review the prevalence of physical activity participation and trends over time in industrialized countries. Part 3 makes clear that there has been considerable recent progress in defining and assessing physical activity as a behavior. There has also been progress in applying that knowledge by systematically monitoring levels of physical activity participation and trends over time.

Recommended Amounts
of Physical Activity

The health benefits of physical activity have been recognized in many cultures for centuries. Physical activity is part of the medical traditions of cultures as diverse as Chinese, Indian, Native American, and African, as well as throughout the history of Greco-Roman Western civilization (U.S. Department of Health and Human Services [DHHS], 1996). There is a long history of general recommendations to be physically active, but those recommendations have not provided specific guidelines about exactly how much activity should be done.

In this review of physical activity recommendations, we focus on health-related guidelines rather than on those designed to enhance sport performance. We also emphasize recommendations for the general population rather than for people with specific medical conditions.

Early Recommendations to Promote Fitness

Efforts to determine the precise amount of physical activity needed to achieve different health outcomes are recent. The first major effort to define the amount of physical activity needed to improve aerobic fitness and body composition in healthy adults was sponsored by the American College of Sports Medicine (ACSM) and appeared in 1978. Based on an extensive review of the literature, "The Recommended Quantity and Quality of Exercise for Developing and Maintaining Fitness in Healthy Adults" was published (ACSM, 1978). The following guidelines were issued: frequency of exercise training, 3 to 5 days per week; intensity of training, 60% to 90% of maximum heart rate reserve or 50% to 85% of maximum oxygen uptake; duration of training, 15 to 60 minutes per session; and the type of activity, "aerobic" or rhythmic use of large muscle groups in activities such as running or jogging, walking, swimming, cycling, cross-country skiing, rope jumping, and various endurance games and sports.

The 1978 guidelines provided the first quantitative guidelines for physical activity for fitness or health outcomes, so they had a major influence on research and practice among exercise scientists as well as health professionals. Researchers began assessing whether study participants were doing the recommended amount, and practitioners began recommending this much activity as part of preventive and therapeutic programs. Public policy was influenced by these guidelines as shown by the inclusion of similar guidelines in the 1990 disease prevention and health promotion objectives in the United States (U.S. Public Health Service, 1980). The general public also became familiar with the 1978 ACSM guidelines through innumerable articles in the popular press. This guideline became the standard physical activity recommendation throughout most of the world.

The 1978 guideline produced several benefits. First, this relatively simple-to-understand guideline provided a yardstick for deciding whether a given person was active enough. It could be used by health professionals and the lay public alike. Second, the guideline helped raise public awareness of the desirability of being physically active. Third, the message that a person should do this specific amount of exercise probably helped trigger the "fitness boom" in the late 1970s and well into the 1980s. Entire industries of manufacturers and service providers sprang up or greatly expanded to help people achieve this recommended goal.

However, there were several problems with the 1978 guideline. First, it was developed based on how much activity is needed to promote aerobic fitness in sedentary adults, but it was quickly interpreted as being the amount of activity needed to ensure good health. Second, most of the studies on which the guidelines were based were conducted with young, Caucasian males.

Nevertheless, the guidelines were generalized to women, children, the elderly, and all ethnic and racial groups. Not enough consideration was given to whether the guidelines should be applied to these other groups. Third, the aerobic exercises specified in the guidelines were not attractive to the vast majority of adults in Westernized nations. Most adults did not find it appealing to jog, swim, bike, or do aerobic dance 3 to 5 days per week. Thus, the vast majority of adults did not follow the guidelines and to some extent felt like failures. As new research refined our understanding of the effects of different types and amounts of physical activity on various health outcomes, pressure grew to revise the original 1978 guidelines.

Developing Recommendations to Promote Health

One of the steps on the road to guidelines focused on health benefits was a review article by Haskell and colleagues (Haskell, Montoye, & Orenstein, 1985) that emphasized the documented benefits of physical activity performed at lower intensities than those recommended in the 1978 ACSM guidelines. This article, based on the first workshop in the United States to comprehensively examine physical activity and public health, was influential in stimulating debate about the limitations of the 1978 ACSM recommendations.

In 1990, the ACSM's position statement was revised (ACSM, 1990). The most significant change was to add a major objective of developing muscular strength and endurance. There were only minor changes in the recommendations for enhancing aerobic fitness. It was reiterated that the guidelines were based on data related to the dose of exercise needed to enhance fitness and body composition. For the first time, the 1990 statement recognized a distinction between physical activity to enhance fitness versus health outcomes. The authors emphasized that the guidelines were well supported by scientific data related to fitness development, but they acknowledged the epidemiological studies showing that less intensive physical activity may reduce the risk for some chronic diseases. The position statement did not, however, provide specific health-related guidelines.

The growing realization that different amounts and intensities of physical activity may be needed for health and fitness gains prompted researchers to reexamine results of both laboratory and epidemiological studies. As shown by Haskell (1994a), most laboratory-based exercise training studies demonstrated that lower intensities, durations, and frequencies of exercise than those recommended in the ACSM guidelines produced improvements in fitness. Following the guidelines led to faster and somewhat greater increases in fitness than exercise done at lower levels.

Examination of the major epidemiological studies also demonstrated that moderate levels of physical activity and fitness were sufficient to provide important protection from cardiovascular diseases and all-cause mortality. The consistent pattern of results is that the greatest risk reduction occurs when moving from the least active or fit group to the middle activity or fitness group. There is less improvement when moving from the middle group to the highly active or fit group.

This pattern can be seen in the data shown in Figure 2.1 in Chapter 2. The interpretation of those results is that the greatest improvements in health can be obtained by helping the least active and fit group become a bit more active and fit. This goal of targeting moderate increases in activity among the low-active group was well articulated by Blair and colleagues (Blair, Kohl, Gordon, & Paffenbarger, 1992).

The ACSM guidelines were intended to produce large increases or nearly optimal levels of physical fitness. There was a strong movement in the late 1980s to reinterpret the same studies to determine the minimal amount of physical activity needed to produce smaller but meaningful improvements in health and fitness. Part of the motivation to reexamine the studies in an attempt to develop different recommendations was the fact that the general public was not following the ACSM recommendations. As detailed in Chapter 6, the vast majority of adults in industrialized nations do not meet the ACSM guidelines, and in some countries, there was little or no increase in the percentage of adults who exercised. It was reasoned that vigorous exercise was unacceptable to many people, so it may be more effective to encourage people to engage in less vigorous activities that still provide substantial health benefits.

Experts gradually reached a consensus that a great deal of health benefits could be derived from performing moderate-intensity physical activity on a regular basis. This consensus in the field led to new recommendations that are part of public health policy in several nations.

Recommendations for Moderate-Intensity Physical Activity and Health

One of the first official recommendations to reflect the new focus on moderate-intensity activities was in *Healthy People 2000*, the statement of

U.S. health promotion and disease prevention objectives (U.S. DHHS, 1991). *Healthy People 2000* included a comprehensive set of recommendations related to physical activity and inactivity. The moderate-intensity objective provided a guideline of 30 minutes of light to moderate physical activity daily. The objectives also included vigorous exercise similar to the ACSM recommendations, as well as activities to promote muscular strength, muscular endurance, and flexibility. In recognition of the severe risks of leading very sedentary lives, an objective was included to reduce the proportion of people who engage in no leisure time physical activity. The objectives from *Healthy People 2000* are listed in Table 4.1. They have served as models for several other nations as well as international groups. For example, a general physical activity recommendation has been included in the Australian goals and targets to improve health (Commonwealth Department of Human Services and Health, 1994). In an important position statement, the World Health Organization and International Federation of Sports Medicine recommends that adults should perform at least 30 minutes of moderate-intensity physical activity every day (Blair, Booth, et al., 1995).

There have been some misunderstandings about the guidelines for moderate-intensity physical activity. Many people believe that they do not have to do as much activity if they follow the moderate guidelines rather than the more vigorous ACSM guidelines. This is not true, because the overall energy expenditure is very similar. Because the intensity is reduced in the moderate-intensity guidelines, the frequency has been increased from 3 days per week to *preferably* every day. The main difference from the vigorous activity guideline is intensity of the activities. If one were to jog for 30 minutes, 3 times per week, at a 10-minute mile, this would amount to about 9 miles per week. At 100 kilocalories (kcals) per mile, this is 900 kcals per week of vigorous exercise. If one were to walk for 30 minutes, 5 times per week, at a 15-minute mile, this would be about 10 miles per week. Although the intensity of activity would be lower, the overall energy expenditure is about 1,000 kcal, or more than for the vigorous exercise recommendation.

The second major misconception is that moderate-intensity activities require little or no exertion. For young and middle-aged adults, this is not the case. Moderate intensity is considered brisk walking, or about 3 to 4 miles per hour. This requires more effort than the kind of strolling most people do while window-shopping, for example. Still another incorrect assumption is that the new moderate guideline means that vigorous activity is no longer recommended. In fact, the evidence still indicates that for many health and

Table 4.1 National and International Recommendations Related to Physical Activity and Health

Source	*Physical Activity Recommendations*
Healthy People 2000 (U.S. DHHS, 1991)— United States	• Increase to at least 30% the proportion of people aged 7 and older who engage regularly, preferably daily, in light to moderate physical activity for at least 30 minutes per day.
	• Increase to at least 20% the proportion of people aged 18 and older and to at least 75% the proportion of children and adolescents aged 6 through 18 who engage in vigorous physical activity that promotes the development of cardiorespiratory fitness 3 or more days per week for 20 minutes per occasion.
	• Reduce to no more than 15% the proportion of people aged 6 and older who engage in no leisure time physical activity.
	• Increase to at least 40% the proportion of people aged 6 and older who regularly perform physical activities that enhance and maintain muscular strength, muscular endurance, and flexibility.
Better Health Outcomes for Australians (Commonwealth Department of Human Services and Health, 1994)—Australia	• Increase participation in physical activity. Based on the percentage of adults who, in the past 2 weeks, did not engage in vigorous exercise, moderate exercise, or walking for recreation or exercise.
Centers for Disease Control and American College of Sports Medicine (Pate, Pratt, et al., 1995)— United States	• Every U.S. adult should accumulate 30 minutes or more of moderate-intensity physical activity on most, preferably all, days of the week.
International Perspectives on Promoting Physical Activity (Killoran, Fentem, & Caspersen, 1994)—United Kingdom	• To reduce by at least 10% the proportion of men and women aged 16 to 74 taking no occasion of moderate-intensity physical activity of at least 30 minutes each week by 2005. Ideally, this 30 minutes should be one sustained period of activity but may be accumulated through the day in bouts of at least 15 minutes on the same day.

(continued)

Table 4.1 Continued

Source	Physical Activity Recommendations
International Perspectives on Promoting Physical Activity (Killoran, Fentem, & Caspersen, 1994)—United Kingdom	• To increase the proportion of men and women aged 16 to 74 who take a minimum of 30 minutes of at least moderate-intensity physical activity on 5 days a week or more by at least 15% by 2005. Ideally, this 30 minutes should be one period of sustained activity but may be accumulated through the day in bouts of at least 15 minutes. • To increase the proportion of men and women aged 16 to 64 taking on average three periods of vigorous physical activity of 20 minutes duration a week by at least 10% by 2005.
U.S. Surgeon General's Report (U.S. Department of Health and Human Services, 1996)— United States	• Significant health benefits can be obtained by including a moderate amount of physical activity (e.g., 30 minutes of brisk walking or raking leaves, 15 minutes of running, or 45 minutes of playing volleyball) on most, if not all, days of the week. • Additional health benefits can be gained through greater amounts of physical activity. People who can maintain a regular regimen of activity that is of longer duration or of more vigorous intensity are likely to derive greater benefit.
World Health Organization and International Federation of Sports Medicine (Blair, Booth, et al., 1995)—International	• Adults should be encouraged to increase habitual activity gradually, aiming to carry out every day at least 30 minutes of physical activity of moderate intensity (e.g., brisk walking and stair climbing). More strenuous activities such as slow jogging, cycling, field and court games (soccer, tennis, etc.) and swimming could provide additional benefits. • Specific population groups mentioned include children and adolescents, women, the elderly, the disabled, and those with chronic diseases.

Table 4.1 Continued	
Source	*Physical Activity Recommendations*
International Consensus Conference on Physical Activity Guidelines for Adolescents (Sallis & Patrick, 1994)— International	• All adolescents should be physically active daily, or nearly every day, as part of play, games, sports, work, transportation, recreation, physical education, or planned exercise, in the context of family, school, and community activities.
	• Adolescents should engage in three or more sessions per week of activities that last 20 minutes or more at a time and that require moderate to vigorous levels of exertion.
Health Education Authority (Biddle, Sallis, & Cavill, 1998)— United Kingdom	• All young people should participate in physical activity of at least moderate intensity for 1 hour per day.
	• Young people who currently do little activity should participate in physical activity of at least moderate intensity for at least half an hour per day.
	• At least twice a week, some of these activities should help to enhance and maintain muscular strength and flexibility and bone health.

fitness outcomes, more benefits are gained from vigorous activity, so it is still the preferred activity recommendation. For those who do not do regular vigorous exercise, it is important to work to meet the moderate-intensity guidelines.

A major refinement of the moderate-activity guideline occurred in 1995 when a panel of U.S. experts introduced the concept that the activity could be accumulated over the course of the day rather than performed continuously in a single session (Pate, Pratt, et al., 1995). This change was motivated in part by the difficulties reported by many people in trying to find 30 minutes in their days for continuous physical activity. There were indications that people who could not regularly meet this goal simply stopped their attempts to be physically active.

Two types of data indicated that physical activity did not need to be continuous. The first set of evidence was the epidemiological studies, showing that the most common activities that helped reduce risk of death were walking, climbing stairs, gardening, and doing household chores (e.g., Leon, Connett, Jacobs, & Rauramaa, 1987). Among these, only walking is likely to be performed continuously, suggesting that substantial amounts of intermittent activity can be beneficial. The second set of supportive evidence came from controlled studies in which three 10-minute sessions of activity produced nearly the same amount of health benefit as a single 30-minute session (DeBusk, Stenestrand, Sheehan, & Haskell, 1990). Although direct support for the idea of accumulating physical activity throughout the day is limited, the expert panel believed the existing evidence justified a recommendation that might encourage more people to do some physical activity (Pate, Pratt, et al., 1995). Another examination of the evidence led to the adoption of similar guidelines in England (Killoran, Fentem, & Caspersen, 1994). The British recommendation to the public provided additional clarification not found in the U.S. version:

> Take 30 minutes of moderate intensity physical activity, such as a sustained brisk walk, on at least five days of the week. Aim for a total of 30 minutes of physical activity on each of these days. Ideally take this in one period, but you can also make up this total from bouts of 15 minutes, if this is easier for you. Build up gently.
>   Moderate intensity physical activities are those that raise the heart rate sufficiently to leave you warm and slightly out of breath, such as brisk walking, climbing stairs, swimming, social dancing, exercise, heavy DIY [do it yourself], heavy gardening, and heavy housework. (Killoran et al., 1994, p. 215)

The moderate-intensity recommendation was adopted almost verbatim by the National Institutes of Health Consensus Development Panel on Physical Activity and Cardiovascular Health (1996). This panel of professionals from a variety of health fields examined the evidence and confirmed the likely benefits of moderate-intensity physical activity in treating and preventing cardiovascular diseases. This group broadened the recommendations to apply to children as well as adults.

It is too early to determine how these new guidelines are being received by the public and whether they will encourage people to engage in more physical activity. It is expected that people will like the message that it is easier to fit physical activity into their day than they were previously told. On the other hand, people may believe they already accumulate 30 minutes of activity each day by walking around. This is probably not true for many people, because most casual walking is low intensity, and as discussed in Chapter 1, modern societies have been successful in eliminating a great deal of walking from daily lives.

A further evolution of recommendations was contained in the 1996 U.S. Surgeon General's report, *Physical Activity and Health* (U.S. DHHS, 1996). Although it is often reported that overall amount of physical activity (a combination of frequency, duration, and intensity) is related to health and longevity, the difference in kcal expenditure between activity groups has not often been calculated. Based on a review of several epidemiological studies, it was concluded that an increase of about 150 kcals per day, or 1,000 kcals per week, over sedentary levels, was sufficient to improve health. Vigorous activity was not required for these effects.

The U.S. Surgeon General's report included the recommendation that "significant health benefits can be obtained by including a moderate amount of physical activity . . . on most, if not all, days of the week" (U.S. DHHS, 1996, p. 4). The value of this recommendation emphasizing *moderate* amounts of physical activity is that it allows great flexibility in how one achieves the goal. Less intense activities can be done for a longer time (e.g., 45 minutes of playing volleyball) or more intense activities can be done for a shorter time (e.g., 15 minutes of running). The guiding principle is to do 150 kcals of physical activity every day, and activities can vary from day to day. Some examples of activities that will burn 150 Calories are shown in Table 4.2. The disadvantage of this recommendation is that most people do not routinely translate their physical activity into kcals expended. It may be easier for people to set goals for minutes per day, rather than kilocalories per day.

The U.S. Surgeon General's report concludes that the benefits of physical activity are related to the effort that one devotes to activity, and there are additional advantages of vigorous activities: "People who can maintain a regular regimen of activity that is of longer duration or of more vigorous intensity are likely to derive greater benefit" (U.S. DHHS, 1996, p. 4). People who have been doing vigorous physical activity that meets the original ACSM guidelines are encouraged to continue to do so. However, for those who are sedentary, it is expected that the new guidelines promoting moderate amounts of physical activity are more realistic goals.

Physical activities that enhance components of physical fitness other than cardiorespiratory endurance are also believed to have health benefits. However, the health effects of activities that increase muscular strength and

Table 4.2 Ways of Meeting the Moderate Activity Guidelines

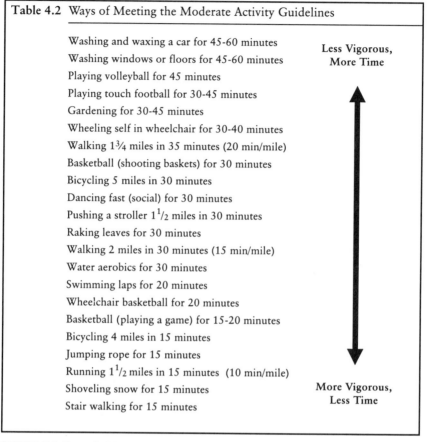

Washing and waxing a car for 45-60 minutes

Washing windows or floors for 45-60 minutes

Playing volleyball for 45 minutes

Playing touch football for 30-45 minutes

Gardening for 30-45 minutes

Wheeling self in wheelchair for 30-40 minutes

Walking 1¾ miles in 35 minutes (20 min/mile)

Basketball (shooting baskets) for 30 minutes

Bicycling 5 miles in 30 minutes

Dancing fast (social) for 30 minutes

Pushing a stroller 1½ miles in 30 minutes

Raking leaves for 30 minutes

Walking 2 miles in 30 minutes (15 min/mile)

Water aerobics for 30 minutes

Swimming laps for 20 minutes

Wheelchair basketball for 20 minutes

Basketball (playing a game) for 15-20 minutes

Bicycling 4 miles in 15 minutes

Jumping rope for 15 minutes

Running 1½ miles in 15 minutes (10 min/mile)

Shoveling snow for 15 minutes

Stair walking for 15 minutes

Less Vigorous, More Time

More Vigorous, Less Time

SOURCE: U.S. Centers for Disease Control and Prevention.
NOTE: A moderate amount of physical activity is roughly equivalent to physical activity that uses approximately 150 Calories (kcal) of energy per day, or 1,000 Calories per week. Some activities can be performed at various intensities; the suggested durations correspond to expected intensity of effort.

flexibility have not been extensively studied. Experts have hesitated to provide explicit health-related guidelines for activities that increase muscular strength (such as weight training) and flexibility (such as stretching and hatha yoga), because of the lack of data. Studies of these activities have begun to accumulate, prompting the following conclusion in the U.S. Surgeon General's report: "Recent recommendations from experts also suggest that cardiorespiratory endurance activity should be supplemented with strength-developing exercises at least twice per week for adults . . . " (U.S. DHHS, 1996 p. 37). It is likely that recommendations for strength and flexibility exercises will undergo an evolution over the next few years as additional studies are reported.

The development of guidelines for the minimal and optimal amounts of physical activity for health benefits is an ongoing challenge. The task of developing guidelines is complicated by the emerging findings that different health outcomes are related to different types and amounts of physical activity. Thus, a great deal of further research is needed to develop a firm empirical basis for guidelines for the public. Continued research on the dose of physical activity needed to achieve various health outcomes is of great public health importance. Additional research is needed on the effects of guidelines, to determine if they make any difference to people's perceptions and behaviors and if they influence the actions of policymakers.

Physical Activity Guidelines for Young People

The physical activity recommendations discussed above are based on extensive documentation from hundreds of studies of adults. Recommendations for physical activity in children and adolescents have generally been an afterthought, if they were considered at all. When recommendations are provided for youth, there has been no attempt to base them on studies of physical activity and health variables in young people. Instead, adult guidelines are assumed to apply to youth. This process has not generated confidence in the existing physical activity recommendations for youth.

In 1994, two guidelines on physical activity for adolescents were published based on extensive reviews of the literature concerning adolescents (Sallis & Patrick, 1994). Seven literature reviews determined that regular physical activity produced important health benefits during adolescence (i.e., psychological health, obesity management, and aerobic fitness) and influenced risk factors related to chronic diseases in adulthood (i.e., bone health, blood pressure, blood lipids). Adolescents were defined as ages 11 to 21, and children were not included in these reviews because of a lack of scientific data.

The resulting physical activity guidelines for adolescents were surprisingly consistent with the guidelines for adults. The first guideline, shown in Table 4.1, is similar to the moderate-intensity guideline for adults and states that adolescents should be active every day (Sallis & Patrick, 1994). Daily activity, regardless of intensity, appears to have several positive health effects.

Even brief, daily, weight-bearing activities can promote greater bone density. Substantial amounts of daily physical activity are expected to reduce risk of obesity by increasing energy expenditure. Although the studies of adolescents did not support specific conclusions about the length of the activity, the 30-minute guideline for moderate physical activity from *Healthy People 2000* (U.S. DHHS, 1991) was adopted.

The second adolescent guideline was similar to the 1990 ACSM recommendation. Studies of adolescents clearly showed that moderate to vigorous exercise increased aerobic fitness and improved psychological health in the general population. In adolescents with "at-risk" levels, physical activity reduced blood pressure and increased high-density lipoprotein cholesterol. The consensus group recognized that these guidelines also apply to adolescents with special needs such as medical conditions or mobility limitations.

In 1997, an international group convened by the Health Education Authority in the United Kingdom reexamined physical activity recommendations for youth (Biddle, Sallis, & Cavill, 1998). The goal of the conference—and the resulting book—was to review a broad range of literature on youth physical activity and health, develop physical activity recommendations, and create a framework for policies and programs to promote youth physical activity throughout the United Kingdom.

There are some important differences from the 1994 guidelines for adolescents (Sallis & Patrick, 1994). Although the Health Education Authority recommended 30 minutes of "physical activity of at least moderate intensity" every day for those who are inactive, the primary recommendation was for 1 hour per day. Maintaining the 30-minute recommendation as a minimal standard keeps the recommendation for youth consistent with the adult guidelines. However, two specific findings led to the preferred recommendation of 1 hour per day: (a) Most young people are already active 30 minutes per day, but (b) the prevalence of obesity is increasing in the United Kingdom and other developed nations (Biddle et al., 1998).

Young people are also encouraged to include activities that enhance muscular strength, flexibility, and bone health at least 2 days per week. There continues to be little empirical evidence of the health benefits of strength and flexibility exercises in youth, but the consensus of the group strongly supported the specific promotion of activities that should affect these fitness components (Biddle et al., 1998).

The Health Education Authority recommendations do not specifically recommend 20 minutes of structured moderate-to-vigorous physical activity for 3 or more days each week (Biddle et al., 1998), so this is a major departure from the 1994 adolescent guidelines (Sallis & Patrick, 1994). The reason for deleting this recommendation was the finding from heart rate monitoring studies that very few young people engage in continuous physical activity, although survey studies find that many young people report this pattern of physical activity (see Chapter 6). The Health Education Authority group decided it was counterproductive to recommend a pattern of physical activity that young people are unlikely to achieve.

Public health experts are motivated to produce health-related physical activity guidelines for young people because of anticipated positive effects on current physical and psychological health, as well as the possibility of reducing risk for chronic diseases of adulthood. However, the limited scientific literature linking physical activity and health outcomes in youth means that recommendations must rely heavily on the consensus of experts. It is hoped these recommendations for youth will encourage the development of programs to promote physical activity in young people and stimulate more research to provide a scientific basis for refining current guidelines.

SUMMARY

As physical activity is adopted as a public health priority by various nations, it is important to inform people how much physical activity they need to do to maintain good health. Initial guidelines were based on exercise needed to enhance fitness, but in the past few years, recommendations have explicitly been designed to promote health in entire populations. There are at least two motivating factors behind the recent statements about physical activity guidelines and their continuing revision. The first motivator is the recognition that large proportions of adults in the industrialized world are too sedentary to preserve health and well-being. Providing clear guidelines about how much activity is needed to prevent disease may lead some people to increase their activity. The second motivator is that specific guidelines are needed so that health promotion programs can be developed to help people become adequately active and policymakers can determine whether programs are working.

It may be easy to get confused by the array of physical activity guidelines from various sources, but the basic message can be simply stated. The current approach to improving health through physical activity recommendations is summarized well in the British consensus document: "The strategic aim has to be one of making more people, more active, more often" (Killoran et al., 1994, p. 213).

FURTHER READING

Killoran, A., Fentem, P., & Caspersen, C. (Eds.). (1994). *International perspectives on promoting physical activity.* London: Health Education Authority.

A careful literature review documents the empirical basis of the moderate physical activity guidelines that were adopted for the United Kingdom.

Pate, R. R., Pratt, M., Blair, S. N., Haskell, W. L., Macera, C. A., Bouchard, C., Buchner, D., Ettinger, W., Heath, G. W., King, A. C., Kriska, A., Leon, A. S., Marcus, B. H., Morris, J., Paffenbarger, R. S., Patrick, K., Pollock, M. L., Rippe, J. M., Sallis, J., & Wilmore, J. H. (1995). Physical activity and public health: A recommendation from the Centers for Disease Control and Prevention and the American College of Sports Medicine. *Journal of the American Medical Association, 273,* 402-407.

This article describes and provides the justification for public health recommendations in the United States.

Sallis, J. F., & Patrick, K. (1994). Physical activity guidelines for adolescents: Consensus statement. *Pediatric Exercise Science, 6,* 302-314.

These are the first physical activity guidelines for young people to be specifically based on a review of studies of youth.

U.S. Department of Health and Human Services. (1991). *Healthy People 2000: National health promotion and disease prevention objectives* (DHHS Publication No. PHS 91-50212). Washington, DC: Government Printing Office.

Healthy People 2000 contains comprehensive recommendations for physical activity to promote all components of health-related fitness.

Measuring Physical Activity

Physical activity is difficult to measure because it is a complex behavior. It is, in fact, an entire class of behaviors that theoretically includes all bodily movement, ranging from fidgeting to participating in triathlons. The basic dimensions are commonly referred to by the acronym FITT: frequency, intensity, time, and type. Exercise recommendations are often given in FITT, and each dimension of FITT may affect different health outcomes.

For some purposes, it is desirable to assess all the FITT dimensions. You would need to assess at least frequency, intensity, and time to determine how many people in a population are meeting the Centers for Disease Control/American College of Sports Medicine recommendations of 30 minutes of daily moderate physical activity (see Chapter 4). For other purposes, it is sufficient to assess the overall amount, or volume, of physical activity. The most common measure of volume is kilocalorie (kcal) expenditure, a useful measure for weight control studies or programs.

Most of the health benefits are the result of physical activity over a period of weeks, months, or years. Many researchers are interested in characterizing "habitual" physical activity that reflects long-term patterns. However, many people may have no habitual level of physical activity. This is because types and amounts of physical activity differ from day to day, season to season, and year to year.

One way to assess habitual physical activity is to ask people to recall their "usual" or "typical" activity patterns. Assessing habitual physical activity in this way almost always oversimplifies a complex behavior, but these measures are useful for some purposes. Another strategy is to measure physical activity more accurately over several days. This can be done with self-reports or objective measures. How many days of physical activity must be assessed before the habitual level can be estimated? One study assessed young children with heart rate monitors and direct observation over several days. The researchers calculated that, depending on the heart rate measure used, between 2 and 20 days of monitoring were needed before a reliable estimate of habitual physical activity could be obtained (DuRant et al., 1993). Not surprisingly, few studies are able to measure study participants for large numbers of days. Because adults have less variation in their activity patterns than children, it may take many fewer days to estimate habitual physical activity in adults.

There is increasing interest in assessing specific sedentary behaviors, or levels of inactivity, because inactivity is part of the activity spectrum. Inactive time, such as hours of television viewing, has been associated with negative health effects, such as obesity (see Chapter 6), so it is an important topic for behavioral medicine. However, measurement of inactivity or sedentary behaviors is not well developed.

This chapter describes the major types of physical activity measures and provides examples of each type. The strengths and limitations of each type of measure are summarized.

Measurement of Adults' Physical Activity by Self-Report

To accurately determine the prevalence of physical activity (and inactivity) in the population, to assess the effect of an intervention program, or to identify the relationships between activity and various health outcomes or measures of human performance, self-report measures are the most frequently used.

Self-report questionnaires generally require respondents to recall their activities over a particular time frame (anywhere between 24 hours and 1 year) and may be administered by personal interview or telephone; they may be self-administered in person or through the mail. Respondents may be asked to recall leisure time activities only or both leisure time and occupational activities. They may be asked to recall varying levels of detail, with a less detailed approach asking for the frequency of participation in broad classes of activity (e.g., activities that cause sweating and breathlessness). In a more detailed assessment, respondents can be asked to recall the frequency, duration, and intensity of each activity in which the respondent participated every hour of the recall period.

The Harvard Alumni Activity Survey (HAAS) was originally developed for use in a study of the relationship between physical activity and heart attack risk (Paffenbarger, Wing, & Hyde, 1978). It is described in detail by Paffenbarger, Blair, Lee, and Hyde (1993). This instrument is self-administered through the mail and asks respondents the number of flights of stairs climbed, city blocks walked, and sports played (type and number of hours) over the previous 7 days. Sports are classified as strenuous (e.g., basketball, running) or light (boating, dancing, yard work). Each type of activity is ascribed an energy expenditure value; one flight of stairs climbed (4 kcal • min^{-1}), one block walked (8 kcal • min^{-1}), strenuous sports (10 kcal • min^{-1}), light sports (5 kcal • min^{-1}). Leisure time physical activity energy expenditure per week is calculated and expressed as total kcal.

Booth, Owen, Bauman, and Gore (1996a, 1996b) describe two types of interviewer-administered measures of physical activity that can also be used in a self-administered format. Both measures have been used in population surveys of physical activity participation in Australia. The first self-report measure asked respondents about their participation in broad classes of activity (vigorous, moderate, and walking) over the previous 2 weeks:

a. "In the past two weeks, did you engage in vigorous exercise—exercise which made you breathe harder or puff and pant (e.g., vigorous sports such as football, netball, tennis, squash, athletics, jogging or running, keep-fit exercises, vigorous swimming etc.)?"

b. "In the past two weeks did you engage in less vigorous exercise for recreation, sport, or health-fitness purposes which did not make you breathe harder or puff and pant?"

c. "In the past two weeks, did you walk for recreation or exercise?"

Those responding "yes" to the questions on moderate activity and walking were then asked to report the number of sessions of each type of activity. An index of total activity was established by summing the number of sessions of participation in vigorous and moderate activities and in walking. The responses for each level of activity and for total activity were transformed to produce three categories of frequency of participation: none, one to two times a week, and three or more times a week. By doing so, the data for this measure can be analyzed in both continuous and categorical form.

For the second self-report measure, respondents were presented with a list of 20 common leisure time physical activities (Table 5.1). They were asked, in reference to the activities they had undertaken over the last two weeks, to

a. identify up to five activities in which they had participated,
b. state the frequency of participation in each activity,
c. state the average duration of participation in each activity, and
d. state the usual intensity for each activity among the categories (very vigorous, fairly vigorous, not very vigorous, not at all vigorous).

The rate of energy expenditure for each intensity of participation for each activity, in metabolic equivalents or METS (Table 5.1), was multiplied by the total time engaged in the activity over the last 2 weeks. The resultant values were energy expenditures due to each activity and were expressed as kcal • kg^{-1} • day^{-1}. These data were summed to yield total energy expenditure owing to leisure time physical activity. Each activity was classified as very hard, hard, or moderate in intensity (Table 5.1) according to a compendium of intensity values for physical activities (Ainsworth et al., 1993) and the categorization of Blair and colleagues (Blair et al., 1985).

Respondents were also classified into one of four activity categories: vigorous, moderate, low, or sedentary. The criteria for each category were defined as follows:

Vigorous activity is considered participation in an aerobic activity (Table 5.1) at least six times over the last 2 weeks for a minimum of 20 minutes per session and a total energy expenditure value of greater than or equal to 3.8 kcal • kg^{-1} • day^{-1}. Respondents could participate in any combination of aerobic activities to meet the criteria. For example, two sessions of swimming, two of jogging, and two of bicycling. The two criteria of aerobic-type activity and energy expenditure value were used because respondents who engaged in extensive low-intensity activity (walking is the best example) could achieve a high energy expenditure without their exercising heart rate entering the

Table 5.1 Metabolic Equivalents (METS) for Leisure Time Activities at Four Self-Reported Intensities

Activity Type	Type & Intensity Codes	How vigorous was the activity?			
		Very	*Fairly*	*Not very*	*Not at all*
Athletics	a,vh	8	6	4	2
Table tennis	m	4	3	2	1
Sailing/boating	m	4	3	2	1
Cricket/football	a,vh	12	8	6	4
Snow skiing	vh	12	8	6	4
Water skiing	h	12	8	6	4
Ice skating	vh	12	8	6	4
Lawn bowls	m	4	3	2	1
Walking	a,m	7	4	2	1
Jogging	a,vh	13	10	7	4
Calisthenics	a,h	12	9	7	4
Aerobics	a,vh	12	8	4	2
Weight training	m	4	3	2	1
Circuit training	a,vh	12	8	4	2
Swimming	a,h	10	6	3	1
Bicycling	a,m	9	6	3	1
Netball/basketball	a,vh	12	8	4	2
Golf	m	4	3	2	1
Tennis	vh	8	6	4	2
Squash	a,vh	13	10	7	4

SOURCE: Based on Booth et al. (1996a, 1996b).
NOTE: One MET is the amount of energy expended by an adult of average weight while sleeping and is approximately equivalent to one kilocalorie $\bullet$ kg^{-1} $\bullet$ hr^{-1}).
KEY: a = aerobic activities; vh = very hard activities; h = hard activities; m = moderate activities.

training range. The criterion of 3.8 kcal $\bullet$ kg^{-1} $\bullet$ day^{-1} is approximately equivalent to 1,600 kcal $\bullet$ 2 weeks^{-1} (Bauman & Owen, 1991).

Moderate activity is a total energy expenditure value greater than or equal to 1.8 kcal $\bullet$ kg^{-1} $\bullet$ day^{-1} and not included in the "Aerobic" category. *Low-level activity* is a total energy expenditure value of 0.12 to 1.79 kcal $\bullet$ kg$^{-1}\bullet$ day^{-1}, inclusive. *Sedentary* is a total energy expenditure value less than 0.12 kcal $\bullet$ kg^{-1} $\bullet$ day^{-1}.

These four categories of activity have been shown in a cross-sectional study to be correlated with a number of biological indices of cardiovascular disease risk (Bauman & Owen, 1991), and those classified as being in the sedentary category have been shown to have sociodemographic characteristics that in other studies have been indicative of physical inactivity (e.g., Owen & Bauman, 1992; also see Chapter 6 of this volume).

The measures described above are examples of typical adult self-report physical activity measures used in epidemiologic studies. The quality of such measures must be examined critically, because poor measurement will produce (a) inaccurate population-prevalence estimates, which we describe in Chapter 6; (b) incorrect conclusions about the outcomes of the individual and community-level interventions, described in Chapters 8 and 9; and (c) poor-quality data on which to base policy initiatives, described in Chapter 9. Good-quality measurement is fundamental to all research on physical activity.

Criteria for evaluating measures include (a) reliability, (b) validity, (c) sensitivity to change, or responsiveness, (d) being nonreactive (not influencing respondent's behavior), (e) being acceptable to the respondent, and (f) having an acceptable cost of administration. LaPorte, Montoye, and Caspersen (1985) identified more than 30 different methods of assessing physical activity and concluded that none of the available methods met all of the criteria. That conclusion is still valid today. The method of physical activity assessment selected, then, must depend on the type of information required by the researcher and the resources available. Whatever the method selected, its limitations should be kept in mind when interpreting the findings of any study.

The type of self-report, or recall, methods described earlier generally meet three of the six criteria described above: They tend to be nonreactive, to be acceptable to respondents, and to have reasonable costs of administration.

Reliability and Validity of Measures of Adults' Self-Reported Physical Activity

Reliability, or repeatability, is the consistency with which an instrument assesses the object of measurement. Reliability is usually assessed in terms of agreement between different observers or instruments (interrater reliability) or between different measurement occasions using the same method (test-retest reliability).

Godin and Shephard (1985) employed a simple, self-administered questionnaire that asked respondents to report the number of times, on average, they engaged in strenuous, moderate, and light activities in their free time for at least 15 minutes. Arbitrary exercise units were created by multiplying the estimated rate of energy expenditure for each level of activity (9, 5, and 3 METS for strenuous, moderate, and light activity, respectively) by the reported frequency of participation in each level of activity. Total leisure time activity was calculated as the sum of the three activity measures. Test-retest reliabilities were 0.94, 0.46, 0.48 and 0.74 for strenuous, moderate, light, and total activity, respectively.

The Seven-Day Recall questionnaire administered by interview was developed for use in the Stanford Five-City Study and assesses both occupational and leisure time physical activities (Sallis et al., 1985). Respondents are asked to identify the activities in which they participated over the previous 7 days and to report the total amount of time spent at each activity. They were also asked to report the average number of hours of sleep per night. The activities were classified as moderate, hard, and very hard, and MET values were assigned to each classification (4, 6, and 10 METS, respectively). Sleep has a MET value of 1. The time spent at light activities was determined by subtraction and was given a MET value of 1.5. Total energy expenditure was calculated by multiplying the hours spent at each activity by the appropriate MET value, then taking the sum of the products, expressed as either kcal • kg^{-1} • day^{-1} or kcal • day^{-1}. This measure has since been modified, and a structured training program for interviewers was evaluated. The reliability of two interviewers who independently interviewed the same subject on the same day was $r = .86$, indicating that interviewers can be trained to a high standard (Gross, Sallis, Buono, Roby, & Nelson, 1990).

Folsom, Jacobs, Caspersen, Gomez-Marin, and Knudsen (1986) examined the test-retest reliability of the Minnesota Leisure Time Physical Activity Questionnaire. During a structured interview, respondents were asked to recall their participation in 63 leisure time physical activities over the preceding 12 months. Typical energy expenditure values for each type of activity were multiplied by the total duration of participation in each activity, then summed to provide total leisure time activity energy expenditure (expressed as kcal • day^{-1}). Energy expenditure for light (2.0-4.0 kcal • min^{-1}), moderate (4.5-5.5 kcal • min^{-1}), and heavy (> 6.0 kcal • min^{-1}) activities were also calculated. Test-retest correlations were lowest for light activity ($r = .79$) and highest for total energy expenditure ($r = .88$).

There are some inherent problems in assessing the reliability of physical activity by self-report (Booth et al., 1996b). For example, a large proportion of respondents may report no involvement at both test and retest measurements. Those respondents would have identical values (usually zero) on both measurement occasions, thus inflating the reliability of the measure of physical activity. An assumption of studies of repeatability is that the behavior is fairly stable over time. In the case of self-reported physical activity measures with a short recall period (often 7 days or 2 weeks), low reliability could be due to either true variation in the activities reported or poor measurement characteristics of the instrument, or both.

Validity, or accuracy, of measures is *the* key issue in the assessment of adults' physical activity levels. The latter sections of this chapter describe promising objective measures of physical activity that can be used as criterion or "gold standard" measures for evaluating self-reports. These objective measures include activity and heart rate monitors, direct observation methods, physiological markers, and an expensive but highly reliable and valid energy expenditure measure—doubly labeled water. Although most of these should be considered "silver" or even "bronze" standards, validity can usefully be assessed by examining the extent to which a self-report measure relates to some more objective measure of activity or fitness. We prefer objective measures of physical activity rather than fitness tests as validity criteria, because fitness levels have a strong genetic component, which may be related to genetic aspects of physical activity (Perusse, Tremblay, LeBlanc, & Bouchard, 1989).

Montoye, Kemper, Saris, and Washburn (1996) compiled tables of validity results of all published studies using a variety of validity criteria. Eight validity studies of the Harvard Alumni Questionnaire were summarized (Montoye et al., 1996, p. 48). One study using doubly labeled water, the best measure of energy expenditure, was correlated $r = .39$ with the survey. Three studies that used the Caltrac accelerometer (a motion sensor) produced a wide range of correlations (r's $= -.03$, .30, and .70). Moderate correlations with aerobic fitness have also been reported. In general, the validity of the Harvard Alumni Survey is strongly supported, but because there is inaccuracy in both the self-report and the criterion, there are often inconsistencies across studies.

The Stanford 7-day recall interview has been examined for validity in 11 studies (Montoye et al., 1996). The correlation with doubly labeled water was $r = .30$. Correlations with the Caltrac accelerometer varied, but almost all were significant (r's $= .12, .14, .33, .37, .49, .57$, and $.79$). Physical fitness also correlates with the 7-day recall, so this widely used measure also shows good evidence of validity.

The Minnesota Leisure Time Questionnaire has been evaluated in five studies (Montoye et al., 1996, p. 46). The correlation with doubly labeled water was $r = .26$. Correlations with the Caltrac accelerometer were lower than for the previous self-reports ($r = -.06, .18,$ and $.40$), but the correlation with another activity monitor was $r = .45$. Correlations with aerobic fitness were generally supportive of validity. Because fitness measures should reflect activity over an extended period, they may be particularly appropriate validity criteria for long-term recalls such as the Minnesota 12-month recall.

All of these commonly used measures of physical activity have substantial evidence of validity. However, none of the correlations with any of the objective criteria were high. That means that even these best self-report measures have considerable error. These error-prone measures are still able to show strong associations with health outcomes, so they are very useful in indicating which people are more active and less active. However, it is unknown how accurately adults can report their absolute level of physical activity. The technology has only recently become available to objectively assess the minutes spent at different intensities of physical activity, so these new monitors can be used to determine how accurately people can report minutes spent in moderate and vigorous intensity activity.

Child Self-Reports

Self-reports are widely used in children because of their low cost and convenience of administration. The lack of valid objective measures that are affordable and suit investigators' needs also encourages a reliance on self-reports. There are several types of child physical activity self-reports, including self-administered recall, interviewer-administered recall, diary, and proxy reports, in which parents and/or teachers report on the child's physical activity (Sallis, 1991). These types of measures vary in cost of implementation, adherence rate, and validity. Self-administered recalls are the least costly, because they can be given to entire classes of students in school. Diaries may be the most accurate, but they require the cooperation of the children and are limited to use by children with good reading and writing skills. Interviewer-administered recalls are expensive because they require one-to-one interviews. Most proxy reports of children's physical activity have not been shown to be valid, probably because neither parents nor teachers are able to observe children all day. The most commonly used methods are self- and interviewer-administered recalls, so examples of these are described here.

Baranowski (1988) discussed the considerable cognitive demands placed on children when they are asked to recall specific events. The accuracy of the recalls depends in part on the detail that is requested, the format of the question, pretraining before the recall, and the use of prompting questions and probes. Even more so, the validity of recalls depends on the cognitive development and age of the child.

A critical question is, How old does a child have to be before he or she can accurately recall physical activity? This question was addressed by a study that evaluated the reliability and validity of the 7-day recall interview in three age groups of children and adolescents (Sallis, Buono, Roby, Micale, & Nelson, 1993). This is the same 7-day recall used for adults. It is a semistructured interview during which the interviewer asks the respondent to recall the time spent in sleep and moderate, hard, and very hard physical activities for each of the past 7 days. The interview was repeated twice within a 7-day period, and reliability was based on the correlation of days that were recalled on both interviews. As expected, the test-retest reliability increased with age: $r = .47$ for 5th graders, .59 for 8th graders, and .81 for 11th graders. All of these correlations were statistically significant, but only the 11th graders had a reliability correlation that would be considered acceptable for adult measures. Validity was assessed by comparing reported time in high-intensity activities with minutes of high heart rates (i.e., greater than 140 beats per minute) on the same days. There was a large variation in validity correlations by age: $r = .29$ for 5th graders, .45 for 8th graders, and .72 for 11th graders. This study indicates that 5th- and 8th-grade children are limited in their ability to recall their physical activity. Based on this study and other data, it is recommended that physical activity recalls should not be used at all with children in less than the 4th grade (Sallis, 1991). Reliability and validity of children's self-reports are limited until they reach high school.

It could be argued that self-reports should not be used at all until children are 15 or 16 years old. However, validity correlations are usually significant in fourth- and fifth-grade samples, and many investigators do not have other physical activity measures available to them. Each investigator needs to decide if the accuracy of children's physical activity recalls is sufficient to adequately answer the research question.

Recalling physical activity is a difficult task for children, but it appears to be easier if they are asked to recall over a short time period. In the study of the 7-day recall, children completed two recalls in less than a 7-day period, so some days were recalled twice (Sallis, Buono, et al., 1993). The correlations of overall physical activity scores on matched days were computed for short (2-3 days) and long (4-6 days) intervals between recalls. Across all ages, when children had to remember only the past 2 to 3 days, the reliability of recall was $r = .79$. When children had to remember the past 4 to 6 days, the reliability was $r = .45$. This finding that length of recall makes a big difference in accuracy has led to an emphasis on brief recalls, especially for younger children. For maximal accuracy, 1-day recalls are preferred.

The validity of 1-day recalls was assessed in fifth-grade students from four regions of the United States (Sallis, Strikmiller, et al., 1996). This study also directly compared versions that were individually interviewer administered or self-administered to entire classrooms of children. In the self-administered version, assessment staff read the items out loud and answered questions. Both versions used checklists of common physical activities to aid children's memories, and children reported the minutes they spent doing these physical activities the previous day. See Figure 5.1 for the data collection form. Selected sedentary behaviors, such as watching television and playing computer games, were also assessed. Before administering the tests, children received brief training in defining physical activities and in estimating time spent in activities. Validity was assessed by correlations with heart rate and activity monitoring data that were gathered the day before the recall.

Surprisingly, the self-administered and interviewer-administered versions had similar levels of validity. The score from the self-administered recall correlated .59 with heart rate and .32 with accelerometer variables, and the interviewer-administered version correlated .54 with heart rate and .38 with accelerometer. These validity correlations are somewhat higher than those for the 7-day recall with similar age children (Sallis, Buono, et al., 1993), possibly because of the improved recall over 1 day. The validity of both 1-day recalls was supported by correlations with two objective measures, but the self-administered version is recommended for further use, because it can be administered to large numbers of children at low cost.

Correlations demonstrate validity only in the limited sense that children who report more activity have higher scores on objective measures. A more stringent test is to examine the absolute accuracy of reports. In the study of 1-day recalls (Sallis et al., 1996), this was done by comparing reported activity minutes with an estimate of 43 minutes from heart rate monitoring data. Fifth graders reported 73 minutes on the interviewer-administered recall and 94 minutes on the self-administered recall. Thus, the self-reports of total activity appeared to be overestimates of 67% and 112%. These results

Section B. Activities

A. Activity	B. Before School	N S M	D. During School	N S M	F. After School	N S M	
	C. None, Some, Most		E. None, Some, Most		G. None, Some, Most		
1 Bicycling							1
2 Swimming laps							2
3 Gymnastics: bars, beam, tumbling, trampoline							3
4 Exercise: push-ups, sit-ups, jumping jacks							4
5 Basketball							5
6 Baseball/softball							6
7 Football							7
8 Soccer							8
9 Volleyball							9
10 Racket sports: badminton, tennis							10
11 Ball playing: four square, dodge ball, kickball							11
12 Games: chase, tag, hopscotch							12
13 Outdoor play: climbing trees, hide-and-seek							13
14 Water play: swimming pool, ocean, or lake							14
15 Jump rope							15
16 Dance							16
17 Outdoor chores: mowing, raking, gardening							17
18 Indoor chores: mopping, vacuuming, sweeping							18
19 Mixed walking/running							19
20 Walking							20
21 Running							21
22 Other: physical activity classes, lessons, or teams							22
23							23
24							24
25							25

(continued)

	Before School	*After School*
T.V./Video	H.1 _____ hours _____ minutes	H.2 _____ hours _____ minutes
Video games & computer games . . .	H.3 _____ hours _____ minutes	H.4 _____ hours _____ minutes

Figure 5.1. Form used for one-day recall of physical activities, suitable for use with older primary school age children.

SOURCE: Sallis, Strikmiller, et al. (1996). SAPAC/PACI DATA FORM. Reprinted with permission.

indicate that children's reports of activity minutes should not be taken at face value, which calls into question prevalence rates of physical activity patterns based on self-reports.

For some purposes, it is important to obtain an indication of habitual physical activity, and older adolescents may be able to provide adequate reports. A 1-year self-administered physical activity recall was developed and evaluated for adolescents by Aaron et al. (1995). The survey used a list of activities, and respondents reported the frequency and duration of each activity that was done 10 times or more over the past year. An evaluation was conducted with one hundred 15- to 18-year-olds. For the validity measure, four 7-day recall surveys were collected at 3-month intervals. The correlation between the 1-year recall and mean of four 1-week recalls was $r = .83$. This shows that adolescents can reliably recall their physical activity over the past year, but correlations with other self-reports are very weak evidence of validity. However, reports of participating in specific organized activities were validated by rosters in 86% to 100% of cases.

In summary, self-reported physical activity should not be used in children younger than 9 or 10 years old. From age 9 until about 15, self-reports should be used cautiously, and adolescents about age 15 or older should be expected to provide reports of the same quality as adults. Recalls of brief periods are more valid than recalls of longer periods at any age, but adolescents can reliably report activity patterns over the past year. Reports of absolute physical activity minutes have not been validated for any age. Continuing challenges for physical activity self-reports of youth are to validate assessments of moderate- and vigorous-intensity activities. A general recommendation is to use self-reports to supplement data from the objective measures described below.

Activity and Heart Rate Monitors

Activity and heart rate monitors have the promise of substantial benefits over self-report measures of physical activity, because they avoid the biases and inaccuracies of recalls, provide quantitative data on both physical activity and energy expenditure, and provide comparable data across ages and population groups. There are limitations of both types of measures, so they cannot be considered the "ultimate solution" to physical activity measurement.

Accelerometers and pedometers are the most commonly used activity monitors. Pedometers have been used since the 1920s to count steps while walking and running, and mechanical and electronic models are now available. The mechanical devices are known to have low validity and a great deal of interinstrument variability, so they are not used for research (Bassett et al., 1996).

A study comparing five electronic pedometers found some to be more valid than others. Pedometers can either count steps or estimate distance walked, if stride length is estimated. Based on number of steps taken, the Yamax Digi-Walker had less than 1% error, compared with up to 14% error from other devices (Bassett et al., 1996). This device had less interinstrument variability than all the others, based on comparisons of pedometers on left and right hips. The Digi-Walker was also more accurate than others at slow speeds, although all pedometers functioned better at faster walking speeds.

The most commonly used activity monitor is the accelerometer. The unidimensional accelerometers that are commercially available assess vertical movement of the trunk. When the body moves vertically, a lever is displaced that generates electrical current proportional to the energy of the acceleration. This current can be used as a raw number to indicate movement, or it can be entered into a formula with age, sex, height, and weight to estimate energy expenditure. The Caltrac accelerometer used in most studies was made by Hemokinetics (Madison, Wisconsin), but a modified device is now available from Muscle Dynamics (Torrance, California).

The Caltrac has high interinstrument reliability when two devices are worn at the same time ($r = .89-.94$; Montoye et al., 1996, p. 83). Several studies have shown that Caltracs worn on the waist are highly correlated with either workload or energy expenditure on treadmills for children and adults. Typical correlations are in the range of $r = .70$ to $.90$. Validity studies conducted in the field produce more variable results, because of the different criterion measures used. As examples, Caltrac correlated $r = .54$ with heart rate recording, $r = .55$ with doubly labeled water, $r = .69$ with direct observation of adults, and $r = .40$ with direct observation of children (Montoye et al., 1996, p. 87).

The benefits of the Caltrac are its small size, relatively low cost, and lack of interference with ongoing activity. It is a valid measure of movement with an important vertical component, which characterizes the vast majority of activities and sports that involve walking and running. On the other hand, many activities are not assessed well by the device. Bicycling, weight lifting, skating, swimming, and some calisthenics are common examples. Even on a treadmill, accelerometers are not sensitive to changes in grade or carrying heavy objects. Another limitation is the display that shows only cumulative counts or kcals. Unfortunately, it impossible to tell whether a low score is due to sedentariness or failure to wear the instrument.

Some of the limitations of the Caltrac have been overcome by the CSA accelerometer (Computer Science and Applications, Shalimar, Florida). This instrument has a memory that stores activity counts for user-defined periods that can be as short as 1 second (Melanson & Freedson, 1995). This allows an investigator to examine the pattern of activity, assess time spent in activities of different intensities, and verify that the instrument was actually being worn. Data are downloaded directly to a computer. The CSA and Caltrac were found to have similar validity in a treadmill study of university students (Melanson & Freedson, 1995), and there were correlations ranging from $r = .50$ to .74 with heart rate monitoring in children (Janz, 1994).

Other limitations of unidimensional accelerometers may be overcome by the newer triaxial accelerometers. Three accelerometers detect vertical, horizontal, and lateral movements, but this theoretical advantage has not been shown convincingly to improve sensitivity to the entire range of physical activities. The Tritrac R3D (Hemokinetics, Madison, Wisconsin) features separate or combined data from the three accelerometers, storage of output for user-defined periods, and storage of raw counts and energy expenditure. This device can collect minute-by-minute data up to 21 days at a time, but it is substantially larger than the Caltrac or CSA monitor ($11.1 \times 6.7 \times 3.2$ cm). The larger size may make some participants reluctant to wear it, and it may interfere with activities in younger children. In one study of children, Tritrac was highly correlated with Caltrac scores ($r = .88$) and moderately correlated with heart rate data (r = .58) (Welk & Corbin, 1995). A study of obese children reported high correlations between Tritrac and heart rate monitoring (r = .71) (Coleman, Saelens, Wiedrich-Smith, Finn, & Epstein, 1997).

Heart Rate Monitoring

Heart rate is highly correlated with oxygen uptake, especially during exercise. This means that heart rate can be used to estimate workload or intensity of activity. However, a given heart rate for one person does not indicate the same amount of work as the same heart rate for another person. This means that energy expenditure cannot be estimated from heart rate recordings unless the individual's heart rate/oxygen uptake curve has been determined during a fitness test. In most studies of habitual physical activity, heart rate throughout the day is used as an index of physical activity intensity.

Small, affordable heart rate telemetry units have been used with a wide variety of populations. The Sport Tester PE 3000 (Polar Electro OY, Kempel, Finland) has been used in many studies. It consists of a strap around the chest that contains electrodes and a transmitter. A receiving unit is worn like a wristwatch, and it has a memory that can store minute-by-minute data for up to 16 hours of monitoring. The data are downloaded directly to a computer. The heart rate telemetry devices are extremely valid, with about a 2% error rate (Montoye et al., 1996). Compared with other objective measures of physical activity, correlations have varied from r = .73 with doubly labeled water in adults to r = .64 with observation of children during physical education classes (Montoye et al., 1996, pp. 106-107).

The advantages of heart rate recording include high validity and the sensitivity of heart rates to activity intensity. A major disadvantage is the inability of heart rates to distinguish light- and moderate-intensity activities. Elevated heart rates can be produced by mental stress in the absence of physical activity, and this is a particular problem because most activity is in the light to moderate range. Only high-intensity activity produces high heart rates, so this method is most appropriate for assessing vigorous physical activity. Another disadvantage is the inconvenience of using the telemetry equipment. Especially in children, the chest strap slips down when they sweat, stopping the recording. Consecutive days of monitoring are difficult or impossible because the chest electrodes cause irritation and occasional rashes. Various electronic devices, including televisions, microwaves, and other telemetric transmitters, interfere with the receiver and cause lost data.

Combined Activity and Heart Rate Monitors

The combination of activity and heart rate monitors has the potential to overcome the weaknesses of both. Activity monitors are not sensitive to additional energy expenditure due to carrying loads or moving up an incline, and monitors on the trunk cannot detect stationary activities or those with extensive arm or leg movements. Heart rate monitoring is not sensitive to activity at lower-intensity levels. If activity monitors were placed on arm, leg, and trunk, and individual heart rate/oxygen uptake curves were computed, a combination monitor system should be able to provide an accurate measure of a wide variety of types of physical activity (Haskell, Yee, Evans, & Irby, 1993).

A combination activity and heart rate monitor, called the Vitalog, has undergone initial evaluation (Haskell et al., 1993). The Vitalog was effective in assessing activities such as stationary cycling, arm cranking, bench stepping, walking, and running. A difficulty of a combination system is integrating the results from all sensors. However, a multiple regression equation was able to account for .73 of the variance in oxygen uptake across all activities.

The Vitalog is a promising system, but it awaits advances in technology to reduce the size and weight of its components. A combination monitor system that requires sensors on the arm, leg, and trunk, in addition to heart rate electrodes, will be cumbersome to use, and it is likely to be expensive. However, the development of a commercially available system will provide the first objective measure of physical activity that can provide data on the frequency, intensity, duration, and type (e.g., involvement of legs or arms).

Observational Measures Used With Children

Children's physical activity is well suited to assessment by direct observation, because the behavior is overt and often done in public places. Direct observation has the advantage of assessing multiple dimensions of physical activity. Activity and heart rate monitors can provide data on frequency, intensity, and duration of physical activity, but direct observation can also quantify type of activity, environmental setting, and related social interactions. Children have been observed in many settings, including homes, schools, and playgrounds. Codes are often entered into portable computers, easing some of the logistical problems of collecting this type of data.

Several observation strategies can be used to assess physical activity (McKenzie, 1991). With the momentary time sampling method, activity level is coded at the moment the observation interval ends. This provides a snapshot or sample of activity levels. The partial time-sampling method requires observers to code all activities that occur during a short interval, usually 5 to 20 seconds. In the partial-interval recording, observers code the main activity that occurs during brief intervals, such as 10 seconds. Duration recording requires observers to note the beginning and ending time of each activity. Duration recording is rarely used with children, because they change activities so often.

Direct observation is considered to have high validity if two observers demonstrate high reliability. Thus, it is essential to develop coding systems that can be reliably recorded, and this requirement usually leads to simple systems, with three to six activity categories. Most observation systems have interobserver agreements that range from 85% to 99% (McKenzie, 1991; Montoye et al., 1995). Although direct observation should be seen as a valid objective measure of physical activity, several studies have documented the validity, usually with comparisons to heart rate. In virtually all cases, more vigorous activity categories show higher heart rates (McKenzie, 1991).

Two physical activity observation systems illustrate different approaches. The BEACHES (Behaviors of Eating and Activity for Child Health) system was developed for use with children aged 4 to 9 years (McKenzie et al., 1991). The five activity codes are recorded at the end of each 30-second observation interval: lying, sitting, standing, walking, and very active. Notice that the first three codes are actually body positions that all indicate lack of activity. The very active category includes all activities that require more energy expenditure than walking, and these activities can be done in any body position. For example, wrestling can be done while lying down, and bicycles are ridden while sitting. The 30-second observation interval is followed by a 30-second recording interval, and data are entered into a portable computer. Heart rates were highly related to activity category, ranging from a mean heart rate of 99 beats per minute in the lying category to 153 beats per minute in the very active category. The BEACHES system as a whole contains 10 codes, so data are simultaneously collected on location, whether eating occurs, the presence of other people, television viewing, and various social interactions related to eating and physical activity. BEACHES was used to assess children at home and school (McKenzie et al., 1991), and the activity codes have been used to evaluate physical education interventions (McKenzie et al., 1996; McKenzie et al., 1993).

A different approach was taken in developing activity categories for the Children's Activity Rating Scale (CARS) (Puhl, Greaves, Hoyt, & Baranowski, 1990). Data are collected each minute, with 30 seconds for observation and 30 seconds for recording. The five activity categories are stationary, no movement; stationary, movement (usually of arms or legs); translocation, easy; translocation, moderate; translocation, strenuous. This system is designed to make finer distinctions between rate of energy expenditure. This is an advantage over the BEACHES; however, the CARS has somewhat lower interobserver reliabilities. The CARS categories are also highly related to heart rate, providing strong evidence of validity.

Observation systems can provide high-quality and rich data on children's activities, but there are important disadvantages. Cost is a major limitation, because multiple observers are needed for each study, and each observer requires extensive initial training and ongoing assessment and retraining. To obtain a thorough assessment of children's physical activity, it is necessary to observe children for most of their waking day, on several days of the year. Few investigators can afford this extent of measurement. The other major limitation is access to study participants. Direct observation has been used most extensively with young children, because they must be supervised by adults anyway, and they do not often object to being observed. Most older children and adults do not allow this type of intrusive measure. For older children and adults, direct observation may be most useful for validating other measures or for assessing physical activity in specific public settings, such as parks, sports venues, or workplaces.

Doubly Labeled Water

The doubly labeled water technique has attracted attention because it appears to be a gold standard for the assessment of energy expenditure (Montoye et al., 1996). Because it assesses all forms of energy expenditure, it is not a specific measure of physical activity. Metabolic rate and thermic effect of food are quite stable, and because the most variable component of energy expenditure is physical activity, it is the major determinant of individual differences. Assessment by doubly labeled water requires that the study participant ingest a known amount of isotopes of hydrogen (^{2}H) and oxygen (^{18}O). These isotopes are not radioactive, so there is no risk to the participant. The isotopes become distributed throughout the body water in a matter of hours, and a baseline reading of their concentration is taken from a urine sample. One to 3 weeks later, participants provide another urine sample, and based on these samples, energy expenditure can be calculated for the entire interval.

Labeled hydrogen leaves the body as water, through urine, sweat, and moisture in respiration. Labeled oxygen leaves the body in the same way, *plus* as carbon dioxide from respiration. Because the amount of carbon dioxide lost through respiration is very closely related to oxygen consumption, energy expenditure can be calculated based on the difference between rates of loss of ^{2}H and ^{18}O.

The advantages of the doubly labeled water method include a very high validity, with most studies showing an error rate of less than 3%. The method can be used in laboratory or field conditions and seems to be equally valid for children and adults. Measures are taken over a 1- to 3-week period, so habitual physical activity is assessed. The method is safe, places little burden on the participant, and is not expected to influence his or her physical activity level.

The primary disadvantage is the cost. Each dose of ^{18}O currently costs several hundred U.S. dollars, although the price is dropping. The analysis of samples requires a mass spectrometer, which costs about U.S.$250,000. Finally, the measure does not provide data on the type, frequency, intensity, or duration of physical activity. Doubly labeled water is valuable for small controlled studies and as a criterion by which to validate other physical activity measures (Montoye et al., 1996).

SUMMARY

Most studies of large groups use questionnaires to assess physical activity. There are many measures available for adults, and several have reasonably good evidence of reliability and validity. The accuracy of reports of the absolute minutes of physical activity reported is suspect, and estimates are likely to be inflated. The age of children is highly related to reliability and validity of self-reported physical activity. Self-reports should not be used with children less than 9 or 10 years of age. Quality of self-reports is limited during the early teen years, and accuracy appears to be higher for short-term recalls. Adolescents aged 15 or 16 and above are able to report their activities as well as adults.

Electronic activity monitors and heart rate monitors are an alternative to self-reports. Newer activity monitors record minute-by-minute patterns of physical activity continuously for several weeks, so time in moderate and vigorous intensity activities can be assessed objectively. There are limitations to both activity and heart rate monitors. Systems that combine both types of monitors are not widely available but are expected to provide highly accurate data on the patterns of physical activity. Objective measures can be used to validate self-reports, but the electronic monitors should also be used to measure physical activity participation in populations and evaluate intervention programs. Doubly labeled water is an expensive but accurate measure of energy expenditure, but it provides no data on physical activity patterns. The search continues for other physiological markers of activity.

FURTHER READING

Ainsworth, B. E., Montoye, H. J., & Leon, A. S. (1994). Methods of assessing physical activity during leisure and work. In C. Bouchard, R. J. Shephard, & T. Stephens (Eds.), *Physical activity, fitness, and health* (pp. 146-159). Champaign, IL: Human Kinetics.

This chapter is an excellent overview of assessment methods, with discussion of issues affecting reliability and validity.

Montoye, H. J., Kemper, H. C. G., Saris, W. H. M., & Washburn, R. A. (1996). *Measuring physical activity and energy expenditure.* Champaign, IL: Human Kinetics.

This book is the definitive review of all assessment methods. It contains tables summarizing all reliability and validity studies.

Pereira, M. A., Fitzgerald, S. J., Gregg, E. W., Joswiak, M. L., Ryan, W. J., Suminski, R. R., Utter, A. C., Zmuda, J. M., Kriska, A. M., & Caspersen, C. J. (1997). A collection of physical activity questionnaires for health-related research. *Medicine and Science in Sports and Exercise, 29* (Suppl. to No. 6), S1-S205.

This is an extremely useful publication that includes reproductions of actual survey instruments, instructions, and scoring directions. Reliability and validity studies are also summarized.

The Descriptive Epidemiology
of Physical Activity

In this chapter, we discuss a key element of the information needed to allow public health researchers and practitioners to proceed from a scientific understanding of the health benefits of more physically active lifestyles to appropriate and effective initiatives to promote physical activity. Descriptive epidemiology deals, in large part, with the distribution of health behaviors and other health risks in the population as a whole and in particular social groups, settings, or localities. Descriptive epidemiology studies of physical activity play a key role in shaping national policy (e.g., Booth, Bauman, Owen, & Gore, 1997; Killoran, Fentem, & Caspersen, 1994).

This chapter describes selected studies that may be characterized as the descriptive epidemiology (or demography) of physical activity and inactivity (e.g., Caspersen & Merritt, 1995; Owen & Bauman, 1992). These studies identify groups of people with relatively high and low levels of physical activity, with an emphasis on demographic characteristics, such as sex, age, ethnicity, socioeconomic status, and location of residence. Within the behavioral epidemiology framework, these data are crucial to planning the public health initiatives encompassed by Phases 4 and 5. The usefulness of these studies depends in large part on the quality of the measures used. Because most of these studies rely on self-reported data, there is error in all the estimates reported in this chapter.

Initiatives and programs to promote physical activity for particular community groups, campaigns directed at the whole population, and public policy innovations to create new activity settings and environments require good descriptive epidemiology data for at least three reasons. First, it is important to know the extent to which physical inactivity has become an integral part of people's lives. If, for example, 90% of the adult population were active consistent with the ACSM (1990) guidelines described in Chapter 4, there would be a weak public health argument for efforts to promote higher levels of exercise participation.

Second, we need to know how physical inactivity is distributed in the population. Are women or men the more active sex? Are older adults more or less active than those who are middle-aged? Are those who are well educated or financially well-off more active than those who are not? Identifying less active groups allows interventions to be developed that are tailored to the needs and situations of these groups.

Third, what are the trends over time in physical activity participation? Are most people more or less active now than they were 10 years ago? This type of information helps determine whether the need for further interventions is increasing or decreasing.

Comparisons of Adult Activity Levels in Industrialized Nations

Measures of self-reported participation in leisure time physical activity (see the section "Measurement of Adults' Physical Activity by Self-Report" in Chapter 5) have been used in population surveys since the early 1980s in a small number of economically developed nations. Such surveys, particularly in the United States, Canada, England, and Australia (Caspersen & Merritt, 1995; Caspersen, Merritt, & Stephens, 1994) have collected data on relatively large samples of the adult population.

Population sampling methods allow physical activity researchers to obtain information that has a high degree of generalizability. The first level of generalizability is the total population estimate: It is possible to be confident that the proportions of active and inactive people found in the sample correspond closely to the whole population from which the sample was drawn. The second level of generalizability is to subgroups. If the sampling methods are designed to adequately recruit members of key groups— for example, age, gender, education, and race and ethnicity subgroups—it is possible to make estimates about each of these subgroups and the differences between them (Drury, 1989). This is very important because activity levels vary widely in different population groups, and different approaches are often needed to effectively intervene with various subgroups.

International comparisons, where they have been possible, have generally demonstrated consistencies between the leisure time physical activity levels of people living in industrialized countries. For example, when similar measures and criteria were used, it was found that about one quarter to one third of adults in the United States, Canada, England, and Australia could be characterized as sedentary in their leisure time physical activity habits (*Allied Dunbar National Fitness Survey,* 1992; Caspersen & Merritt, 1995; Caspersen et al., 1994; Fentem & Walker, 1994). Between 10% and 15% of adults report that they engage in regular vigorous exercise. Chapter 4 ("Patterns and Trends in Physical Activity") of the 1996 U.S. Surgeon General's report *Physical Activity and Health* (U.S. Department of Health and Human Services [DHHS], 1996) provides a detailed summary of the findings from several large surveys of U.S. samples conducted mainly during the 1990s. Table 6.1 shows recent international comparisons of adult physical activity levels.

What stands out, for all countries shown, is the high proportion of total "sedentariness" in the adult populations of these nations and the relatively small proportion who engage in regular, vigorous activity. People are considered sedentary when they report no physical activity in their leisure time. The current scientific and public health consensus is that the totally sedentary are at significantly elevated risk for a number of health problems. This is a major public health concern, given these sedentariness rates of up to 30%.

Although most physical activity guidelines emphasize the health benefits of moderate-intensity physical activity (see Chapter 4), this is difficult to measure. Definitional and measurement issues are discussed by Pate, Pratt, et al. (1995), who identified some of the challenges faced by researchers and practitioners in coming to grips with the relatively new public health agenda of promoting participation in moderate-intensity activities such as walking. Because moderate-intensity physical activities can be accumulated throughout the course of daily routines, it is expected that they are self-reported with

Table 6.1 Definitions, Recent Prevalence Estimates, and Temporal Changes of Physical Activity Levels in Selected Countries

	Physical Activity Level								
	Lowest			Moderate			Highest		
		Prevalence (%)			Prevalence (%)			Prevalence (%)	
Country, Survey Name, and Years of Surveillance	*Description of Activity Definition*	*Most Recent*	*Total Change*	*Description of Activity Definition*	*Most Recent*	*Total Change*	*Description of Activity Definition*	*Most Recent*	*Total Change*
Australia									
Department of Arts, Sport, Environment, Tourism and Territories (1984-1987)	No aerobic physical activity reported over 2 weeks	26.5	−5	> 0 to < 1,600 kcal/week over 2 weeks	56	+1.5	> 1,600 kcal/week over 2 weeks of aerobic activity	17.5	+3.5
Canada									
Canada Fitness Survey (1981-1988)	0-1.4 kcal/kg/day (< 600 kcal/week)	43	−15	1.5-2.9 kcal/kg/day of any intensity activity (> 600 to < 1,250 kcal/week)	24	+7	3+ kcal/kg/day of any intensity activity (≥ 1,250 kcal/week)	33	+8
Finland									
National Public Health Institute (1982-1991)	A few times a year or less of physical activity to produce light sweating, or cannot exercise	16.1	−6.6	1 time/week or 2-3 times/month of physical activity to produce light sweating	33.3	−0.7	2+ times/week and 30+ min/occasion of physical activity to produce light sweating	51.3	+7.3

Table 6.1 Continued

Country, Survey Name, and Years of Surveillance	Physical Activity Level								
	Lowest			Moderate			Highest		
	Description of Activity Definition	Prevalence (%)		Description of Activity Definition	Prevalence (%)		Description of Activity Definition	Prevalence (%)	
		Most Recent	Total Change		Most Recent	Total Change		Most Recent	Total Change
United States									
Behavioral Risk Factor Surveillance System (26 states) (1989-1990)	No physical activity reported during the past month	30.5	−2.3	3+ times/week and 20+ min/occasion of physical activity either not reaching 60% of age- and sex-specific maximum cardiorespiratory capacity or not involving rhythmic contractions of large muscle groups	31.9	+0.5	3+ times/week and 20+ min/occasion of physical activity at 60% + of age- and sex-specific maximum cardiorespiratory capacity involving rhythmic contractions of large muscle groups	9.1	+2.1
England									
Allied Dunbar National Fitness Survey (1990)	0-4 occasions of physical activity during the past month	33.5	na	energy cost 5.0+ kcal/min or mixed vigorous and moderate; 20+ min, 12+ times in past month	36	na	energy cost 7.5+ kcal/min; 20+ min, 12+ times in past month	9	na

SOURCE: Adapted from Caspersen, Merritt, and Stephens (1994, Figure 3.2, pp. 78-79; Allied Dunbar National Fitness Survey, 1992).

more error than vigorous activities, which are more easily remembered. Because moderate-intensity physical activities are not assessed very well, and existing measures are not comparable across countries, the comparisons of moderate levels of physical activity shown in Table 6.1 are expected to be less precise than the other estimates.

Additional health benefits accrue from regular participation in vigorous-intensity physical activity, and several nations have included similar measures in their population surveys. The fact that only 10% to 15% of adults in industrialized countries meet the regular vigorous physical activity criterion is a concern.

Trends in Adult Physical Activity Participation

Data on changes in physical activity participation over time are needed to determine whether people are becoming more or less active. Trend data can suggest, for example, whether there are already changes in a favorable direction that can be built on. Trend studies can also indicate that specific subgroups may be reducing their activity levels, indicating a need for imme-diate action. Population data on physical activity started to become available only during the 1980s, so what data we have are very recent. A major problem with interpreting trend data is that most nations have not used the same measures of physical activity across different surveys (Caspersen et al., 1994). Thus, it is not clear whether observed changes are due to true changes in physical activity or to inconsistent measurement methods.

What do we know about population trends in exercise participation since the early 1980s? An examination of Australian surveys conducted through the mid-1980s found suggestions that the levels of complete sedentariness (which average around 30% for adult Australians) may have declined slightly between 1984 and 1987 (Bauman, Owen, & Rushworth, 1990). An analysis of 1983 to 1989 and 1989-1990 to 1994-1995 data from two of Australia's major health surveys suggests that the proportion of adult Australians who report taking any type of recreational activity may be increasing. Table 6.2 shows the proportions of 25- to 64-year-old Australians undertaking any physical exercise for sport or recreation in the late 1980s and early 1990s.

There is evidence from the United States that suggests small but signifi-cant increases during the late 1980s in the proportion of the adult population that is active during leisure time. Data from 26 states between 1986 and 1992 show a 4% decrease in the proportion of adults reporting no participation

Table 6.2 Proportion of 25- to 64-Year-Old Australians Undertaking Any Physical Exercise for Sport or Recreation (in percentages)

	National Health Foundation Risk Factor Prevalence Surveys		National Health Surveys	
	1983	*1989*	*1989-90*	*1994-95*
Men	68.0%	71.0%	62.4%	62.7%
Women	68.0%	71.3%	64.1%	67.4%

SOURCE: Abraham, d'Espaignet, and Stevenson (1995).

in leisure time physical activity (Caspersen & Merritt, 1995). However, there was no increase in prevalence of vigorous exercise during this time.

These recent trend data from Australia and the United States illustrate the limitations of the current state of knowledge about trends in physical activity participation. There are few time points to examine, and these time points are from recent years. What the data suggest is that there may well be a trend for adults to become more physically active in their leisure time, as indicated by a decrease in the percentage reporting no physical activity. As physical activity behaviors are tracked through the 1990s in population surveys such as those we have described here, it will become clear whether these apparent trends have continued.

Demographic Variations in Adult Activity Levels

The questions raised at the beginning of this chapter about age, sex, education, and race and ethnic differences in leisure time physical activity participation are keys to the development of properly targeted programs, public campaigns, and policies. The information we examine in this section informs our examination, in Chapters 8 and 9, of ways to involve more people in more activity. We focus on estimates of inactivity, because when people report that they are doing no physical activity, we can have high confidence that they lead a sedentary lifestyle.

Chapter 4 of the U.S. Surgeon General's report *Physical Activity and Health* (U.S. DHHS, 1996) gives an account of the demographics of physical inactivity from recent population studies: (a) Women are more likely to be inactive than men; (b) physical inactivity increases with increasing age; and (c) the prevalence of inactivity decreases with increasing levels of education

Table 6.3 Predictors of Physical Inactivity in an Australian Population Sample

Predictor Variables	Percentage Sedentary	Odds Ratio
Age (years)		
< 25	13.9	1.0
25-39	24.1	2.18
40-54	34.2	3.25
55 plus	45.4	4.35
Sex		
Male	28.2	1.0
Female	31.3	1.06[a]
Education		
< 10 years	41.8	1.0
10-12 years	27.4	0.63
College	19.2	0.43
Income (per year)		
< $15,000	36.5	1.0
> $15,000	25.8	0.81

SOURCE: Owen and Bauman (1992).
a. Not statistically significant.

and income. Surveys from the United States show racial and ethnic differences. For example, non-Hispanic whites had lower rates of inactivity in leisure time than non-Hispanic blacks and Hispanics.

Sociodemographic differences in levels of physical inactivity have been found in Australian population surveys. Some of the findings are similar to those from the United States. Table 6.3 shows demographic variation of physical inactivity (sedentariness), based on data from a series of national population surveys conducted through the mid-1980s (Owen & Bauman, 1992). The physically inactive were more likely to be older, to be less well educated, and to have lower incomes. Although women tended to report less activity than men, the difference was not statistically significant.

The odds ratios (shown in the right-hand data column in Table 6.3) are used by epidemiologists to determine the extent of differences between categories of particular variables, compared with a reference category. The reference group is assigned a value of "1.0," so an odds ratio of "2.0" represents a 100% increase in risk. For example, the odds ratios in Table 6.3

tell us that those over the age of 55 were almost 4.5 times more likely to be physically inactive than those under the age of 25; those with a college education were only 40% as inactive as those who had not finished high school (Owen & Bauman, 1992).

The primary public health focus is to involve those who are sedentary in their leisure time in regular moderate-intensity activity. It is also important to consider the demographic variation of vigorous physical activity participation, which provides health benefits beyond those of moderate intensity activity (U.S. DHHS, 1996). Australian population surveys have found demographic patterns for vigorous activity participation that are the mirror image of those for sedentariness. Vigorously active adults are more likely to be younger, male, and better educated (Bauman et al., 1990). Similar patterns for the United States have been reported in Chapter 4 of the 1996 U.S. Surgeon General's report (U.S. DHHS, 1996).

There are methodological difficulties in analyzing behavioral epidemiology studies of vigorous physical activity (see Caspersen & Merritt, 1995; U.S. DHHS, 1996, chaps. 2 and 5). If vigorous physical activities are classified in terms of their absolute intensity, such as greater than 6 METs, then participation levels clearly decline with increasing age. However, an activity that would be only moderately intense for a young adult (walking, for example) may be rated as quite vigorous for an older adult. That is because activity at a given MET value requires a higher percentage of maximal effort in older adults, because cardiorespiratory capacity declines with age. So if age-related relative-intensity classifications are used, the decline in activity as people age is reversed, and older adults will have a higher rate of vigorous activity than younger adults. As an example, for young and middle-aged adults, brisk walking is considered moderate-intensity activity because it may be only 50% to 60% of their capacity. For an elderly person, this type of walking might be 75% to 80% of their capacity, so it counts as vigorous activity in a relative classification.

One of the problems of using the age-adjusted relative-intensity values is that older people have lower levels of fitness, in part, because they do less physical activity. Therefore, the activity levels of older people are likely to be overestimated when using relative-intensity criteria. Male versus female differences in vigorous-activity participation would also be influenced by the adjustment, because the cardiorespiratory capacity of the average woman is lower than that of the average man (Caspersen & Merritt, 1995). The difference between estimates using absolute versus relative measures of intensity certainly makes more complex the challenge of accurately estimating the prevalence of activity and inactivity in these different groups.

The Descriptive Epidemiology of Physical Activity Participation by Youth

Because of the health benefits of physical activity in youth, it is important to know how active children and adolescents are and how many are meeting current physical activity guidelines. There are much less descriptive epidemiology data on youth than there are for adults. Unfortunately, there are virtually no data on trends across time in youth physical activity. This lack of data has not prevented some people from jumping to conclusions about how inactive children have become. The increasing levels of obesity among U.S. children (Troiano, Flegal, Kuczmarski, Campbell, & Johnson, 1995) *suggest* that children are becoming less active, but we have no direct evidence of this.

What is very clear is that children and adolescents become less physically active as they grow older. This decline in physical activity during the school years is shown in Table 6.4. The table is based on studies from several countries that used heart rate monitoring to estimate activity levels. It is not clear to what extent this decline with age is due to biology or to social influences.

The other observation that can be made from Table 6.4 is that boys are more active than girls at all ages. The sex difference in the table may underestimate the true extent of sex differences. A review of five heart rate studies in youth found that boys, on average, spent 23% more time in physical activity than did girls (Sallis, 1993).

A 14-year longitudinal study conducted in the Netherlands extends our understanding of age and sex differences in the physical activity habits of young people (van Mechelen & Kemper, 1995). The researchers interviewed respondents periodically from the age of 13 to the age of 27 about physical activity, making this a unique study of physical activity. Overall physical activity levels dropped steeply from ages 13 to 16 in boys and girls and less steeply from ages 16 to 27. However, there were important differences in this pattern, depending on the intensity of the activities. For light-intensity activities, girls were consistently higher. Time spent in light activities increased greatly from age 13 to 21, then decreased. For moderate activities, boys and girls reported similar amounts, and there was a substantial decline

Table 6.4 Total Daily Energy Expenditures (Expressed as Kilocalories per Kilogram of Body Weight per Day) for Boys and Girls Aged 6 to 18 Years

	Age in Years						
	6	*8*	*10*	*12*	*14*	*16*	*18*
Boys	82	74	75	58	50	44	44
Girls	76	70	58	53	45	42	42

SOURCE: Adapted from Rowland (1991; Figure 3.1, page 35).

over time. For heavy activities, boys started out with much higher levels than did girls at age 13. As the boys' time spent in vigorous activities declined, the girls stayed at the same low levels. By age 21, boys and girls were similar in their vigorous-activity levels.

It is difficult to determine how much time children and adolescents spend in physical activity, because different studies have used different measures and definitions and there are variations by nation and season. Pate, Long, and Heath (1994) found that estimates of minutes of total physical activity per day for adolescents varied from about 30 minutes to 120 minutes. The lower estimates tended to be based on heart rate monitoring, and the higher estimates on self-report.

Two physical activity guidelines have been established for adolescents (Sallis & Patrick, 1994), and Pate and colleagues (1994) estimated the extent to which adolescents are meeting the guidelines, based on population surveys in the United States. Guideline 1 states that adolescents should be active daily or nearly every day. Adherence estimates were based on obtaining at least 30 minutes per day of physical activity, regardless of intensity. Because the median for all studies was approximately 60 minutes per day, it was estimated that more than 80% of adolescents in the United States are meeting this guideline.

Guideline 2 states that adolescents should engage in three or more sessions per week of activities that last 20 minutes or more at a time and require moderate to vigorous levels of exertion. Based on self-reports, the percentage of high school males in the United States meeting this guideline is about two thirds (62% to 70%), considerably higher than the percentage of high school females meeting the guideline (38% to 51%). The percentage of adolescents meeting this guideline declines from about 60% in the 9th grade to 50% in the 12th grade.

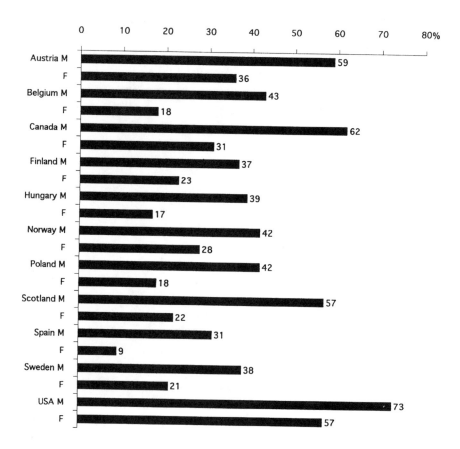

Figure 6.1. International comparisons of 15-year-olds who self-report meeting vigorous physical activity guidelines.

SOURCE: King and Coles (1992, p. 20); U.S. DHHS (1996, p. 191).

The percentage of adolescents who self-report meeting the vigorous physical activity guidelines varies greatly by nation. Data from population studies in 11 nations are shown in Figure 6.1. The reason for the large differences across countries is not known. They are most likely due to differences in measures, sampling biases, cultural variations, and differences in the availability of sports and recreation facilities and programs. Studies using objective measures are needed to verify these differences, so they should be interpreted with caution.

The proportion of adults who are sedentary in their leisure time was examined earlier in this chapter. Because physical activity levels are much higher in children and adolescents, very few can be classified as truly sedentary, although many are not sufficiently active to obtain health benefits. Young people do engage in substantial amounts of sedentary behaviors. Sitting in class, reading, "surfing" the Internet, playing video games, and sitting and socializing are all common sedentary behaviors, and they take up a great deal of young people's time.

The sedentary habit of most concern is watching television. Studies in the United States and Canada indicate that the average adolescent watches more than 20 hours of television per week (Pate et al., 1994), and younger children watch more. There are two health concerns about television. One is that long periods of inactivity and snacking while watching contribute to obesity. This concern is well-founded, because obese children have been shown to watch more television than lean children (Dietz & Gortmaker, 1985). The other concern is that if a child watches television 3 or 4 hours per day, there is little time left for physical activity. The literature is conflicting on this point, but some studies indicate that children who watch television for long periods are only slightly less physically active than children who are less frequent viewers (Robinson et al., 1993).

The results of descriptive epidemiology studies of youth are relevant for the later stages in the behavioral epidemiology framework. Studies are needed to help explain why females are less active than males and why physical activity declines with age among young people. The determinants studies reviewed in Chapter 7 can help answer these questions. The results of descriptive epidemiology studies of youth imply that interventions are particularly needed to promote physical activity in older adolescents and among girls. Interventions are needed at younger ages that will slow or halt the decline in physical activity with age.

SUMMARY

Studies of the descriptive epidemiology of physical activity show that 25% to 30% of adults are sedentary in their leisure time. In several industrialized countries, only 10% to 15% of adults engage in regular vigorous physical activity. Women are less active than men, and older people are less vigorously active and more likely to be inactive than are younger adults. Throughout childhood and adolescence, boys are more active than girls, and physical activity levels decline with age during youth. Although about 80% of adolescents meet the guidelines for daily physical activity, only about two thirds of boys and one half of girls meet the guidelines for regular vigorous activity. These data show that physical activity interventions and public health policy initiatives are needed for people all ages. Females are the highest priority for programs, because they appear to be less active than males at virtually every age.

FURTHER READING

Caspersen, C. J., Merritt, R. K., & Stephens, T. (1994). International physical activity patterns: A methodological perspective. In R. K. Dishman (Ed.), *Advances in exercise adherence* (pp. 73-110). Champaign, IL: Human Kinetics.

This is a thorough discussion of physical activity epidemiology and a comparison of findings, mainly from Australia, Canada, Finland, and the United States.

U.S. Department of Health and Human Services. (1996). *Physical activity and health: A report of the Surgeon General.* Atlanta, GA: Centers for Disease Control and Prevention.

Chapter 5 ("Patterns and Trends in Physical Activity") presents a detailed analysis of U.S. national data on physical activity participation, changes across time, and specific activities of adolescents and adults.

PART
IV

Understanding and Influencing Physical Activity

Section Introduction

Parts 2 and 3 of this book established that physical activity is important for maintenance of physical and mental health, and many people are not active enough to obtain these health benefits. All of this information is interesting, but data on health effects and descriptive epidemiology do not themselves produce improvements in health. They provide the motivation for individuals, health agencies, and governments to act to promote physical activity. But there is a big leap from identifying the problem to solving it.

Part 4 is devoted to solutions, and as usual, we emphasize a systematic scientific approach. In the three chapters of Part 4, we provide an overview of the behavioral research on physical activity. Chapter 7 summarizes descriptive research to improve our understanding of factors that influence physical activity. Because an infinite variety of possible influences can be imagined, theories and models of the influences on behavior are necessary to limit the number of variables studied and to point us in productive directions. Some theories and models are described in Chapter 7 that are commonly applied in studies of physical activity. This chapter introduces several terms that will be unfamiliar to readers with limited background in behavioral science. We hope these are adequately explained so that their meanings are clear. We also hope that the results of these studies of the "determinants" of physical activity can be used to guide the design of effective interventions.

In Chapter 8, we examine the now-extensive literature on physical activity interventions for individuals. These studies have been carried out in a range of different settings and with members of a number of different demographic groups. Chapter 8 makes clear that there has been extensive theory development and applications to successful interventions for individuals and small groups. Although the interventions are not as effective as we would like them to be, theoretically based programs are generally superior to programs developed with less thought and scientific justification.

In Chapter 9, we describe some of the new research findings on interventions to promote physical activity participation in entire communities or the populations of states or nations. Although evidence for the effectiveness of large-scale interventions is not extensive, there are interesting and potentially informative findings from community intervention trials and from studies examining the impact of mass media promotion campaigns on physical activity. Efforts to change behavior in populations are by their nature ambitious, and they are not always effective. However, it is important that we learn how to improve these programs so we can achieve greater public health effects. We offer some ideas for developing innovative programs that are potentially more effective than current approaches.

The material in Chapters 7, 8, and 9 describes the unique knowledge base of the behavioral epidemiology of physical activity and shows how the behavioral and psychological sciences are central to efforts to improve physical activity. These chapters deal with the bottom line for behavioral medicine and physical activity: How can physiological and behavioral research, as well as behavioral theories, be applied to developing interventions to increase physical activity in individuals and populations?

Determinants of Physical Activity

Chapter 6 contains descriptions of how physical activity varies by age, sex, socioeconomic status, and other demographic variables. These biological and other sociodemographic factors are strongly associated with the amount and types of physical activity in youth and adults. These variables do not come close to explaining all the variance in physical activity, so the purpose of Chapter 7 is to explore other variables that might explain why some people are active and others are inactive.

Explaining physical activity is a very challenging task, as is explaining any aspect of human behavior. Because of the serious public health effects of physically inactive lifestyles, it is worth expending intellectual and monetary resources to understand the forces that affect the behavior. The health significance of this line of research is that understanding the factors that control physical activity is expected to provide information that will allow us to intervene more effectively. Research in this field is often called *determinants* or *exercise adherence*. These terms generally refer to observational— that is, without intervention—studies of correlates of physical activity. Thus, determinants is a misnomer because correlational studies cannot lead to conclusions about causation, and exercise adherence is a misnomer because investigators are interested in types of physical activity that go beyond traditional concepts of exercise. Studies reviewed in this chapter assess either cross-sectional correlations or prospective predictions of physical activity.

Because it is impossible to consider all conceivable influences, it is necessary to develop theories, models, and hypotheses to help the researcher focus on variables believed to be among the most highly related to physical activity. One must have some familiarity with the theories to understand physical activity determinants research. Most of the formal theories and models that have been applied to studies of physical activity determinants and interventions are also used to study other behaviors. They are summarized in Table 7.1. This table describes the major variables associated with each theory as well as some of the intervention techniques derived from the theories.

Because the theoretical variables are classified as psychological, social, or physical environment, some of the differences among theories are highlighted. Some of the theories are almost completely psychological in content. The oldest theory, the health belief model (Becker & Maiman, 1975), posits that only psychological variables influence health behaviors. This theory is widely applied in developing knowledge-based interventions for health education, including health risk appraisals. The theory of planned behavior (Ajzen, 1985) is also almost a completely psychologically oriented theory. The only exception is that perceptions of the beliefs of significant others about the behavior are hypothesized to be influential. This theory is sometimes applied in mass communication interventions that attempt to change attitudes. The transtheoretical ("stages of change") model is primarily psychological. However, some of the specific processes of change, measures of perceived benefits ("pros"), and measures of perceived barriers ("cons"), include social and physical environment factors (Prochaska & Marcus, 1994). The broadest models are social cognitive theory (Bandura, 1986) and ecological models (Sallis & Owen, 1997; Stokols, 1992). Social cognitive theory highlights the interactions between intrapersonal, social, and physical environment influences on behavior; a wide range of effective cognitive behavior modification intervention approaches have been developed from this theory. Although ecological models assume multiple levels of influence on behavior, they emphasize the effects of social systems, public policies, and physical environments. Skinner's (1953) principles of operant learning postulate that behavior is controlled by antecedent and consequent stimuli in the

Table 7.1 Theories and Models Used in Physical Activity Research

Theory/ Model	Intrapersonal Variables	Social Variables	Physical Environment Variables	Applications in Interventions
Health Belief Model	Perceived susceptibility; Perceived severity; Perceived benefits; Perceived barriers; Cues to action; Self-efficacy			Knowledge-based programs; health education; risk appraisal
Theory of Planned Behavior	Behavioral intention; Attitude toward the behavior; Perceived behavioral control	Subjective norms: perceptions of beliefs of others and motivation to comply		Attitude change communications
Trans-theoretical Model	Stages of change; Processes of change; Decision balance; Self-efficacy	Some processes of change; Some decision balance variables	Some processes of change; Some decision balance variables	Staged-matched cognitive-behavioral modification
Social Cognitive Theory	Outcome expectations; Behavioral capability; Self-efficacy	Observational learning; Reinforcement	Reinforcement	Cognitive behavior modification
Ecological Models	Multiple levels of influence, including intrapersonal	Interpersonal factors; Institutional factors	Community factors; Public policy factors; Health promotive environments	Multilevel approach

social and physical environments. These principles have been applied to highly effective behavior modification interventions, with positive reinforcement being the most widely used method of change.

Physical activity determinants studies are not always based on these well-known theories. Sometimes investigators hypothesize that new variables will better explain physical activity or that combinations of variables from multiple theories will be most effective. Some studies are atheoretical, and very few have specifically compared one theory against another. Even though studies vary in their application of theories, having a basic understanding of the types of theories often used in this field helps the reader make connections between the theories and the results.

In the reviews of physical activity determinants studies that follow, we hope to provide the reader with an appreciation for the different types of studies that have contributed to this field, some of the challenges of this work, and a summary of the current understanding of physical activity determinants. Studies of youth (including children and adolescents up to the age of 18) and adults (18 and older) are discussed separately. The organization of the reviews reveals our preference for the broader theories, such as social cognitive theory and ecological models, that acknowledge the roles of intrapersonal, social, *and* physical environmental influences on behaviors such as physical activity.

Determinants of Physical Activity in Adults

Overview of Results

This section updates previous reviews of the adult literature on physical activity determinants (Dishman, 1990; Dishman & Sallis, 1994: Dishman, Sallis, & Orenstein, 1985) and adds about 45 studies, most of which were published between 1992 and 1997 (Ainsworth, Berry, Schnyder, & Vickers, 1992; Armstrong, Sallis, Hovell, & Hofstetter, 1993; Bock et al., 1997; Calfas, Sallis, Lovato, & Campbell, 1994; Calfas, Sallis, Oldenburg, & Ffrench, 1997; Courneya, 1995; Courneya & McAuley, 1994; Davis & Fox, 1993; De Weerdt, Visser, Kok, & Van Der Veen, 1990; DiMatteo et al., 1993; Duncan, Duncan, & McAuley, 1993; Emery, Hauck, & Blumenthal, 1992; Emmons, Marcus, Linnan, Rossi, & Abrams, 1994; Godin, Valois, Jobin, & Ross, 1991; Godin, Valois, & Lepage, 1993; Gorely & Gordon, 1995; Haraldsdottir & Andersen, 1994; Hawkes & Holm, 1993; Horne, 1994; Huijbrechts et al., 1997; Jeffery, French, Forster, & Spry 1991; Kelley & Kelley, 1994; Kendzierski & Johnson, 1993; King, Kiernan, Oman, Kraemer, & Ahn, 1997; Klonoff, Annechild, & Landrine, 1994; Kumanyika, Wilson, & Guilford-Davenport, 1993; Lee, 1993; Macera, Croft, Brown, Ferguson, & Lane, 1995; Marcus, Pinto, Simkin, Audrain, & Taylor, 1994; Marcus, Rakowski, & Rossi, 1992; Marcus, Rossi, Selby, Niaura, & Abrams, 1992; Marcus, Simkin, Rossi, & Pinto, 1996; McAuley, 1992, 1993; McAuley, Lox, & Duncan, 1993; Minor & Brown, 1993; Myers & Roth, 1997; Neuberger, Kasal, Smith, Hassanein, & DeViney, 1994; Rudolph & McAuley, 1996; Schnurr, Vaillant, & Vaillant, 1990; Siegel, Brackbill, & Heath, 1995; Simkin

& Gross, 1994; Simoes et al., 1995; Steptoe & Wardle, 1992; Stetson, Rahn, Dubbert, Wilner, & Mercury, 1997; Uitenbroek, 1993). In the late 1980s, Dishman (1988) estimated that more than 200 studies of physical activity determinants had been published. These were reflected in the Dishman (1990) review, and 33 studies were added for the Dishman and Sallis (1994) review, so the current addition of about 45 studies brings to approximately 300 the number of studies summarized in Table 7.2.

We summarized results for studies of physical activity during or after supervised programs separately from studies that typically assessed overall physical activity in all settings. We included studies if the dependent variable was physical activity, exercise, or stage of change, but not if the dependent variable was intention, self-efficacy, or other intermediate measure. When multiple measures of physical activity were used in the study, the measure of vigorous exercise was abstracted, because most studies included this measure, and it appears to be measured with more reliability and validity than other types of physical activity.

An inspection of Table 7.2 reveals consistently documented associations in all categories, which highlights the multiply determined nature of physical activity and supports the broad models such as social cognitive theory and ecological models. No single variable or category explains most adult physical activity or exercise. Different variables are most likely strong influences for different people, and the strength of influences for each person may vary at different stages of change and developmental periods (such as early, middle, and late adulthood).

Demographic and biological factors may be more potent correlates of community-based than of supervised physical activity, but physical environmental characteristics seem to be consistently associated with physical activity in both settings. We examined many psychological and behavioral factors and found that substantial percentages of these variables received no consistent support for associations with physical activity.

It is particularly useful to highlight variables that are subject to modification and that have consistently been associated with physical activity or found to be unrelated to physical activity. Numerous variables from the psychological, behavioral, and social categories were judged to have strong support for their associations with physical activity, including social support, self-efficacy, perceived barriers, perceived benefits, enjoyment of activity, processes of change, intention to exercise, lower intensity of exercise, and

Table 7.2 Associations of Determinants With Physical Activity in Adults

Determinant	Associations With Activity in Supervised Program	Associations With Overall Physical Activity
Demographic and biological factors		
Age	00	– –
Blue-collar occupation	– –	–
Childless		+
Education	+	++
Gender (male)		++
Genetic factors		++
High risk for heart disease	–	–
Income/Socioeconomic status		++
Injury history		+
Marital status	0	
Overweight/obesity	0	00
Race/ethnicity (nonwhite)		– –
Psychological, cognitive, and emotional factors		
Attitudes	+	0
Barriers to exercise	–	– –
Control over exercise		+
Enjoyment of exercise	+	++
Expect benefits	+	++
Health locus of control	0	0
Intention to exercise	0	++
Knowledge of health and exercise	0	00
Lack of time	– –	–
Mood disturbance	–	– –
Normative beliefs	0	00
Perceived health or fitness	++	++
Personality variables		+
Poor body image		–
Psychological health	0	+
Self-efficacy	++	++
Self-motivation	++	++
Self-schemata for exercise		++
Stage of change		++
Stress	0	0
Susceptibility to illness/seriousness of illness		00
Value of exercise outcomes	0	0

(continued)

Table 7.2 Continued

Determinant	Associations With Activity in Supervised Program	Associations With Overall Physical Activity
Behavioral attributes and skills		
Activity history during childhood/youth		00
Activity history during adulthood	++	++
Alcohol		0
Contemporary exercise program	0	0
Dietary habits (quality)	00	++
Past exercise program	++	+
Processes of change		++
School sports	0	00
Skills for coping with barriers		+
Smoking	– –	00
Sports media use		0
Type A behavior pattern	–	+
Decision balance sheet	+	
Social and cultural factors		
Class size	+	
Exercise models		0
Group cohesion	+	
Past family influences		0
Physician influence		++
Social isolation	0	–
Social support from friends/peers	+	++
Social support from spouse/family	++	++
Social support from staff/instructor	+	
Physical environment factors		
Access to facilities: actual	+	+
Access to facilities: perceived	+	00
Climate/season	–	– –
Cost of programs	0	0
Disruptions in routine	–	
Home equipment		0
Physical activity characteristics		
Intensity	– –	–
Perceived effort	– –	– –

KEY: ++ = repeatedly documented positive association with physical activity; + = weak or mixed evidence of positive association with physical activity; 00 = repeatedly documented lack of association with physical activity; 0 = weak or mixed evidence of no association with physical activity; – – = repeatedly documented negative association with physical activity; – = weak or mixed evidence of negative association with physical activity. Blank spaces indicate no data available.

eating habits. A logical next step in research would be to evaluate intervention programs designed to alter those factors that may mediate physical activity.

In contrast, four psychological and behavioral variables were consistently unrelated to physical activity: knowledge, history of exercise during youth, normative beliefs, and susceptibility to illness. These would appear to be poor selections as variables to attempt to change in interventions.

We describe specific studies to illustrate the methodologies used and provide more details about what we believe are some of the most important findings in each category of variables. Highlighting results from specific studies also allows for consideration of the strength of associations, which could not be summarized in Table 7.2.

Intrapersonal Variables

More different types of psychological variables have been examined than any other category in Table 7.2. Many of these variables have been evaluated in only a few studies, so it is difficult to make strong conclusions at this time. We provide an overview of research on some selected variables that have been studied extensively.

Self-Efficacy. In Bandura's (1986) social cognitive theory, self-efficacy is proposed as the most powerful determinant of behavior. It represents the summary of a person's processing of many kinds of information about the behavior. In the physical activity field, self-efficacy is a person's confidence in his or her ability to do specific physical activities in specific circumstances. A person may have high self-efficacy about exercising in good weather, but not in rainy or cold weather. A person might report very different self-efficacy levels for jogging versus walking. Thus, the more specific the measure of self-efficacy, the more highly it should be related to the physical activity outcome. Bandura's theory has been strongly supported, because self-efficacy is the strongest correlate of physical activity in virtually every study that includes it.

In a study of a community sample of 2,053 adults in San Diego, self-efficacy was 1 of 25 potential determinants whose correlations with physical activity were examined (Sallis et al., 1989). The correlation of self-efficacy with vigorous exercise of $r = .48$ was much greater than the next highest correlation ($r = .28$). However, in a cross-sectional study, it is not surprising to find that people who exercise have higher confidence in their ability to exercise than those who are more sedentary. Prospective studies are needed to show that self-efficacy predicts changes in physical activity. Analyses of a 2-year follow-up of these same study participants provided two relevant findings (Sallis, Hovell, Hofstetter, & Barrington, 1992). First, baseline self-efficacy was a strong predictor of subsequent physical activity, indicating that self-efficacy does not merely reflect past physical activity. Second, changes in self-efficacy were associated with changes in physical activity. If physical activity increased over the 2 years, self-efficacy increased. These findings can be applied to interventions. Collecting simple ratings of participants' confidence that they can be physically active in a number of situations can help a group leader or trainer prepare people for situations that they anticipate will make it difficult to be active.

McAuley (1992, 1993) studied 65 middle-aged participants in a group exercise program to examine the role of self-efficacy at different phases in the exercise adoption process. Self-efficacy was measured several times during the 5-month program (McAuley, 1992) and 4 months after the program ended (McAuley, 1993). He hypothesized that self-efficacy is most likely to be correlated when there are numerous barriers to exercise and during transition times. In this case, the most demanding times were expected to be the beginning of the program, when exercise was being adopted, and postprogram, when participants were making the transition to exercise on their own. Exercise self-efficacy assessed near the beginning of the program predicted exercise during the first 2 months of the program. Self-efficacy at the end of the program predicted exercise over the 4 months of follow-up (McAuley, 1993). These are just some of the studies confirming the importance of self-efficacy beliefs in affecting physical activity.

Intention. A psychological variable that has been studied frequently is intention. Ajzen's (1985) theory of planned behavior postulates that intention is the primary determinant of behaviors under personal control, including most types of physical activity. Across 12 studies, the correlation of intention with exercise varied from $r = .19$ to .82, with a mean of $r = .55$ (Godin, 1994). These correlations are substantial and provide support for the theory (Hausenblas, Carron, & Mack, 1997).

Enjoyment. Anecdotally, many people say they do not engage in physical activity simply because they do not enjoy it. Kendzierski and DeCarlo (1991) developed a measure of enjoyment, and its validity was supported when enjoyment ratings predicted which activities participants chose. Using a briefer measure, exercise maintainers had higher scores than those at other stages of change (Calfas et al., 1994). A one-item measure in a scale on exercise barriers ("lack of enjoyment from exercise") was moderately and inversely correlated with exercise frequency (Sallis et al., 1989). Having consistent findings in all three studies using different measures is encouraging and should stimulate future research. If enjoyment is found to be an important determinant, strategies to make physical activity participation more enjoyable will need to be tested.

Barriers. If you have talked informally to people about physical activity, you have no doubt heard lists of reasons for not being active. The all-time winner is "I don't have the time" (Dishman et al., 1985), although that is difficult to take seriously when the average U.S. adult watches 3 hours of television each day. It is not clear whether these lists refer to true reasons or convenient "excuses," but the ubiquity of these reasons makes them important to study. The term used is either *barriers* to physical activity, or *cons* in a decision balance framework (as in pros vs. cons). In a sample of women who were interested in starting exercise, lack of time was again the primary barrier, with reasons for lack of time including work and school (59%), child care (26%), and household duties (18%) (Johnson, Corrigan, Dubbert, & Gramling, 1990). This list would be expected to differ for men. Other barriers endorsed by these women were lack of money (36%), lack of facilities (22%), lack of a partner (21%), and feeling that exercise is boring (lack of enjoyment) (10%). When an 18-item barriers scale was factor analyzed in a group of university students and alumni (Calfas et al., 1994), four factors were found: aversiveness of activity, inconvenience, worries, and competing demands. All of these factors except worries differed significantly by exercise stage of change.

We all experience stressful life events too often, and these can be considered barriers to physical activity. Stetson and colleagues (1997) asked a group of women exercisers to keep track of their stressful life events, levels of perceived stress, and exercise sessions weekly for 8 weeks. They found that both number of stressful events and perceived stress in a week were associated with less physical activity and more missed exercise sessions. During stressful weeks, women had lower self-efficacy in their ability to meet future exercise goals. The women reported that the stressful events were usually minor, but they led to more time pressure to complete their usual tasks, and this restricted their time for physical activity. This study confirms what many people have experienced; stressful life events are barriers to being physically active.

Whether ratings of barriers represent objective or subjective reality, there is a strong and consistent correlation between barriers and exercise. In a 2-year prospective study of determinants, both baseline barriers and change in barriers were related to months of regular exercise (Sallis, Hovell, Hofstetter, et al. 1992); Table 7.2 shows that this is a typical finding. The association of barriers with physical activity is highly relevant to interventions. If the barriers are objective, methods for changing the social and physical environment are needed. If the barriers are more subjective, intervention components to help participants refute these beliefs or think about them less often may be useful.

The Transtheoretical Model

This model is often applied to the study of physical activity (Marcus & Simkin, 1994; Prochaska & Marcus, 1994). The stages of change indicate the steps through which people progress as they make changes, and the processes of change describe the strategies people use to make changes. A major contribution of this model is that people in different stages are shown to use different processes to move to the next stage. For example, precontemplators and contemplators, who are generally sedentary, need to change their thinking if they are to progress. Those in the preparation and action stages already want to be active, so they need behavior change skills to help them be successful in establishing regular habits. Those in the maintenance stage need to use cognitive and behavioral techniques to help them avoid relapses (i.e., stopping exercise) or start back after a relapse. The model was generally supported in a 6-month longitudinal study that found people who increased their stages used more processes and those who relapsed used fewer processes during the follow-up (Marcus et al., 1996). Another study found that behavioral processes were good predictors of success in starting a walking program after brief counseling from a physician (Calfas et al., 1997).

As indicated by its name, the transtheoretical model integrates concepts from multiple theories and models of behavior change. The decisional balance theory from social psychology proposes that a person's evaluations of the pros and cons (or benefits and costs) of a behavior are highly related to behavior change. Perceptions of the pros and cons of exercise vary greatly by stage, indicating that they are important in the change process (Marcus & Simkin, 1994). Self-efficacy, from social learning theory, is also strongly related to stage of change. The theory of planned behavior is also closely related to the transtheoretical model. The primary difference between precontemplators and contemplators is that contemplators intend to change, and intention is a central variable in the theory of planned behavior. Attitude and perceived control also differ by stages of change (Courneya, 1995), further linking the two theories.

Several studies have examined associations of determinants with stages of change rather than associations with direct measures of physical activity (Calfas et al., 1994; Courneya, 1995; Gorely & Gordon, 1995; Marcus & Simkin, 1994). This strategy may permit the identification of key variables that are critical for moving from one stage to another. Both methods have produced similar results. For example, Lee (1993) found that precontemplators were older, had less social support, and perceived fewer benefits of exercise, compared with other groups. These findings echo some of the results summarized in Table 7.2. Lee also found precontemplators to be particularly low in exercise knowledge, which may be a finding specific to this stage. The main difference between contemplators and those in action and maintenance stages is perception of barriers.

Injury and Exercise Relapse

To improve public health, it may be most important to understand determinants of adopting physical activity, because of the large number of sedentary people. However, it is also important to understand why some exercisers relapse or drop out and why others maintain for long periods of time. Two studies point to the critical role of injuries in dropout from vigorous exercise. When people were asked to recall how many times they had stopped exercising for 3 months or more during adulthood, about 20% of both current exercisers and current nonexercisers reported three or more relapses (Sallis et al., 1990). This indicates that relapse is quite common. The most common reason for the last relapse was injury, reported by 40% of current exercisers and 22% of current nonexercisers. Because exercisers were more likely to report injuries, injuries do not seem to lead many people to drop out of exercise completely. The next most frequent reasons for relapsing from exercise were work demands, lack of interest (particularly among the current nonexercisers), and (of course) lack of time.

A rare long-term study of exercisers provides valuable information about reasons for relapse. Koplan, Rothenberg, and Jones (1995) studied a group of participants in a 10K run over 10 years. Results were similar for men and women. Ten years after the original survey of runners, only 56% were still running, but 81% reported doing some kind of regular vigorous exercise. Because most studies of community samples and program participants show about a 50% dropout rate within 1 year, this appears to be a highly committed group of exercisers. However, the primary reason for stopping running permanently was injury (31%), and the knee was the most frequent injury site. Injury was associated with baseline level of exercise, consistent with the well-known risks of overuse. There were a few sex differences in reasons for stopping running. For example, 28% of women, but only 14% of men, stopped running because they chose another form of exercise. Women (11%) were much more likely than men (2%) to stop running because of child care duties. In other hazards of running, about 10% reported being hit by a thrown object or bitten by a dog.

Variables Unrelated to Physical Activity

Several psychological and behavioral variables have repeatedly been found to have no association with exercise participation. These findings contradict some theories and informal hypotheses. Several studies show that knowledge of the health effects of physical activity is not correlated with activity levels, even though the health belief model predicts a relation. To be fair, there are limited data that knowledge may be related to the adoption of moderate-intensity physical activity (Sallis, Hill, et al., 1986). Most people know that exercise is good for health, but many people are not regularly active. The negative results for knowledge indicate that other factors are much more important in controlling physical activity habits and that interventions mainly intended to increase knowledge would not be expected to be effective.

Why is activity level during youth not related to exercise participation in adulthood? Many people expect that if you instill a love of activity and develop habits while children are young, they will naturally carry this good habit into adulthood. Although many studies have yielded null results, most of these studies have been retrospective, so they cannot be considered definitive. The accuracy of recalling physical activities and sports from decades ago is certain to be low. However, a prospective study of physical activity in young people over a period from the ages of 13 to 27 also found nonsignificant correlations ($r = .10$ for boys and $.21$ for girls) over the 15-year period (van Mechelen & Kemper, 1995), supporting the retrospective studies. If the null results are true, it might suggest that involving children in competitive team sports, the dominant mode of youth activity, is not effective in stimulating long-term activity because adults rarely engage in team sports. The concept of "carryover" or "lifetime" activities is that teenagers should be taught some activities that are common in adulthood so that the activities are more likely to be carried over.

Interpersonal Variables

Virtually every study that has included a measure of social influences on physical activity has found a significant association. The most frequently studied variable is social support for exercise from family, friends, or program staff. Support can take the form of direct instrumental support, such as exercising together, watching children, or doing chores while the other is being active. Support can be more indirect, including just talking about activity and encouraging each other (Sallis et al., 1987). Modeling is another form of social influence. Just being in contact with exercisers is believed to provide motivation and information that is useful, especially if one's spouse or significant other is an exerciser. In analyses of different subgroups of a community sample of adults, either social support or presence of exercise models was related to exercise habits in young men and women, older men and women (Sallis et al., 1989), Latinos (Hovell et al., 1991), and the obese (Hovell et al., 1990). Both family and friend social support were associated with changes in exercise in this population over a 2-year period (Sallis, Hovell, Hofstetter, et al., 1992).

These results were expanded upon by a study of health club members (Unger & Johnson, 1995). Exercising with a friend was not correlated with frequency of exercise or skipping sessions in this sample. However, having friends at the club and socializing outside the club with these friends were positively correlated with exercise frequency and negatively correlated with skipping sessions. This study suggests that not all types of support are equally effective.

Environmental Variables

In this section, we apply ecological models to understanding the determinants of physical activity and inactivity. We believe ecological models hold particular promise in explaining these behaviors, but because we are at such an early stage of research in this area, we begin with a conceptual analysis.

There is reason to believe that sedentary lifestyles on a mass basis are a new phenomenon in human history. We strongly suspect that changes in the social and the constructed physical environments are largely responsible for the epidemic of sedentary lifestyles, and without an ecological perspective, we are unlikely to understand the causes of mass sedentary behavior or be able to develop effective solutions to this problem.

Consider how human-constructed environments now make it possible, and even encourage people, to lead extremely sedentary lifestyles: At the beginning of the day, most people do not need to exert themselves in any way to heat up their homes or prepare breakfast. Most people in modern societies go to work in automobiles and drive door to door. Such sedentary daily habits are made possible for the majority of adults by massive societal investments in the manufacture of automobiles and their supplies, as well as the construction of an extensive system of roads and highways. We hypothesize that nations that invest in infrastructures for bicycles, such as The Netherlands, or in attractive public transport, have populations that do more physical activity as part of their daily routines.

In past times, "work" for most people required physical activity for extended periods. This is no longer the case in industrialized nations. Most work is sedentary and is becoming more so. Computers do much of the work for white-collar workers, and machinery does most of the work for blue-collar workers.

In the suburbs, it is necessary to drive everywhere because most homes are out of easy walking distance to common destinations such as shops and workplaces. In many suburbs, the parks and open spaces are small and scattered, providing children and adults with limited facilities for physical activity outdoors. Suburbs are designed for automobile use, so it is inconvenient to use other forms of transportation such as walking and cycling.

The large entertainment industries provide us with many ways to enjoy being sedentary. The average adult in the United States spends more than 25 hours each week watching television, videos, and movies (Singer, 1983). Newer interactive forms of entertainment, such as video games, CD-ROMs, and the Internet, still require the person to be sedentary. A long list of other inventions and mass-scale technological innovations are now part of daily environments designed to help us avoid physical activity, including elevators, escalators, riding lawn mowers, golf carts, food processors, electric can openers, and remote controls for televisions and stereo equipment.

Those who want to lead "couch potato" lifestyles find a great deal of support from companies and government policies. Those who want to lead physically active lifestyles find many environmental barriers to overcome. Almost all workplaces provide convenient parking for employees' automobiles, but few provide showers on-site or parking for bicycles. Those who want to do some physical activity during the workday by taking stairs are often discouraged, because stairs are often difficult to find, have restricted access, or are unpleasant. Funding for public recreation programs and school physical education are declining in the United States, reducing opportunities for children to be active.

The reader can probably think of other aspects of the social and physical environments that discourage physical activity in all but the most committed. The ecological determinants of sedentary behavior that we have described are so ubiquitous, and so woven into the texture of people's lives, that they are taken for granted. What do we know about them from research?

Several environments may affect physical activity, because one can be active in a number of settings. One environment is the home, where a person can have exercise equipment or videos. Characteristics of the neighborhood can also be important, because walking, jogging, and biking around the neighborhood are among the most common forms of physical activity. A neighborhood that has sidewalks, streetlights, and enjoyable scenery may be very inviting for physical activity. On the other hand, people may be discouraged from being active in their neighborhood if there are high crime rates, hills, or heavy traffic. Many people use facilities such as health clubs, swimming pools, bike lanes, and parks, so it is important to consider the convenience of these facilities. Self-reported assessments of these three environments (home equipment, neighborhood characteristics, and convenience of facilities) have been developed, and the reliabilities of the measures were good (Sallis, Johnson, Calfas, Caparosa, & Nichols, 1997). As might be expected, socioeconomic status was correlated with all the scales, such that more advantaged people live in environments that make it easier to be physically active.

Number of types of exercise equipment at home was related to both vigorous and strength exercise (Sallis, Johnson, et al., 1997), which confirms findings of two other studies (Jakicic, Wing, Butler, & Jeffery, 1997; Sallis et al., 1989). The neighborhood characteristics scale was not related to any physical activity measure (Sallis, Johnson, et al., 1997). This is in some disagreement with a focus group study that found walking in the neighborhood is influenced by availability of sidewalks, limited traffic, and local shops

(Corti, Donovan, & Holman, 1997). In addition, people reported they were less likely to take walks if they feared crime or dogs (Corti et al., 1997). More studies of neighborhood characteristics are needed to resolve these conflicting findings.

The convenient facilities scale was correlated with frequency of vigorous exercise (Sallis, Johnson, et al., 1997). This is similar to an earlier finding that perceptions of convenient facilities predicted increases in walking for exercise in prospective analyses (Hovell, Hofstetter, Sallis, Rauh, & Barrington, 1992). It is interesting that three perceived-environment variables predicted adoption of vigorous exercise by men but not by women (Sallis, Hovell, & Hofstetter, 1992). Perceptions of physical environments can help explain physical activity habits, but perceptions may not always reflect reality, so objective measures of the environment are also needed.

A more convincing demonstration of association between environmental characteristics and physical activity is derived from objective measures of the environment. An inventory was conducted of specific settings in which adults could exercise in a city. A total of 385 facilities were classified as either free (for example, parks, colleges, and public schools) or for pay (for example, aerobics studios, fitness clubs, and YMCA/YWCAs). A limitation of the list is that it did not include nonspecific locations, such as sidewalks and bike paths. The locations of facilities and home addresses of more than 2,000 survey respondents were plotted on a grid map. The density of facilities within 1 km to 5 km of respondents' homes was calculated. Exercisers had a higher density of pay facilities around their homes than sedentary adults, even after adjusting for age, education, and income. This study suggests that convenient access to exercise facilities may prompt nearby residents to be physically active and supports ecological models of physical activity behavior.

We are just beginning to study the effects of physical environments on physical activity. A thorough understanding is going to require the measurement of people's perceptions as well as objective characteristics of environments. When the study of environmental influences progresses, we can use the results to help decision makers in government and industry create environments that facilitate physical activity.

Determinants for Population Subgroups

Physical activity determinants most likely vary in strength in different population subgroups. A very few studies of heterogeneous samples have examined similar sets of independent variables in subgroups. Although not all the same variables are significant correlates in all subgroups, in general, the variables that have received strong support across all studies (see Table 7.2) are most likely to be significantly associated with physical activity in each subgroup. For example, one large survey study found significant correlations of vigorous exercise with self-efficacy and perceived barriers for most of these subgroups: younger and older men, younger and older women (Sallis et al., 1989), Latinos (Hovell et al., 1991), the obese (Hovell et al., 1990), and some groups with acute or chronic injuries or disabilities (Hofstetter et al., 1991). These results were found to generalize to university students (Calfas et al., 1994) and high school students (Zakarian, Hovell, Hofstetter, Sallis, & Keating, 1994). Some types of social influence, such as friend support, family support, or number of exercise models was also correlated with vigorous exercise in all of these studies. These findings indicate that at least some determinants operate across a wide range of population groups.

There is evidence that social support for exercise may be more influential for women. Among those who were sedentary at baseline, adoption of exercise at follow-up was significantly predicted by social support for women only and by environmental factors (e.g., convenience of facilities) for men only (Sallis, Hovell, & Hofstetter, 1992). In a study of adults in an exercise program, social support predicted attendance for women only (Duncan et al., 1993).

Because principles of behavior change are expected to apply almost universally across groups of people, similar determinants are expected in different population groups. Because people live in a vast range of cultures, socioeconomic strata, geographic locations, and social situations, some differences in the determinants are also likely. For example, in some cultures, a high socioeconomic status is associated with ability to afford a health club membership and high physical activity. In other cultures, only the affluent have cars and sedentary jobs, so there is an inverse relationship with physical activity. More research is needed to provide an understanding of subgroup differences in determinants.

Determinants of Moderate-Intensity Physical Activity

Because of the recently recognized health benefits of moderate intensities and amounts of physical activity (Pate, Pratt, et al., 1995), it is important to understand the determinants of this pattern of physical activity. Current understanding is very limited, because virtually all the determinants studies have used vigorous exercise or a measure of total physical activity as the outcome. Vigorous and moderate physical activity have very different associations with age and sex. Time spent in moderate-intensity activities tends to increase with age, and women are usually found to do more than men (Dishman & Sallis, 1994). This is opposite from the pattern found with vigorous exercise (U.S. Department of Health and Human Services, 1996).

The few cross-sectional (Hovell et al., 1989) and prospective studies (Hovell et al., 1992) conducted to date have explained much less variance in moderate-intensity physical activity, compared with variance explained in vigorous exercise. The reasons for this probably include inadequate measurement of the behavior, lack of specific theories, and lack of measures of determinants designed to explain moderate-intensity physical activity.

Determinants of Physical Activity in Children and Adolescents

Studies of physical activity determinants in children and adolescents have used similar theories and models that have been applied to adults. Studies generally show that significant correlates have been found in all domains: demographic, biological, psychological/emotional, social and cultural, and physical environmental (Sallis, Simons-Morton, et al., 1992). These investigations are complicated by the rapid physical, social, and psychological development during youth. Although determinants are expected to vary in influence with development changes, these variations are not well understood. Because some determinants that are important during adolescence are irrelevant or impossible to measure during early childhood, it is difficult to study developmental changes in their effects. For instance, psychological determinants are rarely studied in preteen children because they are irrelevant or cannot be measured.

Intrapersonal Variables

Age and sex are the two dominant biological determinants of physical activity in youth. As shown in Chapter 6, physical activity declines dramatically with age during youth, and boys are almost always found to be more physically active than girls (Sallis, 1993). Racial and ethnic differences in physical activity of youth are unclear. Three studies found ethnic minority children to be less active than European Americans (Andersen, Crespo, Bartlett, Cheskin, & Pratt, 1998; McKenzie, Sallis, Nader, Broyles, & Nelson, 1992; Trost, Pate, Saunders, et al., 1997), and another study found no ethnic differences (Baranowski, Thompson, DuRant, Baranowski, & Puhl, 1993). A study of high school students found few ethnic differences in overall physical activity, but socioeconomic status (SES) was found to be important (Sallis, Zakarian, Hovell, & Hofstetter, 1996). High SES students had more physical education classes, reported more activity in those classes, and participated more in sports teams and activity-related classes. It appears that more affluent young people have access to more programs both in school and out of school. It is difficult or impossible to separate the effects of ethnicity and SES, but one consistent finding is that African American adolescents watch more television than do other groups (Andersen et al., 1998; Sallis, Zakarian, et al., 1996; Wolf et al., 1993).

A few psychological variables have been shown to be consistently correlated with physical activity in adolescents, and most of them have also been found to be important correlates of adult behavior. In a cross-sectional study of high school students, self-efficacy for exercise was the most highly correlated variable among girls and boys (Zakarian et al., 1994). Two prospective studies of youth found that self-efficacy for physical activity strongly predicted change in physical activity (Reynolds et al., 1990; Trost et al., 1997).

Perceived barriers are inversely correlated with physical activity, with similar results for boys and girls (Zakarian et al., 1994). In an interesting parallel to the adult studies, the most important barriers for adolescents are lack of time and lack of interest (Tappe, Duda, & Ehrnwald, 1989). It appears that adolescents are not just acquiring adult patterns of sedentary habits, they are also acquiring adult ways of thinking about exercise, including the usual reasons (or excuses) for not being active.

In a study of 28 potential correlates of physical activity, perceived benefits of physical activity were correlated with exercise participation, and for girls, dislike of physical education was negatively correlated (Zakarian et al., 1994). In the one study that included this variable, enjoyment was a significant correlate for girls and boys (Stucky-Ropp & DiLorenzo, 1993). Thus, specific perceptions of personal benefits, barriers, enjoyment, and self-efficacy related to physical activity tend to be correlated with the behavior, whereas more general beliefs, such as self-esteem, or personality factors are generally not correlated (Sallis, Simons-Morton, et al., 1992).

Social Variables

It is not surprising that social influences on physical activity in youth are documented in most studies that include these variables, because young people do much of their physical activity with teams, classes, and playgroups. Nevertheless, it is reassuring to have the impact of direct participation and encouragement validated in multiple studies (Klesges, Eck, Hanson, Haddock, & Klesges, 1990; Sallis, Nader, et al., 1993; Stucky-Ropp & DiLorenzo, 1993; Zakarian et al., 1994). Parents can influence their children's physical activity in a number of ways (Taylor, Baranowski, & Sallis, 1994), but one study found that transporting the child to a location where he or she could be active was more effective than encouraging or even playing with the child (Sallis, Alcaraz, et al., 1992).

The most studied social influence on youth physical activity is parent activity habits. The hypothesis is simple: Active parents have active children. The results are complex, because this is another area in which several studies find the expected correlation and others find no association (Taylor et al., 1994). The conflicting results may indicate that some active parents support their children's physical activity in more direct ways.

Overall, studies indicate strong social influences on physical activity in youth. Further studies are needed to explain the most important types of support at different ages and to determine who is most likely to provide that support.

Environmental Variables

The strongest evidence that physical environment is closely associated with physical activity comes from observational studies of preschool children. In at least three studies, time spent outdoors was the single best correlate of physical activity (Baranowski et al., 1993; Klesges et al., 1990; Sallis, Nader, et al., 1993). This finding suggests that most opportunities to be active are outdoors, and children are generally prevented from being active indoors at home. The easy way to keep young children active, based on this result, would be to send children outside more. However, many parents keep their children indoors because of concern about safety and the lack of space and facilities near homes.

Those children with more outdoor places to play near their home were found to be more physically active than other children (Sallis, Nader, et al., 1993). A national study shows that children are less active in the winter than other seasons (Ross, Dotson, Gilbert, & Katz, 1985a). Although children spend a great deal of time watching television, there is no consistent association between viewing time and physical activity (Robinson et al., 1993; Sallis, Nader, et al., 1993).

Because having access to appropriate environments is so important for young children, it is useful to understand factors that would encourage and discourage parents from taking their children to these places. One study asked parents of young children what factors were most important in helping them to decide whether to take their children to outdoor play environments (Sallis, McKenzie, Elder, Broyles, & Nader, 1997). Of the 24 factors that were rated, the most important were safety, availability of toilets, drinking water, lighting, and shade. Having these amenities to increase comfort and safety was more important than having supervised activities or specific activity equipment.

A survey of high school students found no aspects of the perceived environment that were related to amount of vigorous exercise (Zakarian et al., 1994). However, the only factors studied were neighborhood safety, neighborhood activity models, and convenient facilities. Other physical environment factors need to be studied using objective methods.

Young people obtain most of their structured physical activity in two behavior settings: school physical education and local community programs and settings. Almost 100% of primary students and 50% of secondary students attend school physical education in the United States (Ross, Dotson, Gilbert, & Katz, 1985b). Although the majority of students have access to this important behavior setting, physical education is not providing adequate physical activity. Observations of classes in primary and middle schools revealed that only 3 minutes in the average 30-minute class were spent doing moderate to vigorous physical activity (Simons-Morton, Taylor, Snider, Huang, & Fulton, 1994).

Children and adolescents obtain most of their activity from structured and unstructured programs and settings in the community (Ross et al.,

1985a). At least one study has shown that participation in community sports programs is associated with high levels of total physical activity (Trost et al., 1997), so it is important that young people of all socioeconomic levels have access to these programs. The amount of physical activity provided by community programs is unknown, and participation in unstructured programs has not been quantified.

Environmental influences on children's physical activity are very strong. In the study by Baranowski and colleagues (1993), the combination of gender, location, and month of the year explained more than 75% of the variance in directly observed physical activity. It is expected that environmental influences will decline in their impact during childhood and adolescence as social and psychological factors become more important.

Relevance of Determinants Research for Designing Interventions

Results of determinants studies can be used in two ways to help design physical activity interventions. The first use is to assist in targeting interventions to high-risk groups. For example, findings that physical activity declines dramatically among female adolescents or that levels are particularly low for low socioeconomic status groups provide rationales for creating special programs for those groups. Observations that physical activity levels are lowest in the winter imply a need for interventions targeting winter activities.

A second use of determinants research is to guide the intervention's content. Interventions do not directly change behaviors. Interventions modify the factors that control behavior, and those changes are expected to lead to improved behavior. The adult determinants research suggests that a successful intervention would promote low- to moderate-intensity physical activity; alter perceptions of benefits, self-efficacy, intentions, and enjoyment; and stimulate more social support for exercise. The youth determinants research suggests that interventions that provide enjoyable activities that build perceptions of competence or self-efficacy, reduce perceptions of barriers, stimulate parental assistance, and increase the time that children spend outdoors will be relatively effective. The literature suggests that these variables may influence physical activity, so changing these mediating variables should produce changes in the behavior. Such an intervention may be far from ideal but in theory should be more effective than a program that targets changes in unsupported mediators such as knowledge and normative beliefs.

Determinants researchers are encouraged to consider how their studies can provide hypotheses and preliminary data for intervention studies and policy changes. Intervention researchers are encouraged to make reasonable extrapolations from the results of determinants studies in the selection of goals and content.

SUMMARY

Determinants are variables that are correlated with physical activity and that may have causal effects. It is necessary to use behavior theories and models to guide studies, and the most promising models hypothesize that behavior is influenced by intrapersonal, social, *and* physical environmental variables. Some determinants, such as age, sex, race and ethnicity, and genetics (Perusse, Tremblay, LeBlanc, & Bouchard, 1989) are not modifiable but can identify groups at risk for being inactive. It may be more important to identify modifiable determinants that can be used to guide the design of interventions. Important modifiable determinants for adults include self-efficacy, perceived barriers, perceived benefits, enjoyment of activity, and social support. These determinants generally apply to all subgroups of the population. Important modifiable determinants for young people include self-efficacy, enjoyment, social support from family and friends, and for young children, time spent outdoors. Physical education, sports teams, and activity classes can provide substantial amounts of physical activity for young people.

FURTHER READING

Dishman, R. K., & Sallis, J. F. (1994). Determinants and interventions for physical activity and exercise. In C. Bouchard, R. J. Shephard, & T. Stephens (Eds.), *Physical activity, fitness, and health: International Proceedings and consensus statement* (pp. 214-238). Champaign, IL: Human Kinetics.

This chapter contains a review of physical activity determinants for adults and provides a discussion of important research needs.

Sallis, J. F., & Hovell, M. F. (1990). Determinants of exercise behavior. In *Exercise and sports sciences reviews* (Vol. 18, pp. 307-330). Baltimore: Williams & Wilkins.

This chapter explains the value of determinants research for public health and summarizes the results of a systematic program of research.

Physical Activity Interventions
With Individuals

Interventions to influence individuals in ways that increase physical activity must be based on good-quality research. Designers of such physical activity interventions should make use of information from all of the phases of the behavioral epidemiology process. Research on physical activity determinants is particularly relevant, because it helps to identify which attributes of people, social systems, or environments may or may not influence physical activity. Interventions do not directly change behaviors. An effective intervention will modify one or more of the factors that control behavior, and such changes are expected to lead to improved behavior. It is said that changes in controlling factors "mediate" changes in the behavior. An intervention that changes documented psychological, social, and environmental mediators may not be as effective as desired, but in theory it should be more effective than a program that targets changes in unsupported mediators, such as knowledge, normative beliefs, and susceptibility to illness.

A wide variety of interventions to promote physical activity have been evaluated. This chapter covers primarily those that aim to change individuals, and Chapter 9 reviews community-wide and environmental interventions designed to change entire populations. Both of these chapters highlight particularly effective or promising recent examples of the major types of interventions. Neither this nor the next chapter is able to comprehensively review studies. Nevertheless, we can give some sense of the breadth of studies and their findings by summarizing a meta-analysis of all published physical activity intervention studies.

Meta-Analysis of Physical Activity Intervention Studies

Dishman and Buckworth (1996) published a meta-analytic review of 127 intervention studies. Meta-analysis allows for a quantitative comparison of different kinds of study designs, intervention approaches, and results in a variety of populations. Although there are dangers in comparing very different studies, a major advantage over narrative reviews is the ability to reduce all results to a common metric, called an effect size. This meta-analysis reports how effect sizes vary by study type, intervention, and population characteristics. More than 130,000 people participated in the studies reviewed. All effect sizes reported here are weighted by sample size, which should reflect the public health impact more accurately than unweighted effect sizes.

Dishman and Buckworth (1996) reported a mean weighted effect size over all studies of .75. Guidelines for interpreting effect sizes are that .10, .30, and .50 are small, medium, and large effects, respectively. Thus, physical activity interventions as a whole have large effects. Because the unweighted mean effect size was .34, the larger studies were shown to be more effective. Some of the main findings of the meta-analysis are presented in Table 8.1.

The type of intervention was strongly related to effect size. Behavior modification had a very large effect size (.92), whereas all other approaches, including cognitive-behavioral modification, health education, and physical education curriculum, had small effect sizes in the range of .10 to .20. Within most of the intervention categories, there was a wide range of effects, indicating that the effectiveness of a particular approach is influenced by other factors, such as the specific design of the program, quality of implementation, nature of the population, and measures used. Surprisingly, mediated interventions (.91) were much more effective than face-to-face or combination programs (.10-.16). Media-based interventions were usu-

Table 8.1 Effect Sizes for Selected Physical Activity Intervention Characteristics	
Intervention Characteristics	*Effect Size*[a]
Intervention type	
Behavior modification	.92
Cognitive behavior modification	.10
Health education/risk appraisal	.10
Physical education curriculum	.21
Intervention delivery	
Face-to-face programs	.16
Mediated interventions	.91
Face-to-face + mediated	.10
Activity goal	
Increasing activity during leisure time	.85
Specific aerobic prescription	.18
Strength training	.46
Unsupervised activity	.78
Low- to moderate-intensity activity	.94
General community settings	.82

SOURCE: Based on a meta-analysis by Dishman and Buckworth (1996).

a. .10 = small effect size; .30 medium effect size; .50 = large effect size.

ally delivered by mail or telephone, with a few examples of mass media programs.

The activity goals of the program also made a difference. The goal with the highest effect size was increasing leisure time physical activity (.85). Specific aerobic exercise prescription (.18) and strength training (.46) were also effective, but not as effective as was promoting active leisure time. The findings that interventions promoting unsupervised activity (.78), those in general community settings (.82), and those emphasizing low- to moderate-intensity activity (.94) were particularly effective suggest a combination of approaches that can be expected to have the most impact.

One difficulty in interpreting results of meta-analyses is that methodological factors can be confounded with intervention characteristics. For example, behavior modification studies may use the best outcome measures or have the shortest follow-ups. Therefore, Dishman and Buckworth (1996) conducted a multiple regression analysis to determine which intervention factors improved effect sizes, after controlling for all other factors. They found a number of independent effects. Large effect sizes were associated with combined ages (compared with specific young or old samples), group programs (as opposed to individual or family), and healthy study participants (compared with those with diseases or risk factors). The most effective intervention characteristics were behavior modification, mediated approaches, low- to moderate-intensity goals, and active leisure. The outcome measure associated with the strongest effect size was attendance or observation, compared with self-report, activity monitors, and fitness testing.

The meta-analysis indicates that physical activity interventions are generally effective, but the specific characteristics of the intervention make a difference. For most types of interventions, examples of effective and ineffective programs can be found. These results provide clues about the intervention approaches likely to be most and least effective. These results could change as more studies are conducted. The remainder of this chapter describes the methods and results of innovative or effective interventions that target individuals.

Health Risk Appraisal, Fitness Testing, and Knowledge-Based Programs

Health risk appraisal and fitness testing are common components of health promotion programs; sometimes they are the only interventions. Some health and fitness professionals believe that confronting people with test results showing risk factors or low fitness levels will lead to increases in habitual activity. Controlled studies generally show little effect if any of giving such feedback. For example, Godin, Desharnais, Jobin, and Cook (1987) investigated the separate and combined effects of fitness testing and health risk appraisal. Although knowledge of fitness test results had a short-term effect on intention to exercise, there was no intervention effect at any time on physical activity. Studies that have combined educational programs with fitness tests and health risk assessment have found small effects on physical activity in the short term, but these effects were not maintained 6 months after the intervention (Daltroy, 1985; Reid & Morgan, 1979). Fitness testing and health risk assessments should be used only as part of a broader program and should not be viewed as interventions in themselves.

Behavioral and Cognitive-Behavioral Interventions

Because behavior modification approaches were found to be the most effective physical activity interventions, it is worthwhile to review some of the specific procedures. These methods of behavior change have been applied successfully to many behaviors. Behavior modification is based on the work of psychologist B. F. Skinner (1953), who emphasized the role of environmental antecedents and consequences in controlling behavior. Changing antecedents is called *stimulus control,* and examples for physical activity include planning specific times and locations for activity, keeping running shoes in the car, having exercise equipment at home, posting written reminders to exercise, living near attractive exercise facilities, and making appointments to do physical activity with others.

Altering consequences is the most powerful method for changing behavior: Consequences that increase behavior are called *reinforcers* (or rewards); these can include socializing while doing activities, monetary incentives for walking or cycling to work, or point systems with certificates or other recognition to promote physical activity in school-age children. When a behavior is followed by a *punisher,* the probability of repeating that behavior is reduced. Common punishers for physical activity can include discomfort during exertion, emotional distress while walking through a crime-infested neighborhood, being laughed at because of poor sports skills, and fear of being hit by a car while cycling on a busy street. Physical activity promotion programs need to provide reinforcers for being active and find ways of removing or reducing punishers. Sometimes behavior modification programs are specified in a contingency contract: One person agrees to provide reinforcers contingent on the other person's meeting specified behavior change goals.

A classic small study demonstrated the efficacy of behavioral contracts (Wysocki, Hall, Iwata, & Riordan, 1979). Study participants deposited several items of personal value with the investigators, and these were returned when participants met goals for aerobic exercise. Exercise increased dramatically during the treatment period, with substantial maintenance over 1 year. Even though contracting may be effective, it may not be practical for large groups of people.

However, contracting is practical for patients with life-threatening diseases who typically receive intensive treatment. Oldridge and Jones (1983) studied the effects of contracting with cardiac rehabilitation patients. Patients could voluntarily sign contracts to receive reinforcers for participating in the exercise program for 6 months. About half of patients in both experimental and control groups dropped out. Not all patients agreed to sign the contract, but those who did sign a contract attended significantly more exercise sessions than nonsigners or controls.

There are a number of constraints on the use of reinforcement programs, with access to meaningful rewards being among the most important. However, a program in which participants reinforced one another with tokens that were traded in for prizes increased exercise frequency more than did a control condition (Noland, 1989). Another program evaluated a lottery system to reinforce exercise by sedentary women (Marcus & Stanton, 1993). This program was not effective, possibly because drawings for sweatshirts were held only every 9 weeks. Reinforcement is more effective when it is frequent and immediately follows the behavior.

Cognitive-behavioral interventions are derived from Bandura's (1986) social cognitive theory. Several behavior change techniques are usually grouped together in treatment packages. Table 8.2 describes common cognitive-behavioral techniques. Most programs include self-monitoring, which requires study participants to record their behavior, along with antecedents and consequences that may influence the behavior. Self-monitoring is used to identify controlling factors as well as to track progress in making changes. Goal setting is most effective when goals are quantifiable and short-term—daily or weekly. In self-reinforcement, the individual develops a self-contract and rewards himself or herself when goals are met. Reinforcers can be privileges such as watching a favorite TV program, material items such as a new paperback book, or even self-praise.

Cognitive interventions are often used. The decisional balance technique involves examining the "pros" and "cons" of being physically active. Changing self-talk involves monitoring the content of thoughts and setting goals to reduce negative self-talk ("I don't like exercise") and increase positive self-talk ("I will find something new to enjoy about physical activity each time I do it"). Because virtually no one adheres perfectly to a physical activity schedule, it is useful to teach people how to prevent relapsing to a sedentary lifestyle (Marlatt & Gordon, 1985). A key concept is for people to understand that it is not helpful to feel guilty when they miss a planned activity session (called a "lapse"), because guilt makes one feel like giving up. A more effective response is to use positive self-talk, such as "I will start back on my program tomorrow." Other cognitive-behavioral procedures include enhancing social

Table 8.2 Cognitive-Behavioral Techniques to Promote Adherence to Physical Activity

- *Self-monitoring.* Keep a diary of activity behaviors or how time is spent while not being active.

- *Goal setting.* Based on results of self-monitoring, goals can be set that increase activity levels gradually. Goals should be specific, quantifiable, and short-term.

- *Self-reinforcement.* Give yourself access to rewards but only after activity goals are met. Reinforcers can include reading a book, watching a favorite television program, phoning a friend, or giving self-praise.

- *Decisional-balance analysis.* Examine the "pros" and "cons" of being more active. You can also consider the pros and cons of remaining sedentary.

- *Changing "self-talk."* We give ourselves instructions through inner dialogue. The goal is to increase positive thoughts about physical activity and decrease negative thoughts.

- *Relapse prevention.* All exercisers have lapses back into being sedentary. Short-term lapses can turn into long-term relapses. To prevent relapses, it is important to have a plan for avoiding situations that lead to lapses. When lapses occur, do not feel guilty about missing exercise sessions, but use positive self-talk to make plans to become active again.

- *Social support.* Family and friends can help you stay active by exercising with you, doing chores while you do your activity, or simply encouraging you to be active.

- *Shaping.* In changing physical activity, it is essential to make gradual rather than abrupt increases. Gradual increases make it easier to change and reduce risk of injury.

support, making gradual changes in behavior (shaping), and various methods of enhancing self-efficacy.

Several cognitive-behavioral components have been tested in short-term studies. Wankel (1984) reported a series of studies showing that adherence to exercise classes was enhanced by the decisional balance sheet method and by providing extensive social support for physical activity. Martin and colleagues (1984) conducted a series of six studies with initially sedentary adults. Each study evaluated the addition of one intervention component to the overall program. Attendance at the twice-weekly sessions was significantly improved by frequent personalized praise and feedback from instructors, flexible goal setting by study participants, and the use of distraction during exercise. For beginning exercisers, it is more effective if they think about something other than exercise. A lottery to reinforce attendance and training to prevent relapse were not effective. Overall, the combined cognitive-behavioral interventions produced attendance rates of 80% or greater, whereas a control group with the most basic program had attendance of only about 50%.

Because the determinants literature shows a strong association between self-efficacy and physical activity, McAuley and coworkers (McAuley, Courneya, Rudolph, & Lox, 1994) conducted an experiment to determine whether increased self-efficacy causes improvements in physical activity. Middle-aged, sedentary adults were randomly assigned to a self-efficacy enhancing program or to a walking program with group sessions not designed to increase self-efficacy. The experimental intervention provided information from all four sources of self-efficacy influence: personal experience of success, social modeling, social persuasion, and interpretation of physiological states. During the fifth month, controls walked 10.4 miles, and intervention participants walked 14.8 miles, almost 50% more. Not only did the study show that a well-designed program can increase perceptions of self-efficacy, but self-efficacy ratings predicted amount of walking.

These studies show that specific cognitive-behavioral components can at least contribute to short-term success of physical activity interventions. Many of the techniques have been incorporated into more comprehensive programs that are described later in this chapter and in Chapter 9.

Programs to Promote Home-Based Physical Activity

Many physical activity interventions are evaluated in exercise classes or fitness centers. However, most people prefer to be active on their own—at home or in their neighborhood. Attending a class or group is inconvenient for many people, and it may be more difficult to get to the class than to do the physical activity. It is expected that more people will participate in programs that do not require face-to-face meetings. Therefore, several studies have been conducted to evaluate interventions that help people do regular physical activity at home or any other place they choose. The following studies deliver the interventions by mail or phone.

The first study in this area relied completely on mailed materials (Owen, Lee, Naccarella, & Haag, 1987). A correspondence course was developed to teach participants several of the cognitive-behavioral skills described above.

Sedentary adults were recruited through the media and assigned to receive the exercise correspondence course in a single package or in a series of seven mailings. Comparison groups included those who refused to be in the group and members of a fitness class. At the completion of the course, those who received the single mailing were exercising more than those who received multiple mailings or refused the course. At a 10-month follow-up, there were no differences among groups. This study illustrates the typical finding that physical activity interventions do not have long-lasting effects. Mailed interventions have the benefit of low cost, but they may not be intensive enough to produce long-term effects.

Interventions delivered by telephone are believed to be effective, because they are convenient to the participant and they provide social support that is likely to be more effective than mailed materials. Lombard, Lombard, and Winett (1995) evaluated a simple telephone intervention to promote walking. The study was designed to determine if the content and the length of the calls made a difference. In the high-content calls, counselors helped participants set goals and gave them feedback on recent performance. In the low-content calls, counselors only "touched base" with participants and provided no feedback. Calls were made either every week or every 3 weeks. All calls were very brief, either 1 or 3 minutes. After 6 months of intervention, it was found that the content of the calls did not make any difference, suggesting that feedback and goal setting were not effective. However, the frequency of the calls was important. Of those receiving weekly calls, 46% were walking regularly, compared with only 13% among those who were called every 3 weeks. These findings suggest that frequent, brief phone calls may be effective in prompting or reminding people to walk.

Only one study has directly compared the effects of group and telephone-based interventions. King, Haskell, Taylor, Kraemer, and DeBusk (1991) compared healthy older adults who were randomly assigned to one of four conditions: (a) higher-intensity group-based exercise, (b) higher-intensity home-based exercise, (c) lower-intensity home-based exercise, and (d) control. Group-based exercise sessions were held at convenient community centers. The home-based intervention consisted of an introductory face-to-face meeting, followed by phone calls that varied in frequency from weekly to monthly. To equalize caloric expenditure, the higher-intensity group was instructed to exercise 3 days per week, compared with 5 days per week for the lower-intensity group. At the 1-year assessment, both home-based groups were exercising more and had higher fitness levels than the group-based participants or controls. There seemed to be fewer barriers to exercising at home than in a group. This result also supports the effectiveness of telephone interventions.

The results were different at the 2-year assessment (King, Haskell, Young, Oka, & Stefanick, 1995). The higher-intensity home-based group was exercising more than all the other groups. It appears that it was easier to schedule three sessions of vigorous exercise per week than to find 5 days to do moderate-intensity exercise. This apparent effect of a "trade-off" between intensity and time required should be studied in more detail.

Promoting physical activity at home through mail and telephone interventions is a promising low-cost strategy. Providing social support through these convenient media has been consistently found to be effective (Dishman & Buckworth, 1996). Further work is needed to develop systems for delivering programs such as these to large numbers of people.

Programs to Promote Lifestyle Physical Activity

Programs are needed to help people meet the Centers for Disease Control/American College of Sports Medicine (CDC/ACSM) public health recommendation of accumulating 30 minutes of moderate-intensity physical activity on most or all days of the week (Pate, Pratt, et al., 1995). Studies of programs targeting moderate-intensity activity are beginning to be reported. The randomized controlled Project Active, reported by Dunn and colleagues (1997), compared a lifestyle physical activity program with a structured health club-based program. In the structured exercise program, participants were asked to perform vigorous aerobic exercise and to work out up to 5 days per week. They were given free membership to a well-equipped health club with multiple choices for exercise modes.

The lifestyle intervention's goal was to accumulate 30 minutes of moderate physical activity daily, with the activity integrated into each individual's daily routines to increase convenience. Participants met in groups to learn how to apply cognitive and behavioral skills to help increase physical activity. This intervention was based on the transtheoretical model of behavior change, with groups designed to help participants develop individual plans for increasing physical activity in their daily lives. For example, some participants walked while talking on the phone, and others took brisk walks while their children engaged in sporting events.

After 6 months in their respective programs the 116 men and 119 women, who were all initially sedentary, were assessed. Seventy-eight percent of lifestyle participants were meeting the CDC/ACSM recommendation, as were 85% of the structured participants. Both groups had similar and significant increases in cardiorespiratory fitness as well as similar and significant decreases in total cholesterol, total cholesterol/HDL-C ratio, diastolic blood pressure, and percentage of body fat.

Project Active demonstrated that programs targeting moderate-intensity activity are as effective as vigorous exercise programs in changing behavioral and physiological outcomes. This gives sedentary adults choices for increasing their physical activity. Both programs in Project Active appeared to be effective, in part because they increased self-efficacy and because participants used more of the cognitive and behavioral skills that were taught (Dunn et al., 1997).

Programs in Health Care Settings

Although most health care systems are currently oriented to providing care for existing medical problems, these systems have great potential for helping achieve prevention goals. Primary care physicians have contact with large proportions of the population each year, and patients desire more guidance regarding health behaviors such as physical activity from health care professionals. However, there are substantial barriers to physical activity counseling in health care settings. Most physicians receive no training about physical activity or behavior change counseling in medical school. The major barriers to counseling appear to be time pressures during patient visits and a lack of reimbursement for preventive activities, which is a powerful disincentive (Pender, Sallis, Long, & Calfas, 1994). Despite these barriers, the U.S. Preventive Services Task Force (1996), *Healthy People 2000* (U.S. Department of Health and Human Services, 1991), and other organizations recommend physical activity counseling by health care professionals as part of routine preventive care for adults and young people.

A small number of studies have been conducted to examine the effects of physician-based interventions for physical activity (Ockene, McBride, Sallis, Bonollo, & Ockene, 1997). Two studies included physical activity counseling as part of a multicomponent program. In the United States, the INSURE program used medical education seminars, reimbursement for preventive counseling visits, and reminders to increase the quantity and quality of counseling for several health behaviors (Logsdon, Lazaro, & Meir, 1989). Over a 1-year period, 34% of patients who received the intervention started to exercise, compared with 24% of controls.

In Australia, the Fresh Start program for general practitioners relied mainly on self-help booklets and videos to help patients change multiple risk behaviors (Graham-Clarke & Oldenburg, 1994). The main role of physicians was to assess patients, interpret results, and provide appropriate materials, so most of the counseling was delivered by the media materials. This intervention had no effect on physical activity habits, assessed at either 4 or 12 months after baseline. However, it is likely that many patients did not receive the physical activity component, and continued intervention may be needed to promote long-term behavior change.

PACE (patient-centered assessment and counseling for exercise) is a program for primary health care providers that targets only physical activity. Providers are trained in effective counseling techniques that can be accomplished in 2 to 5 minutes. The counseling is guided by printed worksheets, and patients leave with a record of the main points of their counseling session. The emphasis is on encouraging moderate-intensity activities, such as walking. Similar to the Fresh Start program above, a simplified stages-of-change approach is used that includes structured counseling worksheets specific for each of three stages (Patrick et al., 1994). The protocol for precontemplators prompts patients to consider their personal benefits for being active and to identify barriers. The goal is merely for these patients to think about being active. For contemplators, the goal is to develop a specific and realistic physical activity program that includes short-term goals and social support. For those who are already active, the provider praises them and assists in making plans to prevent relapses. To aid the provider in allotting his or her time, it is recommended that the most counseling time be devoted to contemplators, who are ready to make a change. The PACE program was feasible in office settings, the materials and training were acceptable to providers, and the counseling was highly valued by patients (Long et al., 1996).

A short-term controlled study documented the efficacy of the PACE program (Calfas et al., 1996). Only contemplators were recruited for the study, because they were the only ones likely to make changes during a short-term study. Physicians in a variety of primary care specialties were recruited for the study, and intervention and control practices were matched on specialty, setting, and patient population. Patients were assessed prior to a scheduled visit and reassessed 4 to 6 weeks after the visit. At posttest, 52% of intervention patients reported being in the action stage, compared with only 12% of control patients. Self-report minutes of walking for exercise each week nearly doubled in the intervention group (37 vs. 75 minutes), whereas the control patients made little change (34 vs. 42 minutes). These self-reports were supported by the results of activity monitoring in a subset of patients. It was concluded that brief counseling from a health care provider can lead to important increases in physical activity over the short term. Additional intervention components are needed to promote long-term changes.

Programs for Specific Populations

Patients With Clinical Conditions

Regular physical activity is a central focus of cardiac rehabilitation programs, although most programs also intervene on other factors and behaviors, such as nutrition, smoking, stress reduction, and hypertension control. A meta-analysis found programs that emphasized exercise more than other risk factors reduced deaths from all causes by 31%, which was slightly better than the 19% reduction in programs that emphasized risk factor reduction over exercise (Oldridge, Guyatt, Fischer, & Rimm, 1988). Adherence to exercise is low, even among cardiac patients, so it is surprising that few studies have been conducted to identify interventions to enhance adherence in this group.

The MULTIFIT trial (DeBusk et al., 1994) attempted to reduce the costs of cardiac rehabilitation and increase convenience of physical activity by employing nurses to monitor home-based exercise. In this randomized controlled trial, the nurse-delivered program provided education and counseling for multiple risk behaviors for 1 year, mainly by telephone and mail. After 12 months, 71% of patients were still exercising an average of five times per week. In typical cardiac rehabilitation programs, 50% of patients drop out by the 12-month point (DeBusk et al., 1994).

It is expected that similar behavior change programs will be effective for both healthy and diseased patients. In fact, a few studies have shown that physical activity interventions that include components such as education, goal setting, and social support with renal patients (Painter & Moore, 1994), arthritis patients (Allegrante et al., 1993), and diabetic patients (Schneider et al., 1992) can be effective. More research is needed to determine optimal physical activity interventions for patients with different diseases.

The Obese

Physical activity, either alone or in combination with dietary restrictions, typically has only a small effect on initial weight loss in obese participants. This is believed to be mainly because of the limited caloric expenditure reported in most studies (Hill, Drougas, & Peters, 1994). However, physical activity during weight loss tends to have the favorable effects of promoting fat loss while preserving lean body mass. The data provide much stronger support for the effects of physical activity on weight loss maintenance (Hill et al., 1994), and physical activity is often the only predictor of long-term maintenance of weight loss.

Specific interventions are needed to promote physical activity after initial weight loss. A study by Perri and colleagues (1988) showed that a self-management exercise program needed to be added to a general maintenance program to increase adherence to physical activity. Another study compared maintenance programs to enhance diet or physical activity after a 1-year weight loss intervention (King, Frey-Hewitt, Dreon, & Wood, 1989). Participants in the diet or exercise weight loss programs were randomly assigned to receive no intervention after the initial year or to receive periodic contacts by mail and telephone. The maintenance intervention was more effective in keeping weight off for the exercisers than for the dieters. During the maintenance year, the exercise intervention group had regained only 0.8 kg, compared with 3.9 kg for exercisers with no maintenance intervention and 3.2 kg for dieters with a maintenance program. The exercise maintenance group both ate more calories and exercised more than did the diet maintenance group, showing that exercisers do not have to be as careful with their dietary restrictions.

The Elderly

It is commonly believed that many problems associated with aging can be attributed to lack of physical activity. Loss of the ability to do simple tasks such as get out of a chair, carry the groceries, and clean one's home can interfere substantially with quality of life in older people. Much of this loss of function may be due to simple muscle atrophy resulting from years of inactivity. A groundbreaking study found that it is possible even for the very elderly to increase their strength and function through strenuous resistance training (Fiatarone et al., 1994). The results were dramatic and suggest that resistance training is both safe and effective for the very old.

Mayer and colleagues (1994) conducted a study to evaluate the effects of a variety of prevention interventions on health and medical care costs for the elderly. Elderly Medicare beneficiaries were assigned to either a control condition or a 2-year prevention program, including health risk assessment, educational sessions, and behavioral goal setting. The intervention produced increases in physical activity as well as cost savings.

Physical Activity Interventions for Youth and Families

It can be argued that physical activity interventions are a lower priority for young people because children are the most active age group. However, physical activity levels decline significantly throughout the school years, and by high school most adolescents do not meet the guidelines for vigorous physical activity (see Chapter 6). All of the individually based interventions described in this section are actually family programs. Family approaches are an obvious choice, because parents control children's access to facilities and programs, and families can support each other and do physical activities together.

Two similar programs targeted physical activity and dietary change in healthy families of diverse ethnic groups. Baranowski and colleagues (1990) developed a program for African American families with children in the fifth through seventh grades. The 14-week program was held at a facility that was cherished by the community. One educational and two fitness sessions were held each week. Families exercised to music together, and the educational approach was designed to convey both information and behavior change skills. Incentives were used to promote attendance and participation.

Largely because of the 20% attendance rate at meetings, the program was not successful in improving physical activity or fitness compared with controls (Baranowski et al., 1990). Going to a center adds a further barrier to the many preexisting barriers to being physically active. Most families reported numerous conflicts because of work and school.

Nader and colleagues (1989) reported the results of a physical activity and nutrition intervention for healthy Mexican American and European

American families. Families with fifth- or sixth-grade children were recruited from schools and randomly assigned to intervention or control conditions. The yearlong intervention consisted of 12 weekly sessions followed by 6 more monthly or bimonthly sessions. During each session, families exercised together, participated in educational activities to teach behavior change skills, and set goals to be active.

The intervention led to changes in several dietary, blood pressure, and blood lipid variables over a 2-year period, but these changes were mainly seen in adults (Nader et al., 1989). No significant intervention effects on physical activity or physical fitness were observed in either children or adults. Attendance was about 60% during the weekly sessions and 40% in the maintenance sessions, which might not have been sufficient to lead to increased physical activity. Both of these studies in healthy families lead to the conclusion that educational programs are not effective in promoting physical activity in children. Other approaches for intervening with young people are described in the next chapter on community interventions.

Studies of Obese Children

A number of creative studies of promoting physical activity in obese children have been conducted by Leonard Epstein and colleagues. Although it is unknown how these findings from studies of obese children apply to other groups, these studies raise some important questions and challenge some common assumptions about the best way to increase physical activity in young people.

Until recently, most physical activity interventions promoted vigorous exercise. A study by Epstein, Wing, Koeske, and Valoski (1985) was one of the first to evaluate alternative approaches. All children in the study received assistance in adhering to a weight loss diet, but they were randomized to programmed exercise, lifestyle activity integrated into daily routines, or calisthenics. At the 1-year measurement, children in the lifestyle group lost the most weight, suggesting that children were more successful in adhering to lifestyle activities than to the other exercises (Epstein et al., 1985). However, at the 5- and 10-year follow-ups, both programmed and lifestyle exercise groups had reduced their percentage of being overweight, whereas the calisthenics group increased their percentage of being overweight (Epstein, Valoski, Wing, & McCurley, 1994). This study has led to a closer examination of the benefits of promoting activities conducted as part of one's daily routine.

Epstein, Saelens, and O'Brien (1995) conducted a study based on behavioral economic theory, which deals with people's choices among alternatives. Children must often choose between physical activity and sedentary behaviors, and this study manipulated choices by reinforcing (i.e., rewarding) obese children for either increasing their physical activity or decreasing their sedentary behaviors. On 6 days, children came to the laboratory and had access to equipment and supplies for four active (e.g., jump rope, exercise machine) and four inactive (e.g., videocassette recorder, coloring) behaviors. Children in the increasing-activity group earned points for each minute they used the activity equipment, and children in the decreasing-sedentary behavior group earned points for each minute they did not take part in their most preferred sedentary behaviors. Activity time was coded by observers. Both reinforcement conditions led to large increases in physical activity and large decreases in sedentary behavior during 45-minute laboratory sessions, compared with controls (Epstein, Saelens, et al., 1995).

The promising results of the laboratory study led to the application of similar techniques to treating childhood obesity. Epstein, Valoski, and colleagues (1995) randomly assigned families to increase activity, to decrease sedentary behavior, or to combination conditions. Both parents and children were reinforced for behavior changes. After 1 year of treatment, the group that was reinforced for decreasing sedentary behavior lost significantly more body fat than the other two groups. The decreasing sedentary behavior group also improved their preference for high-intensity activities.

These two studies suggest that reinforcing children for reducing sedentary behaviors may be as effective, or even more effective, than directly reinforcing physical activities. These findings are of particular interest because they seem to contradict the cross-sectional studies (reviewed in Chapter 7) showing little or no correlation between TV viewing and physical activity. We hope that these studies will lead to a closer examination of how children make activity-related choices and how these choices can be altered for the general population of children. Another key issue for research is to better understand how the behavioral choice model might be used to give insights into the patterns of sedentary behavior that are now so common among adults.

SUMMARY

Considerable progress has been made in understanding the types of physical activity interventions that may be used to influence individuals, both adults and children. Education and information have only a very limited impact. Behavior modification interventions that directly alter environmental variables controlling physical activity are particularly successful, but it is sometimes difficult to control the antecedents and consequences. Trials of cognitive-behavioral interventions such as goal-setting and self-reward show these techniques to be effective. Interventions delivered by mail and phone that help people be active in or near their home tend to be more effective than programs that require participants to travel to group sessions. Children's habitual activity can be significantly influenced by reducing reinforcers for sedentary behaviors and making activity more rewarding. However, family programs that do not include direct reinforcement for physical activity have not been effective. Interventions targeting moderate-intensity or lifestyle activities seem to be effective for children and adults.

FURTHER READING

Annesi, J. J. (1996). *Enhancing exercise motivation.* Los Angeles: Leisure Publications.

For those who would like a practical description of how theory-based behavior change techniques can be applied to individual clients, this book will be very helpful. It is written as a step-by-step guide for practitioners.

Dishman, R. K., & Buckworth, J. (1996). Increasing physical activity: A quantitative synthesis. *Medicine and Science in Sports and Exercise, 28,* 706-719.

This is a comprehensive examination of the physical activity intervention literature. The meta-analysis approach allows the authors to determine which interventions are most effective. The reference list itself is a valuable resource.

U.S. Department of Health and Human Services. (1996). *Physical activity and health: A report of the Surgeon General.* Atlanta, GA: Centers for Disease Control and Prevention.

Chapter 6 provides examples of effective programs that have been evaluated for a variety of populations of young people and adults.

Interventions to Promote
Physical Activity in Communities
and Populations

The public health goal of reducing the proportion of the adult population that is sedentary will not be addressed in any satisfactory manner by strategies directed only at individuals or small groups. This is because physical inactivity is a population-wide problem, so strategies must be developed to affect entire populations. The major objective of current population-based physical activity promotion efforts is to assist physically inactive people to adopt and maintain regular, moderate-intensity activity (see Chapter 4). If a stages-of-change model is adopted (Prochaska & Marcus, 1994), the objective is to move people to higher stages of change. This would include moving precontemplators into contemplation. Although physical activity counseling initiatives through physicians (for example, Project PACE; also see Chapter 8, this volume) and other health care providers can potentially reach large numbers of people for face-to-face assessment and advice, such efforts are not likely to have a major impact in reducing the overall population prevalence of inactivity. Similarly, the impact of exercise classes or group-based activity programs is likely to be very modest on a population-wide basis, even if many such programs are implemented. However, these individual-based programs can be seen as components of more comprehensive population-based approaches that also include mass reach strategies and programs for whole communities.

The preceding chapter examined individual- and group-based behavior change approaches. In this chapter, we deal with mass reach efforts to promote more widespread participation in physical activity. In particular, we consider school- and worksite-based programs as examples of strategies in particular settings. We also describe the two major components of mass reach approaches directed at whole communities or populations: (a) programs in which mass media are a major component and (b) environmental and policy changes that can make physical activity a more accessible option for most people.

School-Based Physical Activity Programs

In most nations, schools are the primary societal institution with respon- sibility for promoting physical activity in young people. Thus, it is essential to examine the extent to which school programs, primarily physical educa- tion (PE), are helping meet health-related physical activity objectives. The potential of PE to reach virtually all children makes it a uniquely important resource. In the United States, 97% of primary schools have PE (Ross & Gilbert, 1985), but only about half of middle and junior high schools and one quarter of high schools require PE in all years (Pate, Small, et al., 1995). The declining availability of PE at the upper grades is a cause of concern. Many health professionals have argued that PE should not only provide physical activity during school but should prepare children for a lifetime of physical activity (Corbin, 1994; Sallis & McKenzie, 1991). Courses that teach behavior change skills relevant to this goal are most appropriate near the end of high school, but only 26% of U.S. states require high school courses in lifetime physical activity (Pate, Small, et al., 1995). There is some evidence that college courses designed to promote lifetime physical activity may have long-term effects (Brynteson & Adams, 1993), but studies are needed to develop effective courses for the high school level.

Many goals have been proposed for PE, including cognitive, motor, social, emotional, and sports skills development. Not everyone has accepted health-related goals, although there is a strong movement to adopt health promotion as the primary mission of PE (Pate & Hohn, 1994). To achieve any of the goals, except for cognitive goals, it is necessary for children to be active. Students cannot improve their motor skills by watching others, nor can they improve their sports skills by listening to a lecture. Thus, when it is shown that children engage in very little physical activity during PE, it is clear that there are major problems with existing programs.

Extensive observations of classes in primary and middle schools taught by certified PE specialists revealed that children were vigorously active only about 3 minutes of every half-hour class, or about 10% of the time (Simons-Morton, Taylor, Snider, Huang, & Fulton, 1994). A larger study of primary schools in four states found that children spent about 30 minutes per week (about 34% of class time) doing any physical activity during PE (McKenzie et al., 1996). These studies provide good evidence that children are sedentary for the majority of PE time, and there is a need to improve programs. Studies of U.S. PE programs may or may not be representative of PE in other nations, but studies with objective measures from other countries could not be located.

Several studies in primary schools have shown that it is possible to improve the quality of physical education by changing the curriculum and by training teachers. Health-related PE curricula emphasize activities that children can do for a lifetime, that they can do outside of school, and that do not require teams. Examples of lifetime activities include walking, jogging, tennis, Frisbee games, and aerobic dancing. Health-related PE strives to keep all children as physically active as possible by having enough equipment for everyone, avoiding relay games, and playing games with small teams. Enjoyment of physical activity is enhanced by frequent encouragement and praise, de-emphasis on winning, avoidance of having students select teams, and prohibition of using exercise as punishment.

The Go for Health Study, conducted in Texas, demonstrated that training PE teachers and encouraging their own physical activity led to substantial increases in children's physical activity. After 2 years of the program, children were active for 40% of PE class time, compared with 10% in control schools (Simons-Morton, Parcel, Baranowski, Forthofer, & O'Hara, 1991).

The SPARK (Sports, Play and Active Recreation for Kids) program trained both classroom teachers and PE specialists in Southern California to implement a health-related PE curriculum. Observations of PE classes showed improvements in total minutes of PE per week, minutes of physical activity during PE, and use of quality teaching methods by teachers, compared with controls (Sallis, McKenzie, Alcaraz, et al., 1997). Quality teaching methods included encouraging fitness activities, general instruction, and demonstrating activities. The effects of the SPARK program on minutes of physical activity per week can be seen in Figure 9.1, which shows that trained

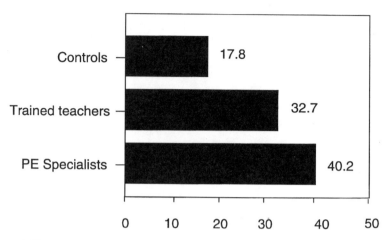

Minutes per week of observed physical activity during PE classes

Figure 9.1. The effects of the SPARK program on minutes per week of physical activity in physical education classes.
SOURCE: Adapted from Sallis, McKenzie, Alcaraz, et al. (1997).

classroom teachers improved their students' physical activity a great deal in comparison with untrained teachers, but PE specialists produced even better results.

A follow-up of SPARK schools 1.5 years after termination of the intervention indicates that health-related physical education programs can have long-term effects on teachers and students (McKenzie, Sallis, Kolody, & Faucette, 1997). The study suggests which strategies are needed to produce these long-term results. When classroom teachers were trained and supported on-site during the main study, they continued to provide high levels of physical education after external support was withdrawn. For example, students of trained teachers continued to be 88% as physically active in physical education classes as they were during the main study. In schools where physical education specialists were provided during the main study, and classroom teachers were trained after the study but did not receive on-site support, physical education classes were no better than controls. These results suggest that physical education specialists provide the best classes. However, classroom teachers who receive the combination of training and on-site support can improve the quality and quantity of their physical education classes.

The largest evaluation of a PE program was the CATCH (Child and Adolescent Trial for Cardiovascular Health) study, carried out in 96 schools in four states (Luepker et al., 1996). After 3 academic years of training and assistance in using the health-related curriculum, intervention students were active 51% of PE class time, compared with 42% for control students (McKenzie et al., 1996).

An example of tailoring physical education for specific ethnic groups is the Dance for Health program, designed for African American and Latino adolescents (Flores, 1995). When PE programs are implemented that substantially increase physical activity, beneficial physiological changes have been noted in cardiorespiratory fitness (Sallis, McKenzie, Alcaraz, et al., 1997; Vandongen et al., 1995), body fat (Dwyer, Coonan, Leitch, Hetzel, & Baghurst, 1983) and blood pressure (Vandongen et al., 1995).

Some school-based physical activity promotion programs include classroom curricula that promote physical activity outside of school. This is considered one step on the way to achieving the goal of lifetime physical activity. There have been mixed results of classroom curricula, with some studies of primary school students showing no effect of the program on out-of-school activity (Sallis, McKenzie, Alcaraz, et al., 1997) and others showing significant increases (McKenzie et al., 1996). This is one area in which programs have been studied in secondary schools. Killen and colleagues (1988) found short-term effects of a 7-week curriculum on physical activity, and Kelder, Perry, and Klepp (1993) found long-term effects of a program that combined school and total community intervention over a 7-year period.

Many studies show that PE curricula and teacher training can be highly effective in increasing physical activity at school, which sometimes leads to physiological improvements. Several studies indicate that classroom curricula can be effective in promoting physical activity outside of school, but this is not always found. A review of school-based cardiovascular health promotion studies found that physical activity interventions tended to be less effective than smoking prevention programs, similar in effectiveness to diet change programs, and more effective than programs targeting decreases in adiposity (Resnicow & Robinson, 1997). Despite the strong evidence that school-based programs can be effective, most schools emphasize traditional team sports in PE rather than activities that children are likely to use for a lifetime. Very few

PE teachers (13%) have received training on how to increase children's physical activity outside of PE class (Pate, Small, et al., 1995), so the knowledge that has been developed in research is not being put into practice for the benefit of students.

Efforts to promote lifelong physical activities among young people are also considered to require the participation of several sectors of society. Schools, community agencies, and families may be key players, but it is useful to examine the extent of strategies recommended by the Centers for Disease Control and Prevention (1997). These strategies provide an excellent blueprint for a community-wide approach to promoting physical activity in youth.

- *Policies* should be established that promote lifelong physical activity.
- *Environments,* both social and physical, should be provided that encourage and enable safe and enjoyable physical activity.
- *Physical education* should be designed to promote physical activity in class and for a lifetime.
- *Health education* should have components relevant for promoting lifelong physical activity.
- *Extracurricular activities* should provide physical activities that meet the needs and interests of all students.
- *Parent involvement* is needed to support school and community programs as well as to directly support their children's physical activity.
- *Personnel training* is needed for professionals and volunteers from numerous sectors who can play a role in promoting physical activity among young people.
- *Health services* can be redirected to include interventions to promote lifelong physical activity for young people.
- *Community programs* are needed that provide physical activities that meet the needs and interests of all young people.
- *Evaluation* is needed to monitor the quality of physical activity instruction, programs, and facilities. (Centers for Disease Control and Prevention, 1997)

Most of the research on physical activity interventions for youth has been conducted in schools, but children obtain most of their physical activity in organized programs outside of school (Ross, Dotson, Gilbert, & Katz, 1985a). There are many opportunities for children to be active in community programs, but we have not been able to locate any published studies of interventions in community settings. Millions of children in the United States and elsewhere participate in physical activity through youth sports, YMCAs, YWCAs, Boys and Girls Clubs, religious organizations, sports clubs, dance classes, swimming classes, and parks and recreation departments, among many others. However, we know very little about how many children participate or how much physical activity is provided by different programs. This is an important area in need of research.

Worksite-Based Physical Activity Programs

Worksites have considerable potential as settings for health promotion programs, including physical activity initiatives, for many reasons:

- They provide the potential to reach a large percentage of the total adult population, including blue-collar workers who may not be reached by other channels.
- They can be approached as communities with already established communication systems.
- They contain groups of people who are in contact over long periods of time.
- They can change environments to make it easier for workers to be active.
- They have already existing physical, organizational, and administrative resources, policies, and incentive systems that may be mobilized.
- They often have departments or staff members concerned with medical, safety, personnel, and in-service education (Fielding, 1984; King, Jeffery, et al., 1995; Sallis, Hill, Fortmann, & Flora, 1986).

Reviews by Sallis, Hill, et al. (1986), Glasgow and Terborg (1988), and Shephard (1996) as well as the report of the U.S. Surgeon General (U.S. Department of Health and Human Services, 1996) all indicate that controlled studies of worksite physical activity interventions are rare; most have used rudimentary pretest/posttest, or posttest-only designs. These reviews have identified several problems that reduce the success of interventions and that need to be addressed in future programs: low recruitment of workers, high rates of dropout, and poor maintenance of both the programs and changes in behavior.

Worksite physical activity programs often recruit only 20% to 30% of the workforce, and these tend to be white-collar workers who are better educated, more fit, and more aware of health issues than are nonparticipants (Lovato & Green, 1990). More recent studies incorporating incentives and competition and involving employees and management in planning of programs indicate that these factors can enhance participation (Gomel, Oldenburg, Simpson, & Owen, 1993).

Blake, Caspersen, Crow, Mittlemark, and Ringhofer (1996) describe a worksite-based program, "The Shape Up Challenge," that was part of the Minnesota Heart Health Program (MHHP). Of 365 companies invited to participate, 33% took part, and average employee participation rates ranged from 84% in smaller companies to as low as 16% in large companies. A total of 119 participating companies in two Minnesota communities and 17,626 employees took part. Employees recorded minutes spent daily in aerobic activities during a monthlong competition. Incentives were offered to promote intragroup cooperation and intergroup competition. Companies competed for awards based on average minutes of exercise per employee rather than per program participant.

Blake and associates (1996) concluded that worksite exercise competitions appear to be a viable strategy for promoting employee physical activity, particularly in smaller companies. Because the study was a single-group, posttest-only design, it is not possible to determine whether the interventions actually increased employees' physical activity.

A number of the methodological challenges in worksite intervention were overcome in a study by Gomel and associates (1993), working with the employees of the state ambulance service in Sydney, Australia. Twenty-eight ambulance stations were randomly allocated to one of four intervention conditions: health risk assessment, risk factor education, behavioral counseling, or behavioral counseling plus incentives. Participants were assessed before the intervention and at 3, 6, and 12 months. On average, among all groups, there was a short-term increase in aerobic capacity followed by a return to baseline levels, although there were other positive changes in cardiovascular risk profiles associated with the interventions. This study used some physical activity interventions but did not directly assess physical activity behavior, using aerobic capacity changes as the outcome measure. In Chapter 5, we considered some of the limitations of such measures when the focus of research is on physical activity behavior.

Blair, Piserchia, Wilbur, and Crowder (1986) carried out a 2-year follow-up of participants in the Johnson & Johnson "Live for Life" program, in which employees took part in comprehensive, information-based and participatory physical activity programs. Compared with 7% of women and 19% of men in control worksites, 20% of women and 30% of men in intervention worksites reported beginning a vigorous exercise program. This program is notable because it treated the worksite as a small community and made policy changes as well as implementing educational programs. The excellent results suggest that comprehensive strategies may be needed.

Three research priorities have been defined for this field (Glasgow & Terborg, 1988; King, Jeffery, et al., 1995; Sallis, Hill, et al., 1986). First, controlled studies are needed that permit a rigorous evaluation of programs. Second, more studies are needed of small to moderate-size worksites and those that employ a diversity of ethnic and socioeconomic groups. Third, the interventions themselves need to be more comprehensive and offer more than educational programs.

Community and Mass Media Interventions

The continuing epidemic of cardiovascular disease has led to large-scale evaluations of comprehensive, community-based approaches that emphasize population-wide education but that have also included changes in community organizations, environmental changes, and incentives and contests (Bracht, 1990). All three community trials conducted in the United States during the 1980s targeted changes in biological risk factors (blood pressure, blood cholesterol, body mass index, and rates of cigarette smoking), but they also reported physical activity outcomes. The Stanford and Minnesota programs illustrate the findings from these types of studies.

The Stanford Five-City Project (FCP) included a number of elements designed to increase levels of physical activity participation in the intervention communities. There was heavy reliance on the delivery of information using electronic and print media, along with face-to-face activities such as classes, contests, and school-based initiatives. There was more emphasis in the Stanford FCP on smoking, nutrition, weight control, and blood pressure than there was on physical activity. The concepts used to guide the programs were drawn from social learning theory, diffusion of innovations, community organization, and social marketing. Data on physical activity outcomes were derived from cross-sectional samples and from a cohort of individuals who were measured repeatedly over time. Young, Haskell, Taylor, and Fortmann (1996) report modest but statistically significant changes in physical activity in the intervention communities. The cross-sectional data showed that men in the intervention communities were more likely to take part in at least one vigorous physical activity. Small but significant increases in moderate-intensity activities were noted among women in both the cross-sectional and the cohort samples.

Luepker and associates (1994) report physical activity outcome data from the MHHP. The MHHP had less of a focus on the use of print and broadcast media education than did the Stanford FCP and concentrated more on promoting physical activity through local health professionals and community organizations. Professionals and community leaders were recruited to serve as role models and opinion leaders. There was an adult education component to the MHHP that used personal, intensive, and multiple-contact programs to try to directly influence physical activity behaviors though teaching self-management skills. The MHHP found small but significant physical activity intervention effects in their cross-sectional samples over the first 3 years of their program, which disappeared as their control group became more active in subsequent years (Luepker et al., 1994).

Each of these projects, as well as the Pawtucket Heart Health Project (Carleton et al., 1995), used a different mix of community intervention methods. All have reported weak and inconsistent changes in physical activity associated with their interventions. It should be noted that all three of these trials placed less emphasis on physical activity than they did on other cardiovascular risk factors. In fairness, at the time these projects were initiated there was much less evidence available on the importance of physical activity in the prevention of cardiovascular disease. More intensive physical activity interventions may have led to more changes.

A smaller multirisk factor community intervention that relied on the creation of community coalitions was conducted in Missouri (Brownson et al., 1996). Community groups were organized, and they were able to apply for minigrants to conduct heart health promotion programs in their local areas. Physical activity-related programs included walking clubs, aerobics classes, and festivals that demonstrated exercises and promoted other programs. Some coalitions constructed walking trails. After 2 years of the program, there were significant reductions in the percentage of residents who reported no physical activity. These improvements were only seen in communities with "active" coalitions. This study shows that programs with modest funding can be effective in some communities. More work is needed to learn how to more effectively mobilize community groups.

In the Finnish Healthy Village Study, low-cost community-based health promotion interventions were evaluated in four villages. Interventions included seminars, study groups, and walking campaigns twice a year over 3 years. Kumpusalo and associates (1996) found that the proportion of physically inactive people remained unchanged in the intervention villages over the course of the program. They attribute this lack of impact, in part, to the fact that traditional village life had until recently involved being physically active to meet basic survival needs such as hunting and gathering food. In this context, being deliberately more active for health reasons may have seemed pointless to many villagers, because they valued their newly found sedentary leisure time.

Community-wide interventions have not been shown to be very effective. We conclude that this field is in its infancy, and we need to learn much more about how to effectively increase physical activity in entire populations. It is likely that more intensive and longer-term approaches are required.

National Physical Activity Campaigns in Australia

Two nationwide physical activity campaigns were conducted in Australia by the National Heart Foundation (NHF) and were carefully evaluated. Both campaigns combined community interventions and mass media. In 1990, the slogan was "Exercise: Make It Part of Your Day" (Booth, Bauman, Oldenburg, Owen, & Magnus, 1992), and in 1991, the slogan was "Exercise: Take Another Step" (Owen, Bauman, Booth, Oldenburg, & Magnus, 1995). The campaigns were informed by social learning and social marketing models and emphasized walking as the main activity. The campaigns were designed to promote increases in physical activity among the inactive. For precontemplators, the goal was to enhance intentions to start activity, drawing on the transtheoretical model's stages of behavior change (Prochaska & Marcus, 1994; also see Chapter 7, this volume).

The two campaigns were promoted through paid television advertisements, public service announcements for radio, the distribution of a newspaper, posters, leaflets, stickers, and T-shirts; publicity tours by two heart health experts; magazine articles; and physical activity themes in episodes of two nationally broadcast television drama series. There were promotions of events through electronic and print news coverage, editorials, and feature articles. In addition to national media-based strategies, local initiatives organized by NHF state divisions included special activity days and competitions.

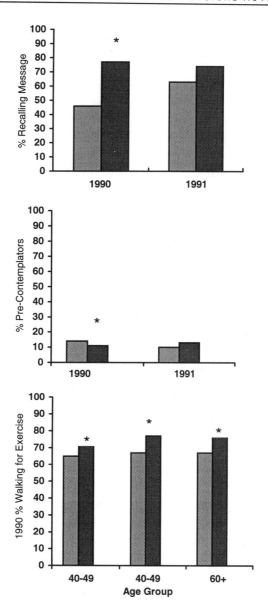

Figure 9.2. Statistically significant pre- to postcampaign differences (*) in message recall, being in precontemplation for exercise and reporting walking for exercise in the previous 2 weeks: 1990 and 1991 Australian Heart Week Campaigns.

SOURCE: Adapted from Owen, Bauman, Booth, Oldenburg, and Marcus (1995).
KEY: Precampaign = light bars; postcampaign = dark bars).

These Australian campaigns provided an opportunity to examine the influence of serial national mass media campaigns directed at increasing levels of participation in physical activity among the inactive. Face-to-face, home-based interviews with a representative national sample were carried out 2 weeks prior to, and 3 to 4 weeks following, each campaign. Results are shown in Figure 9.2. The evaluation of the 1990 campaign (Booth et al., 1992) found statistically significant increases in the prevalence of reports of walking following the campaign. Changes in self-reported walking for exercise were most marked among older people and the least well educated. Awareness of the campaign message increased significantly (46% to 71%). The level of message awareness was still quite high prior to the 1991 campaign (63%), with postcampaign awareness increasing to 74%.

The changes in reported walking for exercise and in readiness to exercise found in 1990 were not repeated in 1991 (Owen et al., 1995). In 1990, the prevalence of reporting *no* intention to do more exercise showed the greatest pre- to postcampaign decreases, suggesting that the campaign may have been most effective in reaching those who were the least active and most resistant to change (i.e., precontemplators). The 1991 campaign message may have reinforced those who had previously adopted activity, but it failed to motivate change in others. Another explanation is that most of those who were able to, or who intended to, change had already done so in response to the 1990 campaign. The studies of the impact of the Australian national campaigns provide some of the few available data on the effects of media-based physical activity campaigns in whole populations.

Strengths and Limitations of Mass Reach Campaigns

Like the other community interventions described earlier, the impact of the Australian media campaign on physical activity was modest. Flora, Maibach, and Maccoby (1989) draw conclusions from mass communication, behavioral science, and marketing theories, as well as the findings of the large-scale, community-based heart disease prevention trials from the United States and Europe in the 1970s and 1980s. They argue that mass media can play four main roles in promoting health behavior change:

1. As an educator to introduce new ideas
2. As a supporter to reinforce old messages or maintain change

3. As a promoter to attract attention to existing programs
4. As a supplement to community-based interventions

The limitations of mass media-based approaches to influencing physical activity are considered by Donovan and Owen (1994), who integrate behavioral epidemiology concepts with a social marketing model. They explain the relevance of the "four Ps" (product, price, place, and promotion) to population strategies for physical activity intervention. Donovan and Owen (1994) use the transtheoretical model (Prochaska & Marcus, 1994) to show how mass media and other strategies may be used for those who are at different stages of change related to physical activity. Media of mass communication are likely to be most effective in influencing the knowledge and attitudes of those who are at the earlier stages of the exercise adoption process, particularly precontemplators and contemplators. Mass media interventions have the potential to play a major role in promoting physical activity, but more studies are needed make that potential a reality.

Interventions With Specific
Ethnic Groups

Several community and worksite intervention trials have included substantial portions of minority group members, but few have examined the impact of the interventions specifically on these groups. An example of a physical activity program directed specifically at low-income minority groups is the PARR project (Physical Activity for Risk Reduction). Lewis and colleagues (1993) developed a program for residents of a low-income African American community living in rental accommodation administered by the Housing Authority of Birmingham, Alabama. There is a particular need for this type of intervention, because lower-income and minority individuals are at high risk for sedentary lifestyles.

In the PARR Project, data collected through focus groups and by a survey of residents' exercise practices were used to inform the development of programs based on a combination of behavioral management and community organization concepts. The programs were implemented and evaluated in six intervention and two control housing developments. Statistically significant increases in physical activity were found in those housing developments where the community provided strong leadership, organization, and commitment to the project. No effects were found where residents did not get actively involved in the program. Data and experiences from the PARR project are likely to be applicable to the delivery of similar types of health-related programs in underserved communities.

Environmental and Policy Interventions to Influence Physical Activity

There is now broad interest in the role of environmental influences in health promotion generally and for physical activity promotion in particular. "Ecological" models of health behaviors, as described by Sallis and Owen (1997), can be used to guide new environmental and policy interventions. It is widely recognized that social and physical environments can influence health behaviors (McLeroy, Bibeau, Steckler, & Glanz, 1988; Stokols, 1992), but few studies have directly applied ecological models to understanding or intervening on physical activity. A key concept that we believe is helpful in understanding the potential impact of social and physical environmental influences is "behavior settings." Behavior settings are especially critical to understanding physical activity, because activities are done in specific places. Some places have characteristics that make it easy for people to be active, and some places make it hard to be active.

The following quotation captures the flavor of ecological models: "People are but one component of the larger behavior-setting system, which restricts the range of their behavior by promoting and sometimes demanding certain actions and by discouraging or prohibiting others" (Wicker, 1979, p. 4). For example, bicycle racks and easily accessible stairs in public places can make it easier for individuals to choose to be more physically active as part of their daily routines.

Because so few studies have documented the effects of environmental interventions on physical activity, we have developed a simple ecological framework that we hope will be useful in stimulating further investigation in this area. At this early stage in the development of the empirical literature, a framework that is specific to the target behavior of physical activity may have more value than the existing general ecological models.

The framework shown in Table 9.1 is based on (a) general ecological principles of the importance of multiple levels of influences; (b) a distinction between social and physical environmental influences, policies, and laws as

Table 9.1 An Ecological Model of Influences on Physical Activity

		Physical Environment Factors	
Intrapersonal Factors	Social Environmental Factors	Natural Environment	Constructed Environment
Demographics	Supportive behaviors	Weather	Information environment
Biological	Social climate	Geography	Urban/suburban environment
Cognitive/ affective	Culture		Architectural environment
Behavioral	Policies governing incentives for activity/inactivity		Transportation environment
	Policies governing resources and infrastructures related to activity/inactivity		Entertainment infrastructure
			Recreation infrastructure

NOTE: Social and physical environments need to be considered within key behavior settings, such as home, neighborhood, school, workplace, parks, recreation and sports facilities, and public buildings.

key aspects of the social environment; (c) the need to study various behavior settings; and (d) the need to acknowledge that the behavior of individuals and groups is also a function of the personal attributes they bring to behavior settings.

The behavior settings listed are the most obvious, and research is needed to determine in which settings people are most likely to be active and in which settings interventions are most likely to be effective. The Social Environment heading provides examples of potential influences on physical activity at varying levels of integration. Supportive behaviors can be provided by individuals, and cultural influences represent influences of cohesive groups. Policies of corporations and government entities are social expressions that can produce incentives or environmental alterations that can affect physical activity and inactivity. The Physical Environment is divided into natural and constructed subdivisions, because both of these seem to be important for physical activity.

Some examples of human-created environments and infrastructures that we hypothesize are related to levels of physical activity and inactivity are also listed. Other environments and infrastructures may be relevant for other health behaviors. One of the benefits of behavior-specific frameworks is that they can give more precise directions to researchers about which variables are most important to study.

The importance of environmental interventions in the promotion of physical activity has been emphasized at various points throughout this book. Such approaches are now being advocated widely and more generally in relation to a range of health-related behaviors. For example, Ebrahim and Smith (1997) conducted a systematic review of randomized controlled trials of multiple risk factor interventions for preventing coronary heart disease. They concluded that such interventions, when they are implemented through standard forms of health education intervention, appear to be limited in their impact on the general population. Educational interventions may be limited in their impact, because even if people are convinced that they should be active, they may not be able to afford a health club membership and they may be fearful of doing physical activity in their high-crime neighborhood. They argue that "health protection" through fiscal and legislative measures may be more effective. Such measures usually involve changes to social and physical environment factors that can influence the behaviors of large numbers of people. We describe examples of such initiatives that have been studied for their effects on physical activity.

Examples of Environmental and
Policy Interventions

King (1994) and King, Jeffery, et al. (1995) provide comprehensive reviews of environmental and policy interventions for promoting physical activity. Policy initiatives can create environmental changes that increase access to and reward physical activity. These environmental changes are likely to have a broader impact on whole populations and to be less costly and more enduring than educationally oriented programs. Ecological principles have been used to guide the development of physical activity promotion policy in Australia (Owen & Lee, 1989) and in England (Owen, 1994), emphasizing the need for appropriate and convenient settings for physical activity.

King, Jeffery, et al. (1995) describe several types of policy and environmental approaches to promoting physical activity and reducing inactivity in populations. One strategy is to target increasing physical activity in each sector of daily life, such as work, domestic life, transportation, and leisure time recreation and sport. Specific interventions are needed to address all of the behavior settings in which these daily activities are conducted. They recommended strategies that do not require overt choice by the individual. Examples of interventions to facilitate activity as part of daily life include making stairways visible, safe, and convenient and having downtown areas open only to pedestrians and bicycle users.

There are resources for physical activity that are underused, and interventions could be aimed at improving access to facilities through the collaboration of health departments with recreation and parks departments, school officials, and others. To implement some of these changes in public policy, it will likely be necessary to educate administrators and community leaders about physical activity and health so that they consider the physical activity impact of policies. Other policy interventions can reduce barriers through liability legislation reform, because fear of legal liability leads some administrators to restrict access to their facilities. Zoning and land use initiatives can significantly increase the range of physical activity options in communities. For example, "greenways" that connect neighborhoods are believed to encourage walking and bicycle use for local transportation.

The approaches summarized above are key elements in ecological strategies for the promotion of physical activity across the whole population. The question that must be asked, however, is, Do such environmental initiatives actually influence people to be more active? Unfortunately, the answer is that we know very little about the effects of environmental and policy interventions on physical activity, because so few studies have been reported.

Four intervention studies are worthy of mention. Brownell, Stunkard, and Albaum (1980) conducted what is probably the first controlled study to increase physical activity using an ecological approach. The study was conducted in a Philadelphia train station in which stairs and escalators were side by side. At baseline, only about 5% of patrons walked up the stairs. The intervention consisted of placing a sign that encouraged people to take the stairs because it is "better for your heart." This modest intervention tripled the number of people who took the stairs, but the posttest rate was still less than 15%. This study suggests that simple environmental changes in key behavior settings may be effective.

Daily commuting to work by walking or cycling is a potential source of regular physical activity that may be subject to intervention. Vuori, Oja, and Paronen (1994) evaluated a multicomponent program. The intervention included information and prompts throughout the target worksite, lotteries to enhance motivation, and improvements in showers and changing facilities.

After 6 months, 7% of employees reported increasing their physically active commuting to work, and 19% increased their overall leisure time physical activity. Although this intervention had modest effects, most employees supported the goals of the program.

Linenger, Chesson, and Nice (1991) examined the impact of a range of settings-based innovations in a naval air station community by comparing intervention and control communities. Extensive environmental changes were made to increase the convenience of physical activity. Bicycle paths were built along roadways; recreation facility hours were extended, new exercise equipment was installed in gymnasiums; a women's fitness center was opened; a number of marked running courses were set up throughout the community; and running and bicycle clubs were organized. These improvements were supplemented by policy changes, such as commanding officers at the air station authorizing release time for activity. There were significant improvements in fitness in the naval community where these social and behavior settings innovations were implemented. Further trials of comprehensive environmental and policy changes in communities would be valuable, especially in nonmilitary settings.

A natural experiment indicates the potential of policy and environmental interventions to increase physical activity. In Belfast, Northern Ireland, 14 new leisure centers were opened in a 7-year period, transforming it from one of the poorest environments for sports and activity into the best served in the United Kingdom (Roberts, Dench, Minten, & York, 1989). This activity-promoting environment was accompanied by a large rise in participation in sports and physical activity among young adults and smaller improvements for other age groups. The usual variation by socioeconomic status was not seen, possibly because many of the new leisure centers were located in disadvantaged areas. Although uncontrolled, this study provides some evidence that environmental interventions can influence population levels of physical activity.

Using Research to Inform Nationwide Programs to Promote Physical Activity

Interventions directed at whole populations or at settings such as schools and workplaces are centerpieces of the overall public health effort to promote higher levels of participation in physical activity. Although these approaches need to be based on relevant theories and models, such as social marketing and ecological models, the same principles of health behavior change used in individual programs have application in population-based programs. General principles to guide public health intervention highlight three themes covered in Chapters 8 and 9:

1. The role of situational and environmental factors in influencing the adoption and maintenance of health-related behaviors (Stokols, 1992)
2. The need for a realistic awareness of what can and cannot be achieved by mass media communication campaigns alone (Redman, Spencer, & Sanson-Fisher, 1990)
3. The usefulness of focusing explicitly on the different stages of behavioral change (Booth et al., 1992)

A broader range of intervention guidelines has been described in ways that are understandable for administrators and policymakers in the original publications (Owen, 1994; Owen & Lee, 1989).

Lessons From Other Fields of Study

Although the state of current knowledge is limited regarding population approaches to promoting physical activity, other areas of public health intervention can be informative. For example, there are potential implications for physical activity promotion in the findings of studies on tobacco control in industrialized countries (Borland, Owen, Hill, & Chapman, 1994; Pierce, Macaskill, & Hill, 1990).

Even with systematic policies, programs, and strategies in place, changes in the overall population prevalence of health-related behaviors can be slow. For example, there was an average 0.8% per annum decrease in smoking prevalence in Australia through the 1980s. What rate of population-wide increases in physical activity participation might we realistically expect to take place if adequately funded and systematic strategies such as those described in this chapter and in Chapter 8 are put in place over the next decade? What would be the effect on physical activity of the population if we could actually implement some of the environmental change initiatives that we have discussed in this chapter (Sallis & Owen, 1997)?

As public awareness about health-related behaviors improves, such changes are likely to influence individuals' decision making and behavioral persistence. That is, people probably start to think and do things differently as they come to believe that other people are thinking and doing things differently. Changes in public awareness and social norms are likely to influence the behaviors of social activists and the political and administrative decision makers who can influence public policy and funding priorities. This should eventually increase political support for environmental and social innovations that can create more settings and opportunities for physical activity. One of the lessons of this chapter should be that those who are already active can make it easier for themselves and others to be active by lobbying policymakers to change community environments so they become more "activity friendly."

SUMMARY

There is great potential for changing physical activity of entire populations through community-based and mass media programs. Currently, we have limited information on what types of large-scale initiatives are likely to be successful. Many of the programs evaluated to date had limited effects, which may be due to an emphasis on educational approaches that are not intensive enough. Programs in schools and worksites that show particular promise alter policies and environments to facilitate physical activity. Social marketing models can be applied more effectively to use mass media approaches to target those who are in the earlier stages of change. Ecological models have barely been applied to physical activity promotion. Research on population interventions for physical activity is especially important, because it can be used directly by decision makers in governments and in the private sector to increase the physical activity, and hence improve the health, of entire populations.

FURTHER READING

Bracht, N. (Ed.). (1990). *Health promotion at the community level.* Newbury Park, CA: Sage.

Written mainly by people who worked on the community heart disease prevention studies in the United States, this book explains theory and methods that can be used in community interventions for many health issues.

Donovan, R. J., & Owen, N. (1994). Social marketing and population interventions. In R. K. Dishman (Ed.), *Advances in exercise adherence* (pp. 249-290). Champaign, Illinois: Human Kinetics.
This chapter describes how social marketing can be applied to physical activity promotion, with an emphasis on media interventions.

King, A. C. (1991). Community intervention for promotion of physical activity and fitness. *Exercise and Sport Science Reviews, 19,* 211-259.
This article not only reviews the studies of community interventions, but it has an excellent description of the key concepts that guide their development.

King, A. C., Jeffery, R. W., Fridinger, F., Dusenbury, L., Provence, S., Hedlund, S. A., & Spangler, K. (1995). Community and policy approaches to cardiovascular disease prevention through physical activity: Issues and opportunities. *Health Education Quarterly, 22,* 499-511.
This is the most comprehensive discussion of how environmental and policy approaches can be used to promote physical activity. Contains many useful examples.

PART
V

Conclusions and
Future Directions

Section Introduction

Using the behavioral epidemiology framework to organize this book, we have emphasized how a logical sequence of research studies can be used to develop effective interventions. We have summarized research on the relationship of different kinds of physical activity to health outcomes, evidence supporting current physical activity guidelines, how to measure physical activity behaviors, factors that help explain why some people are active and others are not, and evaluations of individual- and population-oriented interventions. Knowledge is far from complete in all of these areas, so in the final chapter we look to the future and suggest research priorities that have the greatest potential for improving public health through physical activity.

Even though Chapters 8 and 9 clearly show that many physical activity interventions are not as effective as we would like, there are some effective approaches. As we conduct further research to develop improved interventions, we believe it is wise to implement as widely as possible those programs that have been shown to "work." Chapter 10 contains discussions of why and how to translate research knowledge into public health applications. A key challenge for the future is learning how to ensure that programs used throughout communities rest on a foundation of solid research.

The Future of Physical Activity and Behavioral Medicine
Research and Applications

Using a framework based in behavioral epidemiology and health psychology, in this book we have summarized research related to physical activity and health. We have attempted to show how the behavior of physical activity is related to health and how an interdisciplinary, behavioral medicine approach can lead to improvements in health through effective physical activity interventions. Consistent with a behavioral medicine perspective, the studies have been taken from several scientific disciplines, including exercise physiology, epidemiology, public health, medicine, and health psychology. All of these disciplines have important contributions to make, but no one discipline has all of the answers.

The behavioral epidemiology framework shows that different types of studies are needed for a more complete understanding of physical activity— an understanding that leads to better ways to encourage more people to be more active. The fact that most people in industrialized nations still do not meet physical activity guidelines indicates that much more work needs to be done. In this final part of the book, we suggest priority areas for additional research at several critical steps in the framework. We also speculate on changes that need to be made in societies to reduce the burden that sedentary lifestyles place on the health and well-being of populations.

Key Research Issues

Determining What Types, Amounts, and Intensities of Physical Activity Are Good for Health

One of the priority areas for physical activity research in behavioral medicine is to gain a more detailed understanding of the relationships between physical activity behavior and various health and disease outcomes. Important public health benefits are likely to result from relatively modest increases in moderate-intensity physical activity spread throughout the day (see Chapter 4). The new guidelines raise several research questions:

- Are multiple 8- to 10-minute bouts of physical activity as effective as doing all 30 minutes at once?
- Is overall energy expenditure more important than the intensity of physical activity?
- How much physical activity is needed for different health and physiological outcomes?

Enhanced understanding of the health outcomes of different types and amounts of physical activity can lead to more precise recommendations for the general public and for those with various clinical conditions. This type of physiological research indicates the behaviors that need to be studied more carefully through epidemiological and behavioral research.

Biological Mechanisms of Health Effects

Epidemiological studies primarily inform us about what health outcomes are related to physical activity, but more controlled physiological research can explain the biological mechanisms that control the health outcomes. Research on underlying mechanisms can, for example, examine the role of different types, intensities, and durations of physical activity in altering metabolic functions (including metabolic processes affecting blood lipids and glucose), body composition, diabetes, and other disorders affecting the circulatory system. Physical activity affects a number of other bodily systems and functions, and there are similar needs to more thoroughly understand underlying mechanisms—for example, in relation to bone health, hormonal influences on some cancers, and aspects of immune function.

Understanding the Psychological Effects of Physical Activity

In Chapter 3, we reviewed some of the evidence and research issues in understanding the psychological outcomes of participation in different types of physical activity. Most of these outcomes are beneficial, but there is a limited understanding of the mechanisms that underlie psychological changes, particularly as a result of moderate-intensity and vigorous aerobic activities. Understanding the extent to which psychological benefits are the result of biological changes; of cognitive, affective, or attitudinal mechanisms; or of combinations of these is a fruitful area for future research.

Physical Activity Measurement

In Chapter 5, we described the different methods by which the physical activity levels of children and adults may be assessed. The need for more reliable, valid, and practical measures is relevant for all areas of physical activity research. Improved measures will lead to more accurate prevalence estimates and comparability across nations and better evaluations of interventions. Increasingly, technological advances drive measurement research. New applications of information technology, miniaturization, and biotelemetry are likely to generate many innovations in physical activity measurement over the next several years.

Understanding Population Prevalences and Trends

Although there have been many recent advances in physical activity measurement methods, Chapter 6 clearly shows that there is still relatively limited information by which to compare exercise prevalence rates and trends between different countries. Research in collaboration with the agencies in public health or sport and recreation is needed to develop reliable, valid, consistent, and comparable monitoring systems. Population databases would be more useful for guiding interventions if they were more strongly linked to behavior change and social marketing models (see Chapter 9). A major gap in knowledge relevant to understanding and influencing "incidental" activity is the lack of valid and reliable data to document occupational and domestic physical activity levels. Such data would provide insights into key public health concerns about the physical activity levels of lower-skilled workers and of women who are more likely to be engaged in child rearing and domestic work.

Understanding Physical Activity Determinants

Research has begun to explicate some of the links between physical activity habits and a number of biological, personal, social, and environmental factors. The research on physical activity determinants, reviewed in Chapter 7, is becoming more theory driven rather than mainly descriptive in nature. There is much scope for additional determinants research on physical activity, with a priority on examining factors that influence the different stages of adults' readiness to be more active, and the ways in which environmental and structural factors may influence both sedentary behavior and physical activity participation.

Influencing Individuals to Be More Active

As Chapter 8 illustrates, there is some challenging new research on innovative methods to prompt individuals to adopt and maintain habits of regular physical activity. Trials of home-based and physician-based programs are recent research initiatives, but many other promising approaches are just beginning to be tested. Expert systems delivered by personal computers or over the World Wide Web have considerable potential to be applied to physical activity. Trials of programs tailored to the particular needs or interests of different high-risk or minority groups should also be a research priority.

Developing and Evaluating Community Interventions

Physical inactivity has been clearly identified as a public health problem affecting whole populations as well as large groups of those at higher risk within populations. As shown in Chapter 9, there is an urgent need to develop and test innovative mass reach methods for promoting increased participation in regular physical activity. School-based interventions for children have been repeatedly found to be effective, but studies in secondary schools and other community settings are essentially nonexistent. Small- and large-scale interventions delivered through worksites, community agencies, and the mass media have often not been systematically evaluated, and there is the need to build high-quality measurement into such evaluations. We emphasize the need for developing theory that is relevant to devising environmental and public policy changes that can be used to influence the activity levels of whole populations or community groups.

Translating Research Into Practice

The behavioral epidemiology framework describes how basic and applied research on physical activity and health may be used to inform the development of programs for promoting physical activity interventions and public health policy. We describe five steps of behavioral epidemiology research:

1. Establishing the links between physical activity and health
2. Developing methods for accurately measuring physical activity
3. Identifying factors that influence physical activity habits
4. Evaluating interventions to promote physical activity
5. Translating research into practice

The previous chapters summarized research related to the first four steps, and in this final chapter we comment on the last step.

Behavioral medicine is a very diverse field, but one of its defining features is the application of science to the improvement of health. The bulk of this book is concerned with a scientifically based approach to developing interventions that are effective in promoting physical activity. Several effective interventions have been reported, but these programs do not improve physical activity levels in the population unless they are actually used in practice. The translation of intervention research into intervention practice is a neglected but critical issue.

Unfortunately, there are very few studies of the extent to which effective physical activity interventions are being used at worksites, schools, primary care settings, community organizations, and media outlets. We can only imagine the impact on the population of a country if programs shown to be effective were being implemented in all these settings and were reaching the vast majority of the population. Chapter 6 in the Surgeon General's report, *Physical Activity and Health* (U.S. Department of Health and Human Services, 1996), contains a limited amount of data suggesting that effective programs are probably not being used extensively. On the contrary, approaches known to be ineffective, such as programs that rely on enhancing knowledge, may be in widest use. More systematic research on the application of interventions in field settings is needed.

Translating intervention research into practice may be the most important step in the behavioral epidemiology framework, because of its direct impact on public health. We strongly encourage intervention researchers to study ways of enhancing the adoption of their programs. Studying the diffusion of programs in diverse settings throughout a nation is a difficult research problem, but behavioral medicine researchers have recently developed models and methods to guide this type of research (Oldenburg, Hardcastle, & Kok, 1997). We also encourage professionals involved in implementing physical activity programs in various settings to seek out and adopt interventions shown to be effective in rigorous research.

Understanding and Influencing the Societal Barriers to Physical Activity

This book began with a description of how "we," as a species, have created a post-Industrial Revolution society that has removed the necessity of being physically active in everyday life. We have developed and invested vast amounts of money in machines and elaborate systems that transport us, feed us, do physical labor for us, and entertain us. Sedentary lifestyles are epidemic in industrialized societies because humans have worked hard over the last two centuries to make these lifestyles possible. Thus, it is important to understand that physical inactivity is a societal problem, not just an issue of individual choices.

As we enter the 21st century, we humans are becoming aware that physically inactive lifestyles seriously harm our physical and mental well-being. We are now confronted with making a decision about whether we want to be an active society. One choice is continuing an inactive way of life that leads to 200,000 premature deaths per year (in the United States alone). The other choice is giving up some of the conveniences we have invented, bought in mass quantities, and come to cherish over the years.

What will it take to get us to drive less and walk more for errands? What will it take to get us to use the stairs in buildings? Who will pay to put showers and bicycle lockers at worksites to support employees' physical activity? How much of our transportation budgets are we willing to spend on attractive biking and walking trails? Is it possible to move people away from their television sets for a half hour of activity per day? Are we willing to improve funding for the purchase, upkeep, and supervision of public parks so children have places to play? How can we convince insurance companies to pay for effective physical activity interventions as part of primary care? How can we encourage school officials to improve the quality and quantity of physical education for children throughout the world? How can we educate legislators about the importance of considering the impact on physical activity of laws and policies that affect health care, transportation, building codes, zoning ordinances, and other issues?

Until these questions can be answered, we are unlikely to make large changes in the physical activity levels of populations. Without removing societal barriers and increasing societal supports for physical activity, we are asking people to be active in an environment that discourages physical activity. This is similar to teaching people to swim in a fast-moving river. It can be done, but the chances of success are low. We contend that one reason for the high dropout rate from physical activity is the presence of societal barriers. Individual and community interventions are more likely to be effective in the long run when some of the barriers to physical activity have been eliminated. Unfortunately, as summarized in Chapter 7, there are few studies to document the effects of environmental and policy factors on physical activity. This remains another research priority.

Final Word: Encouragement to Students

Both of us have been doing behavioral medicine research on physical activity for more than 15 years. Not only has this been an enjoyable professional endeavor, but we have witnessed a remarkable increase in the value placed on physical activity by government agencies, the health care system, and the general public. A growing stream of studies documents the multiple and important health benefits of physical activity. These studies have led to (a) the inclusion of physical activity as a prominent health goal for the United States, Australia, England, other nations, and international health organizations; (b) national education campaigns in England and Australia; and (c) the 1996 Surgeon General's report in the United States. These are all historic milestones that demonstrate the vibrancy of research and level of general interest in physical activity and health. This is a healthy and growing field of research, and we encourage students to specialize in this area, because there is a need for more talent.

We believe the challenges for the future are primarily related to Steps 4 and 5 of the behavioral epidemiology framework. It is known that physical activity is critical for maintaining and improving health, and it is well accepted that most young people and adults can benefit from being more active. Thus, the key remaining tasks are developing interventions, documenting their effectiveness, then getting them implemented widely. This is how public health will be improved, and achieving these goals requires the application of sound behavioral science.

It is our experience that there are too few behavioral scientists with expertise in physical activity research. There are job opportunities in several countries for behavioral scientists with competence in studying measurements, determinants, and interventions related to physical activity. These opportunities are likely to increase. We hope this book will stimulate some students to pursue a career in physical activity and behavioral medicine research so that you can contribute to improving the health of people through physical activity. If you do not become a behavioral scientist but are involved in the implementation of physical activity programs, we hope you apply what you have learned in this book to make your programs as effective as possible.

Finally, stay active and *keep this book;* you will want to refer to it in the future and share it with others.

FURTHER READING

Oldenburg, B., Hardcastle, D. M., & Kok, G. (1997). Diffusion of innovations. In K. Glanz, F. M. Lewis, & B. K. Rimer (Eds.), *Health behavior and health education: Theory, research, and practice* (2nd ed., pp. 270-286). San Francisco: Jossey-Bass.

Very little has been written about the need to diffuse effective health promotion programs so that they are widely used. This is the first comprehensive discussion, and the authors present a useful model of diffusion.

U.S. Department of Health and Human Services. (1996). *Physical activity and health: A report of the Surgeon General.* Atlanta, GA: Centers for Disease Control and Prevention.

One section of Chapter 6 (pp. 209-259) contains a description of some of the resources that can be used to promote physical activity as well as a discussion of the limited extent to which effective programs are being used.

References

Aaron, D. J., Kriska, A. M., Dearwater, S. R., Cauley, J. A., Metz, K. F., & LaPorte, R. E. (1995). Reproducibility and validity of an epidemiologic questionnaire to assess past year physical activity in adolescents. *American Journal of Epidemiology, 142,* 191-201.

Abraham, B., d'Espaignet, E. T., & Stevenson, C. (1995). *Australian health trends 1995.* Canberra: Australian Institute of Health and Welfare, AGPS.

Ainsworth, B. E., Berry, C. B., Schnyder, V. N., & Vickers, S. R. (1992). Leisure-time physical activity and aerobic fitness in African-American young adults. *Journal of Adolescent Health, 13,* 606-611.

Ainsworth, B. E., Haskell, W. L., Leon, A. S., Jacobs, D. R., Montoye, H., Sallis, J. F., & Paffenbarger, R. S. (1993). Compendium of physical activities: Classification of energy costs of human physical activities. *Medicine and Science in Sports and Exercise, 25,* 71-80.

Ajzen, I. (1985). From intentions to actions: A theory of planned behavior. In J. Kuhl & J. Beckman (Eds.), *Action-control: From cognition to behavior* (pp. 11-39). Heidelberg, Germany: Springer.

Allegrante, J. P., Kovar, P. A., MacKenzie, C. R., Peterson, M. G. E., & Gutin, B. (1993). A walking education program for patients with osteoarthritis of the knee: Theory and intervention strategies. *Health Education Quarterly, 20,* 63-81.

Allied Dunbar National Fitness Survey. (1992). London: Sports Council and Health Education Authority.

Alpert, B. S., & Wilmore, J. H. (1994). Physical activity and blood pressure in adolescents. *Pediatric Exercise Science, 6,* 361-380.

American College of Sports Medicine. (1978). Position statement on the recommended quantity and quality of exercise for developing and maintaining fitness in healthy adults. *Medicine and Science in Sports and Exercise, 10,* vii-x.

American College of Sports Medicine. (1990). Position stand: The recommended quantity and quality of exercise for developing and maintaining cardiorespiratory and muscular fitness in healthy adults. *Medicine and Science in Sports and Exercise, 22,* 265-274.

Andersen, R. E., Crespo, C. J., Bartlett, S. J., Cheskin, L. J., & Pratt, M. (1998). Relationship of physical activity and television watching with body weight and level of fatness among children: Results from the third National Health and Nutrition Examination Survey. *Journal of the American Medical Association, 279,* 938-942.

Armstrong, C. A., Sallis, J. F., Hovell, M. F., & Hofstetter, C. R. (1993). Stages of change, self-efficacy, and the adoption of vigorous exercise: A prospective analysis. *Journal of Sport and Exercise Psychology, 15,* 390-402.

Armstrong, N., & Simons-Morton, B. (1994). Physical activity and blood lipids in adolescents. *Pediatric Exercise Science, 6,* 381-405.

Bailey, D. A., Faulkner, R. A., & McKay, H. A. (1996). Growth, physical activity, and bone mineral acquisition. *Exercise and Sport Sciences Reviews, 24,* 233-266.

Bailey, D. A., & Martin, A. D. (1994). Physical activity and skeletal health in adolescents. *Pediatric Exercise Science, 6,* 330-347.

Bandura, A. (1986). *Social foundations of thought and action: A social cognitive theory.* Englewood Cliffs, NJ: Prentice Hall.

Baranowski, T. (1988). Validity and reliability of self-report measures of physical activity: An information-processing perspective. *Research Quarterly for Exercise and Sport, 59,* 314-327.

Baranowski, T., Simons-Morton, B., Hooks, P., Henske, J., Tiernan, K., Dunn, J. K., Burkhalter, H., Harper, J., & Palmer, J. (1990). A center-based program for exercise change among Black-American families. *Health Education Quarterly, 17,* 179-196.

Baranowski, T., Thompson, W. O., DuRant, R. H. Baranowski, J., & Puhl, J. (1993). Observations on physical activity in physical locations: Age, gender, ethnicity, and month effects. *Research Quarterly for Exercise and Sport, 64,* 127-133.

Barlow, C. E., Kohl, H. W., Gibbons, L. W., & Blair, S. N. (1995). Physical fitness, mortality, and obesity. *International Journal of Obesity, 19*(Suppl. 4), S41-S44.

Bar-Or, O., & Baranowski, T. (1994). Physical activity, adiposity, and obesity among adolescents. *Pediatric Exercise Science, 6,* 348-360.

Bassett, D. R., Ainsworth, B. E., Leggett, S. R., Mathien, C. A., Main, J. A., Hunter, D. C., & Duncan, G. E. (1996). Accuracy of five electronic pedometers for measuring distance walked. *Medicine and Science in Sports and Exercise, 28,* 1071-1077.

Bauman, A., & Owen, N. (1991). Habitual physical activity and cardiovascular risk factors. *Medical Journal of Australia, 154,* 22-28.

Bauman, A., Owen, N., & Rushworth, R. L. (1990). Recent trends and socio-demographic determinants of exercise participation in Australia. *Community Health Studies* (now *Australian Journal of Public Health, 14,* 19-26.

Becker, M. H., & Maiman, L. A. (1975). Sociobehavioral determinants of compliance with health care and medical care recommendations. *Medical Care, 13,* 10-24.

Berlin, J. A., & Colditz, G. A. (1990). A meta-analysis of physical activity in the prevention of coronary heart disease. *American Journal of Epidemiology, 132,* 612-628.

Biddle, S., Sallis, J. F., & Cavill, N. A. (Eds). (1998). *Young and Active? Young people and health enhancing physical activity: Evidence and implications.* London: Health Education Authority.

Blair, S. N., Booth, M., Gyarfas, I., Iwane, H., Marti, B., Matsudo, V., Morrow, M. S., Noakes, T., & Shephard, R. (1995). Development of public policy and physical activity initiatives internationally. *Sports Medicine, 21,* 157-163.

Blair, S. N., & Connelly, J. C. (1996). How much physical activity should we do? The case for moderate amounts and intensities of physical activity. *Research Quarterly for Exercise and Sport, 67,* 193-205.

Blair, S. N., Haskell, W. L., Ho, P., Paffenbarger, R. S., Vranizan, K. M., Farquhar, J. W., & Wood, P. D. (1985). Assessment of habitual physical activity by a seven-day recall in a community survey and controlled experiments. *American Journal of Epidemiology, 122,* 794-804.

Blair, S. N., Kampert, J. B., Kohl, H. W., Barlow, C. E., Macera, C. A., Paffenbarger, R. S., & Gibbons, L. W. (1996). Influences on cardiorespiratory fitness and other precursors on cardiovascular disease and all-cause mortality in men and women. *Journal of the American Medical Association, 276*, 205-210.

Blair, S. N., Kohl, H. W., Barlow, C. E., Paffenbarger, R. S., Gibbons, L. W., & Macera, C. A. (1995). Changes in physical fitness and all-cause mortality: A prospective study of healthy and unhealthy men. *Journal of the American Medical Association, 273*, 1093-1098.

Blair, S. N., Kohl, H. W., Gordon, N. F., & Paffenbarger, R. S. (1992). How much physical activity is good for health? *Annual Review of Public Health, 13*, 99-126.

Blair, S. N., Kohl, H. W., Paffenbarger, R. S., Clark, D. G., Cooper, K. H., & Gibbons, L. W. (1989). Physical fitness and all-cause mortality: A prospective study of healthy men and women. *Journal of the American Medical Association, 262*, 2395-2401.

Blair, S. N., Piserchia, P. V., Wilbur, C. S., & Crowder, J. H. (1986). A public health intervention model for worksite health promotion. *Journal of the American Medical Association 255*, 921-926.

Blake, S. M., Caspersen, C. J., Crow, R., Mittlemark, M. B., & Ringhofer, K. R. (1996). The Shape Up Challenge: A community-based worksite exercise competition. *American Journal of Health Promotion, 11*, 23-34.

Blumenthal, J. A., Emery, C. F., Madden, D. J., Schniebolk, S., Walsh-Riddle, M., George, L. K., McKee, D. C., Higginbotham, M. B., Cobb, F. R., & Coleman, R. E. (1991). Long-term effects of exercise on psychological functioning in older men and women. *Journal of Gerontology: Psychological Sciences, 46*, 352-361.

Bock, B. C., Albrecht, A. E., Traficante, R. M., Clark, M. M., Pinto, B. M., Tilkemeier, P., & Marcus, B. H. (1997). Predictors of exercise adherence following participation in a cardiac rehabilitation program. *International Journal of Behavioral Medicine, 4*, 60-75.

Booth, M., Bauman, A., Oldenburg, B., Owen, N., & Magnus, P. (1992). Effects of a national mass-media campaign on physical activity participation. *Health Promotion International, 7*, 241-247.

Booth, M., Bauman, A., Owen, N., & Gore, C. J. (1997). Physical activity preferences, preferred sources of assistance, and percieved barriers to increased activity among physically-inactive Australians. *Preventive Medicine, 26*, 131-137.

Booth, M., Owen, N., Bauman, A., & Gore, C. J. (1996a). Relationship between a fourteen-day recall measure of leisure-time physical activity and a sub-maximal test of physical work capacity in a population sample of Australian adults. *Research Quarterly for Exercise and Sport, 67*, 221-227.

Booth, M., Owen, N., Bauman, A., & Gore, C. J. (1996b). Repeatability of self-reported leisure-time physical activity measures for population surveys. *International Journal of Epidemiology, 25*, 153-159.

Borland, R., Owen, N., Hill, D. J., & Chapman, S. (1994). Regulatory innovations, behavior and health: Implications of research on workplace smoking bans. *International Review of Health Psychology, 3*, 167-185.

Bracht, N. (Ed.). (1990). *Health promotion at the community level*. Newbury Park, CA: Sage.

Brownell, K. D., Stunkard, A. J., & Albaum, J. M. (1980). Evaluation and modification of exercise patterns in the natural environment. *American Journal of Psychiatry, 137*, 1540-1545.

Brownson, R. C., Smith, C. A., Pratt, M., Mack, N. E., Jackson-Thompson, J., Dean, C. G., Dabney, S., & Wilkerson, J. C. (1996). Preventing cardiovascular disease through community-based risk reduction: The Bootheel heart health project. *American Journal of Public Health, 86*, 206-213.

Brynteson, P., & Adams, T. M. (1993). The effects of conceptually based physical education programs on attitudes and exercise habits of college alumni after 2 to 11 years of follow-up. *Research Quarterly for Exercise and Sport, 64,* 208-212.

Calfas, K. J., Long, B. J., Sallis, J. F., Wooten, W. J., Pratt, M., & Patrick, K. (1996). A controlled trial of physician counseling to promote the adoption of physical activity. *Preventive Medicine, 25,* 225-233.

Calfas, K. J., Sallis, J. F., Lovato, C. Y., & Campbell, J. (1994). Physical activity and its determinants before and after college graduation. *Medicine, Exercise, Nutrition, and Health, 3,* 323-334.

Calfas, K. J., Sallis, J. F., Oldenburg, B., & Ffrench, M. (1997). Mediators of change in physical activity following an intervention in primary care: PACE. *Preventive Medicine, 26,* 297-304.

Calfas, K. J., & Taylor, W. C. (1994). Effects of physical activity on psychological variables in adolescents. *Pediatric Exercise Science, 6,* 406-423.

Carleton, R. A., Lasater, T. M., Assaf, A. R., Feldman, H. A., & McKinlay, S., & the Pawtucket Heart Health Program Writing Group. (1995). The Pawtucket Heart Health Program: Community changes in cardiovascular risk factors and projected disease risk. *American Journal of Public Health, 85,* 777-785.

Caspersen, C. J., & Merritt, R. K. (1995). Physical activity trends among 26 states, 1986-1990. *Medicine and Science in Sports and Exercise, 27,* 713-720.

Caspersen, C. J., Merritt, R. K., & Stephens, T. (1994). International activity patterns: A methodological perspective. In R. K. Dishman (Ed.), *Advances in exercise adherence* (pp. 73-110). Champaign, IL: Human Kinetics.

Caspersen, C. J., Powell, K. E., & Christenson, G. M. (1985). Physical activity, exercise, and physical fitness: Definition and distinctions for health-related research. *Public Health Reports, 100,* 126-131.

Centers for Disease Control and Prevention. (1997). Guidelines for school and community programs to promote lifelong physical activity among young people. *Morbidity and Mortality Weekly Report, 46*(RR-6), 1-36.

Coen, S. P., & Ogles, B. M. (1993). Psychological characteristics of the obligatory runner: A critical examination of the anorexia analogue hypothesis. *Journal of Sport and Exercise Psychology, 15,* 338-354.

Coleman, K. J., Saelens, B. E., Wiedrich-Smith, M. D., Finn, J. D., & Epstein, L. H. (1997). Relationships between TriTrac-R3D vectors, heart rate, and self-report in obese children. *Medicine and Science in Sports and Exercise, 29,* 1535-1542.

Commonwealth Department of Human Services and Health. (1994). *Better health outcomes for Australians.* Canberra, Australia: Government Publishing Service.

Corbin, C. B. (1994). The fitness curriculum: Climbing the stairway to lifetime fitness. In R. R. Pate & R. C. Hohn (Eds.), *Health and fitness through physical education* (pp. 59-66). Champaign, IL: Human Kinetics.

Corti, B., Donovan, R. J., & Holman, C. D. (1997). Factors influencing the use of physical activity facilities: Results from qualitative research. *Health Promotion Journal of Australia, 7,* 16-21.

Courneya, K. S. (1995). Understanding readiness for regular physical activity in older individuals: An application of the theory of planned behavior. *Health Psychology, 14,* 80-87.

Courneya, K. S., & McAuley, E. (1994). Are there different determinants of the frequency, intensity, and duration of physical activity? *Journal of Behavioral Medicine, 20,* 84-90.

Daltroy, L. H. (1985). Improving cardiac patient adherence to exercise regimens: A clinical trial of health education. *Journal of Cardiopulmonary Rehabilitation, 9,* 846-853.

Davis, C., Brewer, H., & Ratusny, D. (1993). Behavioral frequency and psychological commitment: Necessary concepts in the study of excessive exercising. *Journal of Behavioral Medicine, 16,* 611-628.

Davis, C., & Fox, J. (1993). Excessive exercise and weight preoccupation in women. *Addictive Behaviors, 18,* 201-211.

DeBusk, R. F., Miller, N. H., Superko, H. R., Dennis, C. A., Thomas, R. J., Lew, H. T., Berger, W. E., III, Heller, R. S., Rompf, J., Gee, D., Kraemer, H. C., Bandura, A., Ghandour, G., Clark, M., Fisher, L., & Taylor, C. B. (1994). A case management system for coronary risk factor modification following acute myocardial infarction. *Annals of Internal Medicine, 120,* 721-729.

DeBusk, R. F., Stenestrand, U., Sheehan, M., & Haskell, W. L. (1990). Training effects of long versus short bouts of exercise in healthy subjects. *American Journal of Cardiology, 65,* 1010-1013.

De Weerdt, I., Visser, A. P., Kok, G., & Van Der Veen, E. (1990). Determinants of active self-care behaviour of insulin treated patients with diabetes: Implications for diabetes education. *Social Science and Medicine, 30,* 605-615.

Dietz, W. H., & Gortmaker, S. L. (1985). Do we fatten our children at the television set? Obesity and television viewing in children and adolescents. *Pediatrics, 75,* 807-812.

DiMatteo, M. R., Sherbourne, C. D., Hays, R. D., Ordway, L., Kravitz, R. L., McGlynn, E. A., Kaplan, S., & Rogers, W. H. (1993). Physicians' characteristics influence patients' adherence to medical treatment: Results from the Medical Outcomes Study. *Health Psychology, 12,* 93-102.

DiPietro, L. (1995). Physical activity, body weight, and adiposity: An epidemiologic perspective. *Exercise and Sport Sciences Reviews, 23,* 275-303.

DiPietro, L. (1996). The epidemiology of physical activity and physical function in older people. *Medicine and Science in Sports and Exercise, 28,* 596-600.

Dishman, R. K. (Ed.). (1988). *Exercise adherence: Its impact on public health.* Champaign, IL: Human Kinetics.

Dishman, R. K. (1990). Determinants of participation in physical activity. In C. Bouchard, R. J. Shephard, T. Stephens, J. R. Sutton, & B. D. McPherson (Eds.), *Exercise, fitness, and health: A consensus of current knowledge* (pp. 75-102). Champaign, IL: Human Kinetics.

Dishman, R. K., & Buckworth, J. (1996). Increasing physical activity: A quantitative synthesis. *Medicine and Science in Sports and Exercise, 28,* 706-719.

Dishman, R. K., & Sallis, J. F. (1994). Determinants and interventions for physical activity and exercise. In C. Bouchard, R. J. Shephard, & T. Stephens (Eds.), *Physical activity, fitness, and health: International proceedings and consensus statement* (pp. 214-238). Champaign, IL: Human Kinetics.

Dishman, R. K., Sallis, J. F., & Orenstein, D. R. (1985). The determinants of physical activity and exercise. *Public Health Reports, 100,* 158-171.

Donovan, R. J., & Owen, N. (1994). Social marketing and population interventions. In R. K. Dishman (Ed.), *Advances in exercise adherence* (pp. 249-290). Champaign, IL: Human Kinetics.

Drinkwater, B. L. (1994). Does physical activity play a role in preventing osteoporosis? *Research Quarterly for Exercise and Sport, 65,* 197-206.

Drury, T. F. (Ed.). (1989). *Assessing physical fitness and physical activity in population-based surveys* (DHHS Publication No. PHS 89-1253). Washington, DC: Government Printing Office.

Duncan, T. E., Duncan, S. C., & McAuley, E. (1993). The role of domain and gender-specific provisions of social relations in adherence to a prescribed exercise regimen. *Journal of Sport and Exercise Psychology, 15,* 220-231.

Dunn, A. L., Marcus, B. H., Kampert, J. B., Garcia, M. E., Kohl, H. W., & Blair, S. N. (1997). Reduction in cardiovascular disease risk factors: 6-month results from Project Active. *Preventive Medicine, 26,* 883-892.

DuRant, R. H., Baranowski, T., Davis, H., Rhodes, T., Thompson, W. O., Greaves, K. A., & Puhl, J. (1993). Reliability and variability of indicators of heart-rate monitoring in children. *Medicine and Science in Sports and Exercise, 25,* 389-395.

Durstine, J. L., & Haskell, W. L. (1994). Effects of exercise training on plasma lipids and lipoproteins. *Exercise and Sport Sciences Reviews, 22,* 477-521.

Dwyer, T., Coonan, W. E., Leitch, D. R., Hetzel, B. S., & Baghurst, R. A. (1983). An investigation of the effects of daily physical activity on the health of primary school students in South Australia. *International Journal of Epidemiology, 12,* 308-313.

Dwyer, T., & Grey, J. (1994). The epidemiology of exercise and obesity: An Australian perspective. In A. P. Hills & M. L. Wahlqvist (Eds.), *Exercise and obesity* (pp. 23-31). London: Smith-Gordon.

Ebrahim, S., & Smith, G. D. (1997). Systematic review of randomised controlled trials of multiple risk factor interventions for preventing coronary heart disease. *British Medical Journal, 314,* 1666-1674.

Emery, C. F., Hauck, E. R., & Blumenthal, J. A. (1992). Exercise adherence or maintenance among older adults: 1-year follow-up study. *Psychology and Aging, 7,* 466-470.

Emmons, K. M., Marcus, B. H., Linnan, L., Rossi, J. S., & Abrams, D. B. (1994). Mechanisms in multiple risk factor interventions: Smoking, physical activity, and dietary fat among manufacturing workers. *Preventive Medicine, 23,* 481-489.

Epstein, L. H., Myers, M. D., Raynor, H. A., & Saelens, B. E. (1998). Treatment of pediatric obesity. *Pediatrics, 101*(Suppl.), 554-570.

Epstein, L. H., Saelens, B. E., & O'Brien, J. G. (1995). Effects of reinforcing increases in active behavior versus decreases in sedentary behavior for obese children. *International Journal of Behavioral Medicine, 2,* 41-50.

Epstein, L. H., Valoski, A. M., Vara, L. S., McCurley, J., Wisniewski, L., Kalarchian, M. A., Klein, K. R., & Shrager, L. R. (1995). Effects of decreasing sedentary behavior and increasing activity on weight change in obese children. *Health Psychology, 14,* 109-115.

Epstein, L. H., Valoski, A., Wing, R. R., & McCurley, J. (1994). Ten-year outcomes of behavioral family-based treatment for childhood obesity. *Health Psychology, 13,* 373-383.

Epstein, L. H., Wing, R. R., Koeske, R., & Valoski, A. (1985). A comparison of lifestyle exercise, aerobic exercise, and calisthenics on weight loss in obese children. *Behavior Therapy, 16,* 345-356.

Fagard, R. H., & Tipton, C. M. (1994). Physical activity, fitness, and hypertension. In C. Bouchard, R. J. Shephard, & T. Stephens (Eds.), *Physical activity, fitness, and health: International proceedings and consensus statement* (pp. 633-655). Champaign, IL: Human Kinetics.

Fentem, P., & Walker, A. (1994). Setting targets for England: Challenging, measurable and achievable. In A. Killoran, P. Fentem, & C. J. Caspersen (Eds.), *Moving on: International perspectives on promoting physical activity* (pp. 58-76). London: Health Education Authority.

Fiatarone, M. A., O'Neill, E. F., Ryan, N. D., Clements, K. M., Solares, G. R., Nelson, M. E., Roberts, S. B., Kehayias, J. J., Lipsitz, L. A., & Evans, W. J. (1994). Exercise training and nutritional supplementation for physical frailty in very elderly people. *New England Journal of Medicine, 330,* 1769-1775.

Fielding, J. E. (1984). Health promotion and disease prevention at the worksite. *Annual Review of Public Health, 5,* 237-266.

Fisher, E. B. (1995). The results of the COMMIT Trial. *American Journal of Public Health, 2,* 159-160.

Flora, J. A., Maibach, E. W., & Maccoby, N. (1989). The role of media across four levels of health promotion intervention. *Annual Review of Public Health, 10,* 181-201.

Flores, R. (1995). Dance for health: Improving fitness in African American and Hispanic adolescents. *Public Health Reports, 110,* 189-192.

Folsom, A. R., Jacobs, D. R., Caspersen, C. J., Gomez-Marin, O., & Knudsen, J. (1986). Test-retest reliabilities of the Minnesota Leisure Time Physical Activity Questionnaire. *Journal of Chronic Disease, 39,* 505-511.

Folsom, A. R., Prineas, R. J., Kaye, S. A., & Munger, R. G. (1990). Incidence of hypertension and stroke in relation to body fat distribution and other risk factors in older women. *Stroke, 21,* 701-706.

Friedenreich, C. M., & Rohan, T. E. (1995). A review of physical activity and breast cancer. *Epidemiology, 6,* 311-317.

Glasgow, R. E., & Terborg, J. R. (1988). Occupational health promotion programs to reduce cardiovascular risk. *Journal of Consulting and Clinical Psychology, 56,* 365-373.

Godin, G. (1994). Theories of reasoned action and planned behavior: Usefulness for exercise promotion. *Medicine and Science in Sports and Exercise, 26,* 1391-1394.

Godin, G., Desharnais, R., Jobin, J., & Cook, J. (1987). The impact of physical fitness and health-age appraisal upon exercise intentions and behavior. *Journal of Behavioral Medicine, 10,* 241-250.

Godin, G., & Shephard, R. J. (1985). A simple method to assess exercise behavior in the community. *Canadian Journal of Applied Sport Science, 10,* 141-146.

Godin, G., Valois, P., Jobin, J., & Ross, A. (1991). Prediction of intention to exercise of individuals who have suffered from coronary heart disease. *Journal of Clinical Psychology, 47,* 762-772.

Godin, G., Valois, P., & Lepage, L. (1993). The pattern of influence of perceived behavioral control upon exercising behavior: An application of Ajzen's theory of planned behavior. *Journal of Behavioral Medicine, 16,* 81-102.

Gomel, M., Oldenburg, B., Simpson, J., & Owen, N. (1993). Worksite cardiovascular risk reduction: Randomized trial of health risk assessment, risk factor education, behavioral counseling and incentive strategies. *American Journal of Public Health, 83,* 1231-1238.

Gorely, T., & Gordon, S. (1995). An examination of the transtheoretical model and exercise behavior in older adults. *Journal of Sport and Exercise Psychology, 17,* 312-324.

Graham-Clarke, P., & Oldenburg, B. (1994). The effectiveness of a general-practice-based physical activity intervention on patient physical activity status. *Behavior Change, 11,* 132-144.

Green, J. S., & Crouse, S. F. (1995). The effects of endurance training on functional capacity in the elderly: A meta-analysis. *Medicine and Science in Sports and Exercise, 27,* 920-926.

Greendale, G. A., Barrett-Connor, E., Edelstein, S., Ingles, S., & Haile, R. (1995). Lifetime leisure exercise and osteoporosis: The Rancho Bernardo Study. *American Journal of Epidemiology, 141,* 951-959.

Greist, J. H., Klein, M. H., Eischens, R. R., Gurman, A. S., & Morgan, W. P. (1979). Running as treatment for depression. *Comprehensive Psychiatry, 20,* 41-54.

Grilo, C. M. (1995). The role of physical activity in weight loss and weight loss management. *Medicine, Exercise, Nutrition, and Health, 4,* 60-76.

Gross, L. D., Sallis, J. F., Buono, M. J., Roby, J. J., & Nelson, J. A. (1990). Reliability of interviewers using the seven-day physical activity recall. *Research Quarterly for Exercise and Sport, 61,* 321-325.

Gruber, J. J. (1986). Physical activity and self-esteem development in children: A meta-analysis. In G. A. Stull & H. M. Eckert (Eds.), *Effects of physical activity on children* (pp. 30-48). Champaign, IL: Human Kinetics.

Gudat, W., Berger, M., & Lefebvre, P. J. (1994). Physical activity, fitness, and non-insulin-dependent (Type II) diabetes mellitus. In C. Bouchard, R. J. Shephard, & T. Stephens (Eds.), *Physical activity, fitness, and health: International proceedings and consensus statement* (pp. 669-683). Champaign, IL: Human Kinetics.

Hahn, R. A., Teutsch, S. M., Rothenberg, R. B., & Marks, J. S. (1990). Excess deaths from nine chronic diseases in the United States, 1986. *Journal of the American Medical Association, 264,* 2654-2659.

Haraldsdottir, J., & Andersen, L. B. (1994). Dietary factors related to fitness in young men and women. *Preventive Medicine, 23,* 490-497.

Haskell, W. L. (1994a). Dose-response issues from a biological perspective. In C. Bouchard, R. J. Shephard, & T. Stephens (Eds.), *Physical activity, fitness, and health: International proceedings and consensus statement* (pp. 1030-1039). Champaign, IL: Human Kinetics.

Haskell, W. L. (1994b). Health consequences of physical activity: Understanding and challenges regarding dose-response. *Medicine and Science in Sports and Exercise, 26,* 649-660.

Haskell, W. L., Montoye, H. J., & Orenstein, D. (1985). Physical activity and exercise to achieve health-related physical fitness components. *Public Health Reports, 100,* 202-212.

Haskell, W. L., Yee, M. C., Evans, A., & Irby, P. J. (1993). Simultaneous measurement of heart rate and body motion to quantitate physical activity. *Medicine and Science in Sports and Exercise, 25,* 109-115.

Hausenblas, H. A., Carron, A. V., & Mack, D. E. (1997). Application of theories of reasoned action and planned behavior to exercise behavior: A meta-analysis. *Journal of Sport and Exercise Psychology, 19,* 36-51.

Hawkes, J. M., & Holm, K. (1993). Gender differences in exercise determinants. *Nursing Research, 42,* 166-172.

Hill, J. O., Drougas, H. J., & Peters, J. C. (1994). Physical activity, fitness, and moderate obesity. In C. Bouchard, R. J. Shephard, & T. Stephens (Eds.), *Physical activity, fitness, and health* (pp. 684-695). Champaign, IL: Human Kinetics.

Hofstetter, C. R., Hovell, M. F., Macera, C., Sallis, J. F., Spry, V., Barrington, E., & Callender, C. (1991). Illness, injury, and correlates of aerobic exercise and walking: A community study. *Research Quarterly for Exercise and Sport, 62,* 1-9.

Hopkins, D. R., Murrah, B., Hoeger, W. W. K., & Rhodes, R. C. (1990). Effect of low-impact aerobic dance on the functional fitness of elderly women. *The Gerontologist, 30,* 189-192.

Horne, T. E. (1994). Predictors of physical activity intentions and behaviour for rural homemakers. *Canadian Journal of Public Health, 85,* 132-135.

Hovell, M. F., Barrington, E., Hofstetter, R., Sallis, J. F., Black, D., & Rauh, M. (1990). Correlates of physical activity in overweight and not overweight persons: An assessment. *Journal of the American Dietetic Association, 90,* 1260.

Hovell, M. F., Hofstetter, C. R., Sallis, J. F., Rauh, M. J. D., & Barrington, E. (1992). Correlates of change in walking for exercise: An exploratory analysis. *Research Quarterly for Exercise and Sport, 63,* 425-434.

Hovell, M., Sallis, J., Hofstetter, R., Barrington, E., Hackley, M., Elder, J., Castro, F., & Kilbourne, K. (1991). Identification of correlates of physical activity among Latino adults: An exploratory analysis. *Journal of Community Health, 62,* 23-36.

Hovell, M. F., Sallis, J. F., Hofstetter, C. R., Spry, V. M., Elder, J. P., Faucher, P., & Caspersen, C. J. (1989). Identifying correlates of walking for exercise: An epidemiologic prerequisite for physical activity promotion. *Preventive Medicine, 18,* 856-866.

Huijbrechts, I. P., Erdman, R. A. M., Duivenvoorden, H. J., Deckers, J. W., Leenders, I. C. M., Pop, G. A. M., & Passchier, J. (1997). Modification of physical activity 5 months after myocardial infarction: Relevance of biographic and personality characteristics. *International Journal of Behavioral Medicine, 4,* 76-91.

Jaglal, S. B., Kreiger, N., & Darlington, G. A. (1995). Lifetime occupational physical activity and risk of hip fracture in women. *Annals of Epidemiology, 5,* 321-324.

Jakicic, J. M., Wing, R. R., Butler, B. A., & Jeffery, R. W. (1997). The relationship between presence of exercise equipment in the home and physical activity level. *American Journal of Health Promotion, 11,* 363-365.

Janz, K. F. (1994). Validation of the CSA accelerometer for assessing children's physical activity. *Medicine and Science in Sports and Exercise, 26,* 369-375.

Jeffery, R. W. (1989). Risk behaviors and health: Contrasting individual and population perspectives. *American Psychologist, 44,* 1194-1202.

Jeffery, R. W., French, S. A., Forster, J. L., & Spry, V. M. (1991). Socioeconomic status differences in health behaviors related to obesity: The Healthy Worker Project. *International Journal of Obesity, 15,* 689-696.

Johnson, C. A., Corrigan, S. A., Dubbert, P. M., & Gramling, S. E. (1990). Perceived barriers to exercise and weight control practices in community women. *Women & Health, 16,* 177-191.

Kahn, H. S., Tatham, L. M., Rodriguez, C., Calle, E. E., Thun, M. J., & Heath, G. W. (1997). Stable behaviors associated with adults' 10-year change in body mass index and likelihood of gain at the waist. *American Journal of Public Health, 87,* 747-754.

Kaplan, R. M., & Bush, J. W. (1982). Health-related quality of life measurement for evaluation research and policy analysis. *Health Psychology, 1,* 61-80.

Kayman, S., Bruvold, W., & Stern, J. S. (1990). Maintenance and relapse after weight loss in women: Behavioral aspects. *American Journal of Clinical Nutrition, 52,* 800-807.

Kelder, S. H., Perry, C. L., & Klepp, K. I. (1993). Community-wide youth exercise promotion: Long term outcomes of the Minnesota Heart Health Program and the Class of 1989 study. *Journal of School Health, 63,* 218-223.

Kelley, G. A., & Kelley, K. S. (1994). Physical activity habits of African-American college students. *Research Quarterly for Exercise and Sport, 65,* 207-212.

Kelley, G. A., & McClellan, P. (1994). Antihypertensive effects of aerobic exercise: A brief meta-analytic review of randomized controlled trials. *American Journal of Hypertension, 7,* 115-119.

Kendzierski, D., & DeCarlo, K. J. (1991). Physical activity enjoyment scale: Two validation studies. *Journal of Sport and Exercise Psychology, 13,* 50-64.

Kendzierski, D., & Johnson, W. (1993). Excuses, excuses, excuses: A cognitive behavioral approach to exercise implementation. *Journal of Sport and Exercise Psychology, 15,* 207-219.

Kessler, R. C., McGonagle, K. A., Zhao, S., Nelson, C. B., Hughes, M., Eshleman, S., et al. (1994). Lifetime and 12-month prevalence of DSM-III psychiatric disorders in the United States: Results from the National Comorbidity Survey. *Archives of General Psychiatry, 51,* 3-19.

Killen, J. D., Telch, M. J., Robinson, T. N., Maccoby, N., Taylor, C. B., & Farquhar, J. W. (1988). Cardiovascular disease risk reduction for tenth graders: A multiple-factor school-based approach. *Journal of the American Medical Association, 260,* 1728-1733.

Killoran, A., Fentem, P., & Caspersen, C. J. (Eds.). (1994). *Moving on: International perspectives on promoting physical activity.* London: Health Education Authority.

King, A. C. (1994). Community and public health approaches to the promotion of physical activity. *Medicine and Science in Sports and Exercise, 26,* 1405-1412.

King, A. C., Frey-Hewitt, B., Dreon, D. M., & Wood, P. D. (1989). Diet vs. exercise in weight maintenance: The effects of minimal intervention strategies on long-term outcomes in men. *Archives of Internal Medicine, 149,* 2741-2746.

King, A. C., Haskell, W. L., Taylor, C. B., Kraemer, H. C., & DeBusk, R. F. (1991). Group- vs. home-based exercise training in healthy older men and women. *Journal of the American Medical Association, 266,* 1535-1542.

King, A. C., Haskell, W. L., Young, D. R., Oka, R. K., & Stefanick, M. L. (1995). Long-term effects of varying intensities and formats of physical activity on participation rates, fitness, and lipoproteins in men and women aged 50 to 65 years. *Circulation, 91,* 2596-2604.

King, A. C., Jeffery, R. W., Fridinger, F., Dusenbury, L., Provence, S., Hedlund, S. A., & Spangler, K. (1995). Community and policy approaches to cardiovascular disease prevention through physical activity: Issues and opportunities. *Health Education Quarterly, 22,* 499-511.

King, A. C., Kiernan, M., Oman, R. F., Kraemer, H. C., & Ahn, D. (1997). Can we identify who will adhere to long-term physical activity? Signal detection methodology as a potential aid to clinical decision making. *Health Psychology, 16,* 380-389.

King, A. C., Oman, R. F., Brassington, G. S., Bliwise, D. L., & Haskell, W. L. (1997). Moderate-intensity exercise and self-rated quality of sleep in older adults: A randomized controlled trial. *Journal of the American Medical Association, 277,* 32-37.

King, A. C., Taylor, C. B., Haskell, W. L., & DeBusk, R. F. (1989). Influence of regular aerobic exercise on psychological health: A randomized, controlled trial of healthy middle-aged adults. *Health Psychology, 8,* 305-342.

King, A. J. C., & Coles, B. (1992). *The health of Canada's youth: Views and behaviours of 11-, 13-, and 15-year-olds from 11 countries.* Ottawa, Canada: Minister of National Health and Welfare.

Klesges, R. C., Eck, L. H., Hanson, C. L., Haddock, C. K., & Klesges, L. M. (1990). Effects of obesity, social interactions, and physical environment on physical activity in pre-schoolers. *Health Psychology, 9,* 435-449.

Klonoff, E. A., Annechild, A., & Landrine, H. (1994). Predicting exercise adherence in women: The role of psychological and physiological factors. *Preventive Medicine, 23,* 257-262.

Kohl, H. W., Powell, K. E., Gordon, N. F., Blair, S. N., & Paffenbarger, R. S. (1992). Physical activity, physical fitness, and sudden cardiac death. *Epidemiologic Reviews, 14,* 37-58.

Koplan, J. P., Rothenberg, R. B., & Jones, E. L. (1995). The natural history of exercise: A 10-yr follow-up of a cohort of runners. *Medicine and Science in Sports and Exercise, 27,* 1180-1184.

Kriska, A. M., Blair, S. N., & Pereira, M. A. (1994). The potential role of physical activity in the prevention of non-insulin-dependent diabetes mellitus: The epidemiological evidence. *Exercise and Sport Sciences Reviews, 22,* 121-143.

Kuczmarski, R. J., Flegal, K. M., Campbell, S. M., & Johnson, C. L. (1994). The increasing prevalence of overweight among US adults: The National Health and Nutrition Examination Surveys, 1960 to 1991. *Journal of the American Medical Association, 272,* 205-211.

Kumanyika, S., Wilson, J. F., & Guilford-Davenport, M. (1993). Weight-related attitudes and behaviors of black women. *Journal of the American Dietetic Association, 93,* 416-422.

Kumpusalo, E., Neittaanmaki, L., Halonen, P., Pekkarinen, H., Penttila, I., & Parviainen, M. (1996). Finnish healthy village study: Impact and outcomes of a low-cost health promotion programme. *Health Promotion International, 11,* 105-115.

Landers, D. M., & Petruzzello, S. J. (1994). Physical activity, fitness, and anxiety. In C. Bouchard, R. J. Shephard, & T. Stephens (Eds.), *Physical activity, fitness, and health: International proceedings and consensus statement* (pp. 878-882). Champaign, IL: Human Kinetics.

LaPerriere, A., Ironson, G., Antoni, M. H., Schneiderman, N., Klimas, N., & Fletcher, M. A. (1994). Exercise and psychoneuroimmunology. *Medicine and Science in Sports and Exercise, 26,* 182-190.

LaPorte, R. E., Montoye, H. J., & Caspersen, C. J. (1985). Assessment of physical activity in epidemiological research: Problems and prospects. *Public Health Reports, 100,* 131-146.

Leatt, P., Hattin, H., West C., & Shepard, R. J. (1988). Seven year follow up of employee fitness programme. *Canadian Journal of Public Health, 79,* 20-25.

Lee, C. (1993). Attitudes, knowledge, and stages of change: A survey of exercise patterns in older Australian women. *Health Psychology, 12,* 476-480.

Lee. I-M. (1994). Physical activity, fitness, and cancer. In C. Bouchard, R. J. Shephard, & T. Stephens (Eds.), *Physical activity, fitness, and health* (pp. 814-831). Champaign, IL: Human Kinetics.

Leon, A. S., Connett, J., Jacobs, D. R., & Rauramaa, R. (1987). Leisure-time physical activity levels and risk of coronary heart disease and death: The Multiple Risk Factor Intervention Trial. *Journal of the American Medical Association, 258,* 2388-2395.

Lewis, C. E., Raczynski, J. M., Heath, G. W., Levinson, R., Hilyer, J. C., & Cutter, G. R. (1993). Promoting physical activity in low-income African-American communities: The PARR project. *Ethnicity and Disease, 3,* 106-118.

Linenger, J. M., Chesson, C. V., & Nice, D. S. (1991). Physical fitness gains following simple environmental change. *American Journal of Preventive Medicine, 7,* 298-310.

Lissner, L., Bengtsson, C., Bjorkelund, C., & Wedel, H. (1996). Physical activity levels and changes in relation to longevity: A prospective study of Swedish women. *American Journal of Epidemiology, 143,* 54-62.

Logsdon, D. N., Lazaro, M. A., & Meir, R. V. (1989). The feasibility of behavioral risk reduction in primary medical care. *American Journal of Preventive Medicine, 5,* 249-256.

Lombard, D. N., Lombard, T. N., & Winett, R. A. (1995). Walking to meet health guidelines: The effect of prompting frequency and prompt structure. *Health Psychology, 14,* 164-170.

Long, B. J., Calfas, K. J., Wooten, W. J., Sallis, J. F., Patrick, K. M., Goldstein, M., Marcus, B. H., Schwenk, T. L., Chenoweth, J., Carter, R., Torres, T., Palinkas, L. A., & Heath, G. (1996). A multisite field test of the acceptability of physical activity counseling in primary care: Project PACE. *American Journal of Preventive Medicine, 12,* 73-81.

Lord, S. R., Caplan, G. A., & Ward, J. A. (1993). Balance, reaction time and muscle strength in exercising and non exercising older women. *Archives of Physical Medicine and Rehabilitation, 74,* 837-839.

Lovato, C. Y., & Green, L. W. (1990). Maintaining employee participation in workplace health promotion programs. *Health Education Quarterly, 17,* 73-88.

Luepker, R. V., Murray, D. M., Jacobs, D. R., Mittelmark, M. B., Bracht, N., Carlaw, R., Crow, R., Elmer, P., Finnegan, J., Folsom, A. R., Grimm, R., Hannan, P. J., Jeffery, R., Lando, H., McGovern, P., Mullis, R., Perry, C. L., Pechacek, T., Pirie, P., Sprafka, J. M., Weisbrod, R., & Blackburn, H. (1994). Community education for cardiovascular disease prevention: Risk factor changes in the Minnesota Heart Health Program. *American Journal of Public Health, 84,* 1383-1393.

Luepker, R. V., Perry, C. L., McKinlay, S. M., Nader, P. R., Parcel, G. S., Stone, E. J., Webber, L. S., Elder, J. P., Feldman, H. A., Johnson, C. C., Kelder, S. H., & Wu, M. (1996). Outcomes of a field trial to improve children's dietary patterns and physical activity: The Child and Adolescent Trial for Cardiovascular Health (CATCH). *Journal of the American Medical Association, 275,* 768-776.

Macera, C. A., Croft, J. B., Brown, D. R., Ferguson, J. E., & Lane, M. J. (1995). Predictors of adopting leisure-time physical activity among a biracial community cohort. *American Journal of Epidemiology, 142,* 629-635.

Macera, C. A., & Wooten, W. (1994). Epidemiology of sports and recreation injuries among adolescents. *Pediatric Exercise Science, 6,* 424-433.

Manson, J. E., Nathan, D. M., Krolewski, A. S., Stampfer, M. J., Willett, W. C., & Hennekens, C. H. (1992). A prospective study of exercise and incidence of diabetes among US male physicians. *Journal of the American Medical Association, 268,* 63-67.

Manson, J. E., Rimm, E. B., Stampfer, M. J., Colditz, G. A., Willett, W. C., Krolewski, A. S., Rosner, B., Hennekens, C. H., & Speizer, F. E. (1991). Physical activity and incidence of non-insulin-dependent diabetes mellitus in women. *Lancet, 338,* 774-778.

Marcus, B. H., Pinto, B. M., Simkin, L. R., Audrain, J. E., & Taylor, E. R. (1994). Application of theoretical models to exercise behavior among employed women. *American Journal of Health Promotion, 9,* 49-55.

Marcus, B. H., Rakowski, W., & Rossi, J. S. (1992). Assessing motivational readiness and decision making for exercise. *Health Psychology, 11,* 257-261.

Marcus, B. H., Rossi, J. S., Selby, V. C., Niaura, R. S., & Abrams, D. B. (1992). The stages and processes of exercise adoption and maintenance in a worksite sample. *Health Psychology, 11,* 386-395.

Marcus, B. H., & Simkin, L. R. (1994). The transtheoretical model: Applications to exercise behavior. *Medicine and Science in Sports and Exercise, 11,* 1400-1404.

Marcus, B. H., Simkin, L. R., Rossi, J. S., & Pinto, B. M. (1996). Longitudinal shifts in employees' stages and processes of exercise behavior change. *American Journal of Health Promotion, 10,* 195-200.

Marcus, B. H., & Stanton, A. L. (1993). Evaluation of relapse prevention and reinforcement interventions to promote exercise adherence in sedentary females. *Research Quarterly for Exercise and Sport, 64,* 447-452.

Marlatt, G. A., & Gordon, J. R. (1985). *Relapse prevention: Maintenance strategies in the treatment of addictive behaviors.* New York: Guilford.

Martin, J. E., Dubbert, P. M., Kattell, A. D., Thompson, J. K., Raczynski, J. R., Lake, M., Smith, P. O., Webster, J. S., Sikora, T., & Cohen, R. E. (1984). Behavioral control of exercise in sedentary adults: Studies 1 through 6. *Journal of Consulting and Clinical Psychology, 52,* 795-811.

Martinsen, E. W., & Stephens, T. (1994). Exercise and mental health in clinical and free-living populations. In R. K. Dishman (Ed.), *Advances in exercise adherence* (pp. 55-72). Champaign, IL: Human Kinetics.

Mayer, J. A., Hermanovich, A., Wright, B. L., Elder, J. P., Drew, J. A., & Williams, S. J. (1994). Changes in health behaviors of older adults: The San Diego Medicare Preventive Health Project. *Preventive Medicine, 23,* 127-133.

McAuley, E. (1992). The role of efficacy cognitions in the prediction of exercise behavior in middle-aged adults. *Journal of Behavioral Medicine, 15,* 65-88.

McAuley, E. (1993). Self-efficacy and the maintenance of exercise participation in older adults. *Journal of Behavioral Medicine, 16,* 103-113.

McAuley, E. (1994). Physical activity and psychosocial outcomes. In C. Bouchard, R. J. Shephard, & T. Stephens (Eds.), *Physical activity, fitness, and health: International proceedings and consensus statement* (pp. 551-568). Champaign, IL: Human Kinetics.

McAuley, E., Courneya, K. S., Rudolph, D. L., & Lox, C. L. (1994). Enhancing exercise adherence in middle-aged males and females. *Preventive Medicine, 23,* 498-506.

McAuley, E., Lox, C., & Duncan, T. E. (1993). Long-term maintenance of exercise, self-efficacy, and physiological change in older adults. *Journal of Gerontology: Psychological Sciences, 48,* 218-224.

McAuley, E., & Rudolph, D. (1995). Physical activity, aging, and psychological well-being. *Journal of Aging and Physical Activity, 3,* 67-96.

McKenzie, T. L. (1991). Observational measures of children's physical activity. *Journal of School Health, 61,* 224-227.

McKenzie, T. L., Faucette, F. N., Sallis, J. F., Roby, J. J., & Kolody, B. (1993). Effects of a curriculum and inservice program on the quantity and quality of elementary physical education classes. *Research Quarterly for Exercise and Sport, 64,* 178-187.

McKenzie, T. L., Nader, P. R., Strikmiller, P. K., Yang, M., Stone, E. J., Perry, C. L., Taylor, W. C., Epping, J. N., Feldman, H. A., Luepker, R. V., & Kelder, S. H. (1996). School physical education: Effect of the Child and Adolescent Trial for Cardiovascular Health. *Preventive Medicine, 25,* 423-431.

McKenzie, T. L., Sallis, J. F., Kolody, B., & Faucette, F. N. (1997). Long-term effects of a physical education curriculum and staff development program: SPARK. *Research Quarterly for Exercise and Sport, 68,* 280-291.

McKenzie, T. L., Sallis, J. F., Nader, P. R., Broyles, S. L., & Nelson, J. A. (1992). Anglo- and Mexican-American preschoolers at home and at recess: Activity patterns and environmental influences. *Journal of Developmental and Behavioral Pediatrics, 13,* 173-180.

McKenzie, T. L., Sallis, J. F., Nader, P. R., Patterson, T. L., Elder, J. P., Berry, C. C., Rupp, J. W., Atkins, C. J., Buono, M. J., & Nelson, J. A. (1991). BEACHES: An observational system for assessing children's eating and physical activity behaviors and associated events. *Journal of Applied Behavior Analysis, 24,* 141-151.

McLeroy, K. R., Bibeau, D., Steckler, A., & Glanz, K. (1988). An ecological perspective on health promotion programs. *Health Education Quarterly, 15,* 351-377.

Melanson, E. L., & Freedson, P. S. (1995). Validity of the Computer Science and Applications, Inc. (CSA) monitor. *Medicine and Science in Sports and Exercise, 27,* 934-940.

Minor, M. A., & Brown, J. D. (1993). Exercise maintenance of persons with arthritis after participation in a class experience. *Health Education Quarterly, 20,* 83-95.

Mondin, G. W., Morgan, W. P., Piering, P. N., Stegner, A. J., Stotesbery, C. L., Trine, M. R., & Wu, M. Y. (1996). Psychological consequences of exercise deprivation in habitual exercisers. *Medicine and Science in Sports and Exercise, 28,* 1199-1203.

Montoye, H. J., Kemper, H. C. G., Saris, W. H. M., & Washburn, R. A. (1996). *Measuring physical activity and energy expenditure.* Champaign, IL: Human Kinetics.

Morgan, W. P. (1994). Physical activity, fitness, and depression. In C. Bouchard, R. J. Shephard, & T. Stephens (Eds.), *Physical activity, fitness, and health: International proceedings and consensus statement* (pp. 851-867). Champaign, IL: Human Kinetics.

Morris, J. N., Heady, J. A., Raffle, P. A. B., Roberts, C. G., & Parks, J. A. (1953). Coronary heart disease and physical activity of work. *Lancet, 2,* 1053-1057, 1111-1120.

Morris, M., Steinberg, H., Sykes, E. A., & Salmon, P. (1990). Effects of temporary withdrawal from regular running. *Journal of Psychosomatic Research, 34,* 493-500.

Morrow, J. R., & Freedson, P. S. (1994). Relationship between habitual physical activity and aerobic fitness in adolescents. *Pediatric Exercise Science, 6,* 315-329.

Moses, J., Steptoe, A., Mathews, A., & Edwards, S. (1989). The effects of exercise training on mental well-being in the normal population: A controlled trial. *Journal of Psychosomatic Research, 33,* 47-61.

Myers, R. S., & Roth, D. L. (1997). Perceived benefits of and barriers to exercise and stage of exercise adoption in young adults. *Health Psychology, 16,* 277-283.

Nader, P. R., Sallis, J. F., Patterson, T. L., Abramson, I. S., Rupp, J. W., Senn, K. L., Atkins, C. J., Roppe, B. E., Morris, J. A., Wallace, J. P., & Vega, W. A. (1989). A family approach to cardiovascular risk reduction: Results from the San Diego Family Health Project. *Health Education Quarterly, 16,* 229-244.

National Institutes of Health Consensus Development Panel on Physical Activity and Cardiovascular Health. (1996). Physical activity and cardiovascular health. *Journal of the American Medical Association, 276,* 241-246.

Neuberger, G. B., Kasal, S., Smith, K. V., Hassanein, R., & DeViney, S. (1994). Determinants of exercise and aerobic fitness in outpatients with arthritis. *Nursing Research, 43,* 11-17.

Newman, W. P., Freedman, D. S., Voors, A. W., Good, P. D., Srinivasan, S. R., Cresanta, S. L., Williamson, G. D., Webber, L. S., & Berenson, G. S. (1986). Relation of serum lipoprotein levels and systolic blood pressure to early atherosclerosis: The Bogalusa heart study. *New England Journal of Medicine, 314,* 138-144.

Noland, M. P. (1989). The effects of self-monitoring and reinforcement on exercise adherence. *Research Quarterly for Exercise and Sport, 60,* 216-224.

Ockene, J. K., McBride, P. E., Sallis, J. F., Bonollo, D. P., & Ockene, I. S. (1997). Synthesis of lessons learned from cardiopulmonary preventive interventions in healthcare practice settings. *Annals of Epidemiology, 7*(Suppl.), S32-S45.

O'Connor, P. J., Bryant, C. X., Veltri, J. P., & Gebhardt, S. M. (1993). State anxiety and ambulatory blood pressure following resistance exercise in females. *Medicine and Science in Sports and Exercise, 25,* 516-521.

O'Connor, P. J., & Youngstedt, S. D. (1995). Influence of exercise on human sleep. *Exercise and Sport Sciences Reviews, 23,* 105-134.

O'Dea, K. (1991). Westernization and non-insulin-dependent diabetes in Australian Aborigines. *Ethnicity and Disease, 1,* 171-187.

Oettle, G. J. (1991). Effect of moderate exercise on bowel habit. *Gut, 32,* 941-944.

Oldenburg, B., Hardcastle, D. M., & Kok, G. (1997). Diffusion of innovations. In K. Glanz, F. M. Lewis, & B. K. Rimer (Eds.), *Health behavior and health education: Theory, research, and practice* (2nd ed., pp. 270-286). San Francisco: Jossey-Bass.

Oldridge, N. B., Guyatt, G. H., Fischer, M. E., & Rimm, A. (1988). Cardiac rehabilitation after myocardial infarction: Combined experience of randomized trials. *Journal of the American Medical Association, 260,* 945-950.

Oldridge, N. B., & Jones, N. L. (1983). Improving patient compliance in cardiac exercise rehabilitation: Effects of written agreement and self-monitoring. *Journal of Cardiac Rehabilitation, 3,* 257-262.

Owen, N. (1994). Shaping public policies and programs to promote physical activity. In A. Killoran, P. Fentem, & C. J. Caspersen (Eds.), *Moving on: International perspectives on promoting physical activity* (pp. 194-212). London: Health Education Authority.

Owen, N. (1996). Strategic initiatives to promote participation in physical activity. *Health Promotion International, 11,* 213-218.

Owen, N., & Bauman, A. (1992). The descriptive epidemiology of physical inactivity in adult Australians. *International Journal of Epidemiology, 21,* 305-310.

Owen, N., Bauman, A., Booth, M., Oldenburg, B., & Magnus, P. (1995). Serial mass-media campaigns to promote physical activity: Reinforcing or redundant? *American Journal of Public Health, 85,* 244-248.

Owen, N., & Lee, C. (1989). Development of behaviorally-based policy guidelines for the promotion of exercise. *Journal of Public Health Policy, 10,* 43-61.

Owen, N., Lee, C., Naccarella, L., & Haag, K. (1987). Exercise by mail: A mediated behavior-change program for aerobic exercise. *Journal of Sport Psychology, 9,* 346-357.

Paffenbarger, R. S., Blair, S. N., Lee, I-M., & Hyde, R. T. (1993). Measurement of physical activity to assess health effects in free-living populations. *Medicine and Science in Sports and Exercise, 25,* 60-70.

Paffenbarger, R. S., Hyde, R. T., Wing, A. L., & Hsieh, C-C. (1986). Physical activity, all-cause mortality, and longevity of college alumni. *New England Journal of Medicine, 314,* 605-613.

Paffenbarger, R. S., Hyde, R. T., Wing, A. L., Lee, I., Jung, D. L., & Kampert, J. B. (1993). The association of changes in physical-activity level and other lifestyle characteristics with mortality among men. *New England Journal of Medicine, 328,* 538-545.

Paffenbarger, R. S., Wing, A. L., & Hyde, R. T. (1978). Physical activity as an index of heart attack risk in college alumni. *American Journal of Epidemiology, 108,* 161-175.

Paffenbarger, R. S., Wing, A. L., Hyde, R. T., & Jung, D. L. (1983). Physical activity and incidence of hypertension in college alumni. *American Journal of Epidemiology, 117,* 245-257.

Painter, P., & Moore, G. E. (1994). The impact of recombinant human erythropoietin on exercise capacity in hemodialysis patients. *Advances in Renal Replacement Therapy, 1*(1), 55-65.

Pate, R. R., & Hohn, R. C. (1994). A contemporary mission for physical education. In R. R. Pate & R. C. Hohn (Eds.), *Health and fitness through physical education* (pp. 1-8). Champaign, IL: Human Kinetics.

Pate, R. R., Long, B. J., & Heath, G. (1994). Descriptive epidemiology of physical activity in adolescents. *Pediatric Exercise Science, 6,* 434-447.

Pate, R. R., & Macera, C. A. (1994). Risks of exercising: Musculoskeletal injuries. In C. Bouchard, R. J. Shephard, & T. Stephens (Eds.), *Physical activity, fitness, and health: International proceedings and consensus statement* (pp. 1008-1018). Champaign, IL: Human Kinetics.

Pate, R. R., Pratt, M., Blair, S. N., Haskell, W. L., Macera, C. A., Bouchard, C., Buchner, D., Ettinger, W., Heath, G. W., King, A. C., Kriska, A., Leon, A. S., Marcus, B. H., Morris, J., Paffenbarger, R. S., Patrick, K., Pollock, M. L., Rippe, J. M., Sallis, J., & Wilmore, J. H. (1995). Physical activity and public health: A recommendation from the Centers for Disease Control and Prevention and the American College of Sports Medicine. *Journal of the American Medical Association, 273,* 402-407.

Pate, R. R., Small, M. L., Ross, J. G., Young, J. C., Flint, K. H., & Warren, C. W. (1995). School physical education. *Journal of School Health, 65,* 213-318.

Patrick, K., Sallis, J. F., Long, B., Calfas, K. J., Wooten, W., Heath, G., & Pratt, M. (1994). A new tool for encouraging activity: Project PACE. *The Physician and Sportsmedicine, 22,* 45-55.

Pender, N. J., Sallis, J. F., Long, B. J., & Calfas, K. J. (1994). Health-care provider counseling to promote physical activity. In R. K. Dishman (Ed.), *Advances in exercise adherence* (pp. 213-235). Champaign, IL: Human Kinetics.

Perri, M. G., McAllister, D. A., Gange, J. J., Jordan, R. C., McAdoo, W. G., & Nezu, A. M. (1988). Effects of four maintenance programs on the long-term management of obesity. *Journal of Consulting and Clinical Psychology, 56*, 529-534.

Perusse, L., Tremblay, A., LeBlanc, C., & Bouchard, C. (1989). Genetic and environmental influences on level of habitual physical activity and exercise participation. *American Journal of Epidemiology, 129*, 1012-1022.

Pierce, J. P., Macaskill, P., & Hill, D. (1990). Long-term effectiveness of mass-media led anti-smoking campaigns in Australia. *American Journal of Public Health, 80*, 565-569.

Plowman, S. A. (1992). Physical activity, physical fitness, and low back pain. *Exercise and Sport Sciences Reviews, 20*, 221-242.

Pollock, M. L., & Vincent, K. R. (1996). Resistance training for health. *The President's Council on Physical Fitness and Sports Research Digest, 2*(8), 1-6.

Powell, K. E., & Blair, S. N. (1994). The public health burdens of sedentary living habits: Theoretical but realistic estimates. *Medicine and Science in Sports and Exercise, 26*, 851-856.

Prochaska, J. O., & Marcus, B. H. (1994). The transtheoretical model: Applications to exercise. In R. K. Dishman (Ed.), *Advances in exercise adherence* (pp. 161-180). Champaign, IL: Human Kinetics.

Puhl, J., Greaves, K., Hoyt, M., & Baranowski, T. (1990). Children's activity rating scale (CARS): Description and evaluation. *Research Quarterly for Exercise and Sport, 61*, 26-36.

Raglin, J. S. (1990). Exercise and mental health: Beneficial and detrimental effects. *Sports Medicine, 9*, 323-329.

Redman, S., Spencer, E. A., & Sanson-Fisher, R. W. (1990). The role of mass media in changing health-related behaviour: A critical appraisal of two models. *Health Promotion International, 5*, 85-101.

Reid, E. L., & Morgan, R. W. (1979). Exercise prescription: A clinical trial. *American Journal of Public Health, 69*, 591-595.

Rejeski, W. J., Thompson, A., Brubaker, P. H., & Miller, H. S. (1992). Acute exercise: Buffering psychosocial stress responses in women. *Health Psychology, 11*, 355-362.

Resnicow, K., & Robinson, T. N. (1997). School-based cardiovascular disease prevention studies: Review and synthesis. *Annals of Epidemiology, 7*(Suppl.), S14-S31.

Reynolds, K. D., Killen, J. D., Bryson, S. W., Maron, D. J., Taylor, C. B., Maccoby, N., & Farquhar, J. W. (1990). Psychosocial predictors of physical activity in adolescents. *Preventive Medicine, 19*, 541-551.

Richter, E. A., & Sutton, J. R. (1994). Hormonal adaptation to physical activity. In C. Bouchard, R. J. Shephard, & T. Stephens (Eds.), *Physical activity, fitness, and health: International proceedings and consensus statement* (pp. 331-342). Champaign, IL: Human Kinetics.

Rissanen, A., Heliovaara, M., Knekt, P., Reunanen, A., & Aromaa, A. (1991). Determinants of weight gain and overweight in adult Finns. *European Journal of Clinical Nutrition, 45*, 419-430.

Roberts, K., Dench, S., Minten, J., & York, C. (1989). *Community response to leisure centre provision in Belfast*. London: Sports Council.

Robinson, T. N., Hammer, L. D., Killen, J. D., Kraemer, H. C., Wilson, D. M., Hayward, C., & Taylor, C. B. (1993). Does television viewing increase obesity and reduce physical activity? Cross-sectional and longitudinal analyses among adolescent girls. *Pediatrics, 91*, 273-280.

Ross, J. G., Dotson, C. O., Gilbert, G. G., & Katz, S. J. (1985a). After physical education: Physical activity outside of school physical education programs. *Journal of Physical Education, Recreation, and Dance, 56*(1), 35-39.

Ross, J. G., Dotson, C. O., Gilbert, G. G., & Katz, S. J. (1985b). The National Children and Youth Fitness Study: What are kids doing in school physical education? *Journal of Physical Education, Recreation, and Dance, 56*(1), 73-76.

Ross, J. G., & Gilbert, G. G. (1985). The National Children and Youth Fitness Study: A summary of findings. *Journal of Physical Education, Recreation, and Dance, 56*(1), 45-50.

Rowland, T. W. (1991). *Exercise and children's health.* Champaign, IL: Human Kinetics.

Rudolph, D. L., & McAuley, E. (1996). Self-efficacy and perceptions of effort: A reciprocal relationship. *Journal of Sport and Exercise Psychology, 18,* 216-223.

Sallis, J. F. (1991). Self-report measures of children's physical activity. *Journal of School Health, 61,* 215-219.

Sallis, J. F. (1993). Epidemiology of physical activity and fitness in children and adolescents. *Critical Reviews in Food Science and Nutrition, 33,* 405-408.

Sallis, J. F. (Ed.). (1994). Physical activity guidelines for adolescents [Special issue]. *Pediatric Exercise Science, 6,* 299-463.

Sallis, J. F., Alcaraz, J. E., McKenzie, T. L., Hovell, M. F., Kolody, B., & Nader, P. R. (1992). Parent behavior in relation to physical activity and fitness in 9-year-olds. *American Journal of Diseases of Children, 146,* 1383-1388.

Sallis, J. F., Buono, M. J., Roby, J. J., Micale, F. G., & Nelson, J. A. (1993). Seven-day recall and other physical activity self-reports in children and adolescents. *Medicine and Science in Sports and Exercise, 25,* 99-108.

Sallis, J. F., Grossman, R. M., Pinski, R. B., Patterson, T. L., & Nader, P. R. (1987). The development of scales to measure social support for diet and exercise behaviors. *Preventive Medicine, 16,* 825-836.

Sallis, J. F., Haskell, W. L., Fortmann, S. P., Vranizan, K. M., Taylor, C. B., & Solomon, D. S. (1986). Predictors of adoption and maintenance of physical activity in a community sample. *Preventive Medicine, 15,* 331-341.

Sallis, J. F., Haskell, W. L., Wood, P. D., Fortmann, S. P., Rogers, T., Blair, S. N., & Paffenbarger, R. S. (1985). Physical activity assessment methodology in the Five-City Project. *American Journal of Epidemiology, 121,* 91-106.

Sallis, J. F., Hill, R. D., Fortmann, S. P., & Flora, J. A. (1986). Health behavior change at the worksite: Cardiovascular risk reduction. In M. Hersen, R. M. Eisler, & P. M. Miller (Eds.), *Progress in behavior modification* (Vol. 20, pp. 161-197). New York: Academic Press.

Sallis, J. F., Hovell, M. F., & Hofstetter, C. R. (1992). Predictors of adoption and maintenance of vigorous physical activity in men and women. *Preventive Medicine, 21,* 237-251.

Sallis, J. F., Hovell, M. F., Hofstetter, C. R., & Barrington, E. (1992). Explanation of vigorous physical activity during two years using social learning variables. *Social Science and Medicine, 34,* 25-32.

Sallis, J. F., Hovell, M. F., Hofstetter, C. R., Elder, J. P., Faucher, P., Spry, V. M., Barrington, E., & Hackley, M. (1990). Lifetime history of relapse from exercise. *Addictive Behaviors, 15,* 573-579.

Sallis, J. F., Hovell, M. F., Hofstetter, C. R., Faucher, P., Elder, J. P., Blanchard, J., Caspersen, C. J., Powell, K. E., & Christenson, G. M. (1989). A multivariate study of determinants of vigorous exercise in a community sample. *Preventive Medicine, 18,* 20-34.

Sallis, J. F., Johnson, M. F., Calfas, K. J., Caparosa, S., & Nichols, J. F. (1997). Assessing perceived physical environmental variables that may influence physical activity. *Research Quarterly for Exercise and Sport, 68,* 345-351.

Sallis, J. F., & McKenzie, T. L. (1991). Physical education's role in public health. *Research Quarterly for Exercise and Sport, 62,* 124-137.

Sallis, J. F., McKenzie, T. L., Alcaraz, J. E., Kolody, B., Faucette, N., & Hovell, M. F. (1997). Effects of a two-year health-related physical education program on physical activity and fitness in elementary school students: SPARK. *American Journal of Public Health, 87,* 1328-1334.

Sallis, J. F., McKenzie, T. L., Elder, J. P., Broyles, S. L., & Nader, P. R. (1997). Factors parents use in selecting play spaces for young children. *Archives of Pediatrics and Adolescent Medicine, 151,* 414-417.

Sallis, J. F., Nader, P. R., Broyles, S. L., Berry, C. C., Elder, J. P., McKenzie, T. L., & Nelson, J. A. (1993). Correlates of physical activity at home in Mexican-American and Anglo-American preschool children. *Health Psychology, 12,* 390-398.

Sallis, J. F., & Owen, N. (1997). Ecological models. In K. Glanz, F. M. Lewis, & B. K. Rimer (Eds.), *Health behavior and health education: Theory, research, and practice* (2nd ed., pp. 403-424). San Francisco: Jossey-Bass.

Sallis, J. F., & Patrick, K. (1994). Physical activity guidelines for adolescents: Consensus statement. *Pediatric Exercise Science, 6,* 302-314.

Sallis, J. F., Simons-Morton, B. G., Stone, E. J., Corbin, C. B., Epstein, L. H., Faucette, N., Iannotti, R. J., Killen, J. D., Klesges, R. C., Petray, C. K., Rowland, T. W., & Taylor, W. (1992). Determinants of physical activity and interventions in youth. *Medicine and Science in Sports and Exercise, 24,* S248-S257.

Sallis, J. F., Strikmiller, P. K., Harsha, D. W., Feldman, H. A., Ehlinger, S., Stone, E. J., Williston, B. J., & Woods, S. (1996). Validation of interviewer- and self-administered physical activity checklists for fifth grade students. *Medicine and Science in Sports and Exercise, 28,* 840-851.

Sallis, J. F., Zakarian, J. M., Hovell, M. F., & Hofstetter, C. R. (1996). Ethnic, socioeconomic, and sex differences in physical activity among adolescents. *Journal of Clinical Epidemiology, 49,* 125-134.

Schneider, S. H., Khachadurian, A. K., Amorosa, L. F., Clemow, L., & Ruderman, N. B. (1992). Ten-year experience with an exercise-based outpatient life-style modification program in the treatment of diabetes mellitus. *Diabetes Care, 15,* 1800-1808.

Schnurr, P. P., Vaillant, C. O., & Vaillant, G. E. (1990). Predicting exercise in late midlife from young adult personality characteristics. *International Journal of Aging and Human Development, 30,* 153-160.

Shephard, R. J. (1996). Worksite fitness and exercise programs: A review of methodology and health impact. *American Journal of Health Promotion, 10,* 436-452

Siegel, P. Z., Brackbill, R. M., & Heath, G. W. (1995). The epidemiology of walking for exercise: Implications for promoting activity among sedentary groups. *American Journal of Public Health, 85,* 706-710.

Simkin, L. R., & Gross, A. M. (1994). Assessment of coping with high-risk situations for exercise relapse among healthy women. *Health Psychology, 13,* 274-277.

Simoes, E. J., Byers, T., Coates, R. J., Serdula, M. K., Mokdad, A. H., & Heath, G. W. (1995). The association between leisure-time physical activity and dietary fat in American adults. *American Journal of Public Health, 85,* 240-244.

Simons-Morton, B. G., Parcel, G. S., Baranowski, T., Forthofer, R., & O'Hara, N. M. (1991). Promoting physical activity and a healthful diet among children: Results of a school-based intervention study. *American Journal of Public Health, 81,* 986-991.

Simons-Morton, B. G., Taylor, W. C., Snider, S. A., Huang, I. W., & Fulton, J. E. (1994). Observed levels of elementary and middle school children's physical activity during physical education classes. *Preventive Medicine, 23,* 437-441.

Singer, D. G. (1983). A time to reexamine the role of television in our lives. *American Psychologist, 38,* 815-816.

Skinner, B. F. (1953). *Science and human behavior.* New York: Macmillan.

Stefanick, M. L. (1993). Exercise and weight control. *Exercise and Sport Sciences Reviews, 21,* 363-396.

Stefanick, M. L., & Wood, P. D. (1994). Physical activity, lipid, and lipoprotein metabolism, and lipid transport. In C. Bouchard, R. J. Shephard, & T. Stephens (Eds.), *Physical activity, fitness, and health: International proceedings and consensus statement* (pp. 417-431). Champaign, IL: Human Kinetics.

Stephens, T. (1988). Physical activity and mental health in the United States and Canada: Evidence from four population surveys. *Preventive Medicine, 17,* 35-47.

Steptoe, A., & Bolton, J. (1988). The short-term influence of high and low intensity physical exercise on mood. *Psychology and Health, 2,* 91-106.

Steptoe, A., & Wardle, J. (1992). Cognitive predictors of health behaviour in contrasting regions in Europe. *British Journal of Clinical Psychology, 31,* 485-502.

Stetson, B. A., Rahn, J. M., Dubbert, P. M., Wilner, B. I., & Mercury, M. G. (1997). Prospective evaluation of the effects of stress on exercise adherence in community-residing women. *Health Psychology, 16,* 515-520.

Stewart, A. L., Hays, R. D., Wells, K. B., Rogers, W. H., Spritzer, K. L., & Greenfield, S. (1994). Long-term functioning and well-being outcomes associated with physical activity and exercise in patients with chronic conditions in the Medical Outcomes Study. *Journal of Clinical Epidemiology, 47,* 719-730.

Stokols, D. (1992). Establishing and maintaining healthy environments: Toward a social ecology of health promotion. *American Psychologist, 47,* 6-22.

Stucky-Ropp, R. C., & DiLorenzo, T. M. (1993). Determinants of exercise in children. *Preventive Medicine, 22,* 880-889.

Tappe, M. K., Duda, J. L., & Ehrnwald, P. M. (1989). Perceived barriers to exercise among adolescents. *Journal of School Health, 59,* 153-155.

Taylor, W. C., Baranowski, T., & Sallis, J. F. (1994). Family determinants of childhood physical activity: A social-cognitive model. In R. K. Dishman (Ed.), *Advances in exercise adherence* (pp. 319-342). Champaign, IL: Human Kinetics.

Teegarden, D., Proux, W. R., Kern, M., Sedlock, D., Weaver, C. M., Johnston, C. C., & Lyle, R. M. (1996). Previous physical activity relates to bone mineral measures in young women. *Medicine and Science in Sports and Exercise, 28,* 105-113.

Troiano, R. P., Flegal, K. M., Kuczmarski, R. J., Campbell, S. M., & Johnson, C. L. (1995). Overweight prevalence and trends for children and adolescents: The National Health Examination Surveys, 1963-1991. *Archives of Pediatrics and Adolescent Medicine, 149,* 1085-1091.

Trost, S. G., Pate, R. R., Saunders, R., Ward, D. S., Dowda, M., & Felton, G. (1997). A prospective study of the determinants of physical activity in rural fifth-grade children. *Preventive Medicine, 26,* 257-263.

Tucker, L. A., & Silvester, L. J. (1996). Strength training and hypercholesterolemia: An epidemiologic study of 8499 employed men. *American Journal of Health Promotion, 11,* 35-41.

Uitenbroek, D. G. (1993). Seasonal variation in leisure time physical activity. *Medicine and Science in Sports and Exercise, 25,* 755-760.

Unger, J. B., & Johnson, C. A. (1995). Social relationships and physical activity in health club members. *American Journal of Health Promotion, 9,* 340-343.

U.S. Department of Health and Human Services. (1991). *Healthy People 2000: National health promotion and disease prevention objectives* (DHHS Publication No. PHS 91-50212). Washington, DC: Government Printing Office.

U.S. Department of Health and Human Services. (1996). *Physical activity and health: A report of the Surgeon General.* Atlanta, GA: Centers for Disease Control.

U.S. Preventive Services Task Force. (1996). *Guide to clinical preventive services* (2nd ed.). Baltimore: Williams & Wilkins.

U.S. Public Health Service. (1980). *Promoting health/preventing disease: Objectives for the nation.* Washington, DC: U.S. Department of Health and Human Services.

Vandongen, R., Jenner, D. A., Thompson, C., Taggart, A. C., Spickett, E. E., Burke, V., Beilin, L. J., Milligan, R. A., & Dunbar, D. L. (1995). A controlled evaluation of a fitness and nutrition intervention program on cardiovascular health in 10- to 12-year-old children. *Preventive Medicine, 24,* 9-22.

Van Mechelen, W., & Kemper, H. C. G. (1995). Habitual physical activity in longitudinal perspective. In H. C. G. Kemper (Ed.), *The Amsterdam Growth Study: A longitudinal analysis of health, fitness, and lifestyle* (pp. 135-158). Champaign, IL: Human Kinetics.

Vuori, I. M., Oja, P., & Paronen, O. (1994). Physically active commuting to work: Testing its potential for exercise promotion. *Medicine and Science in Sports and Exercise, 26,* 844-850.

Wadden, T. A., Vogt, R. A., Kuehnel, R. H., Andersen, R. E., Bartlett, S. J., Foster, G. D., Wilk, J., Weinstock, R., Buckenmeyer, P., Berkowitz, R. I., & Steen, S. N. (1997). Exercise in the treatment of obesity: Effects of four interventions on body composition, resting energy expenditure, appetite, and mood. *Journal of Consulting and Clinical Psychology, 64,* 269-277.

Wankel, L. M. (1984). Decision-making and social-support strategies for increasing exercise involvement. *Journal of Cardiac Rehabilitation, 4,* 124-135.

Welk, G. J., & Corbin, C. B. (1995). The validity of the Tritrac-R3D activity monitor for the assessment of physical activity in children. *Research Quarterly for Exercise and Sport, 66,* 202-209.

Wicker, A. W. (1979). *An introduction to ecological psychology.* Monterey, CA: Brooks/Cole.

Williams, P. T. (1996). High-density lipoprotein cholesterol and other risk factors for coronary heart disease in female runners. *New England Journal of Medicine, 334,* 1298-1303.

Williamson, D. F., Madans, J., Anda, R. F., Kleinman, J. C., Kahn, H. S., & Byers, T. (1993). Recreational physical activity and 10-year weight gain in a US national cohort. *International Journal of Obesity, 17,* 279-286.

Wolf, A. M., Gortmaker, S. L., Cheung, L., Gray, H. M., Herzog, D. B., & Colditz, G. A. (1993). Activity, inactivity, and obesity: Racial, ethnic, and age differences among school girls. *American Journal of Public Health, 83,* 1625-1627.

Woods, J. A., & Davis, J. M. (1994). Exercise, monocyte/macrophage function, and cancer. *Medicine and Science in Sports and Exercise, 26,* 147-156.

Wysocki, T., Hall, G., Iwata, B., & Riordan, M. (1979). Behavioral management of exercise: Contracting for aerobic points. *Journal of Applied Behavior Analysis, 12,* 55-64.

Yates, A. (1991). *Compulsive exercise and the eating disorders.* New York: Brunner/Mazel.

Young, D. R., Haskell, W. L., Taylor, C. B., & Fortmann, S. P. (1996). Effect of community health education on physical activity knowledge, attitudes, and behavior: The Stanford five-city project. *American Journal of Epidemiology, 144,* 264-274.

Zakarian, J. M., Hovell, M. F., Hofstetter, C. R., Sallis, J. F., & Keating, K. J. (1994). Correlates of vigorous exercise in a predominantly low SES and minority high school population. *Preventive Medicine, 23,* 314-321.

Index

About the Authors

James F. Sallis has conducted research on the health effects of physical activity, determinants of active lifestyles, and interventions for young people and adults. A current special interest is encouraging wide use of programs found to be effective in research, including SPARK physical education (World Wide Web: http://www.foundation.sdsu.edu/projects/spark/index.html) and the PACE program for primary care (World Wide Web: http://www.shs.sdsu.edu/pace/). He received his doctorate in clinical psychology from the University of Memphis, completed an internship at Brown University, and began his research on behavioral aspects of physical activity while at the Stanford Center for Research on Disease Prevention. He is currently Professor of Psychology at San Diego State University and on the faculty of the Department of Pediatrics at the University of California, San Diego. Dr. Sallis was on the editorial board of the 1996 U.S. Surgeon General's report, *Physical Activity and Health,* and has received an award from the Health Psychology Division of the American Psychological Association. He lectures and consults internationally, has published over 200 scientific articles and chapters, and is coauthor of *Health and Human Behavior* (1993). He enjoys jogging, walking, bicycling, and modest resistance training. He gets a little more physical activity by playing drums in a rock and roll band.

Neville Owen's research has focused on understanding and influencing health-related behaviors, particularly physical activity and cigarette smoking. Recently, he has been interested in workplace influences—through studies of smoking bans and the uses of the workplace setting in promoting behavioral changes to reduce the risk of cardiovascular disease and cancer. He has also been studying the distribution of health-related behaviors in populations and the implementation and impact of large-scale health campaigns. He received his doctorate in experimental psychology from the University of Western Australia in 1972 and then worked as a community clinical psychologist in Vancouver, Canada. Much of his working life was spent at the University of Adelaide in South Australia, where he taught medical students and worked closely with epidemiologists, physical educators, and tobacco control and heart disease prevention groups. He spent 1982 as a Kellogg Foundation Fellow and Visiting Scholar with the Stanford Heart Disease Prevention Program, where he first met Jim Sallis. In 1995, he was appointed Foundation Professor of Human Movement Science at Deakin University in Melbourne, Head of the School of Human Movement, and Director of Research for Deakin University's Faculty of Health and Behavioural Sciences. He has published some 120 scientific articles and chapters, has been actively involved in the research and health promotion initiatives of the National Heart Foundation of Australia and was involved in many aspects of the QUIT campaign and tobacco control generally in South Australia. He is an Academic Associate of the Centre for Behavioural Research in Cancer in Melbourne. His recent involvements have included work on Australia's strategies for the prevention of overweight and obesity, population monitoring of physical activity, and the "Active Australia" strategy. He has a spouse with her own busy career and three young adult children. At the time of writing this book, he was president of the Eastern Suns Basketball Club. What time he can find to be physically active usually involves either walking his two dogs, riding one of his four bicycles, or bouncing and shooting with one of his son's numerous basketballs. All of the above supports his scientific hypothesis that the fundamental determinants of physical activity are competing time demands, proximal environmental cues, and structural elements of the work and family context.